EQUAL OPPORTUNITIES
AND SOCIAL POLICY

LONGMAN SOCIAL POLICY IN MODERN BRITAIN

Series Editor:
Jo Campling

Published Titles:
The Personal Social Services
Robert Adams

Health Policy and the NHS
Judith Allsop

Responding to Poverty
Saul Becker

Housing Problems and Policies
Brian Lund

Crime and Criminal Justice Policy
Tim Newburn

Elderly People and Society
Anthea Tinker

Forthcoming Titles:

New Directions in Educational Policy
Paul Lodge

Lone Mothers
Jane Millar

LONGMAN SOCIAL POLICY IN BRITAIN SERIES

Equal Opportunities and Social Policy: Issues of Gender, Race and Disability

Barbara Bagilhole

Longman

London and New York

Addison Wesley Longman Limited
Edinburgh Gate
Harlow
Essex CM20 2JE
United Kingdom
and Associated Companies throughout the world

*Published in the United States of America
by Addison Wesley Longman, New York*

© Addison Wesley Longman Limited 1997

First published 1997

ISBN 0 582 27951-8

British Library Cataloguing-in-Publication Data
A catalogue record for this book is available from the British Library

Library of Congress Cataloging-in-Publication Data
Bagilhole, Barbara, 1951–
    Equal opportunities and social policy : issues of gender, race,
and disability / Barbara Bagilhole.
       p. cm. – (Longman social policy in Britain series)
    Includes bibliographical references and index.
    ISBN 0–582–27951–8
    1. Great Britain–Social policy. 2. Equality–Great Britain.
3. Women–Government policy–Great Britain. 4. Minorities–
Government policy–Great Britain. 5. Handicapped–Government
policy–Great Britain. I. Title. II. Series.
HN390.B34   1997
361.6'1'0941–dc21   97–3427
                                             CIP

Set by 35 in 10/12 pt Times

Produced through Longman Malaysia, ACM

For George and Ben Bagilhole, my two major productions.

CONTENTS

ACKNOWLEDGEMENTS

I have worked in the field of 'equal opportunities' for over a decade as both an academic and practitioner and have therefore benefited enormously in the development of my ideas from all those with whom I have shared my experiences. Many people have contributed to and developed my ideas, including staff in the Equal Opportunities Department of Derbyshire County Council, community and voluntary groups, and both staff and students at Loughborough University. I should like to thank my friends and colleagues in the Social Policy teaching group for supporting my study leave to complete this book, with particular thanks to Arthur Gould for taking on the task of Course Director earlier than he was scheduled to do so. I should like to thank Viv Dhaliwal for her patient contribution of sorting and printing drafts and the final manuscript, and for holding my hand in times of printer and photocopier crisis. I wish to acknowledge the important contribution of Sandra Jasper, Ruth Lister and Jocey Quinn who read the draft of this book and made such detailed, perceptive and constructive criticisms, and very importantly highly supportive comments. Of course, I accept responsibility for the final outcome. Finally, I should like to thank Rupert, George, Ben and my Mum, Joyce, for their unfailing love and support.

The publishers are grateful to the following for permission to reproduce copyright material:

Commission for Racial Equality for extracts from *Factsheet No 2 RACIAL ATTACKS AND HARASSMENT* (1997) and *Factsheet No 4 EMPLOYMENT AND UNEMPLOYMENT* (1995); Guardian News Services Ltd for an extract from the article 'Putting Women in their place' (Interview with Valerie Amos, Chief Executive of the EOC and Gillian Shephard – Conservative MP for Norfolk South West) from *THE GUARDIAN* 30.12.91. © The Guardian 1991; Macmillan Press Ltd for extracts from UNDERSTANDING DISABILITY: FROM THEORY TO PRACTICE by M. OLIVER (1996) p108; The Women's Press for poem 'Tomorrow I'm Going to Rewrite the English Language' by Lois Keith from *MUSN'T GRUMBLE: Writing by Disabled Women* edited by Lois Keith, first published by The Women's Press, 34 Great Sutton Street, London EC1V ODX.

INTRODUCTION

The ideas of 'equal opportunities' are at the core of social policy. Social policy as a discipline concerns itself with the relation between 'equal opportunities' and the outcome of the welfare services provided. This book examines these issues through three major social and structural divisions within society on which 'equal opportunities' legislation has been based: gender, 'race' and disability.

Although this book will consider gender, 'race' and disability as separate oppressions, it is important to approach 'equal opportunities' as an integrated concept. Despite acknowledging and recognizing that there are important differences between the disadvantage and discrimination experienced by different groups on the grounds of gender, 'race' and disability, there are also many areas that overlap. Women, ethnic minorities and disabled people are often the most vulnerable to changes and the withdrawal and retraction of public resources in the field of welfare. It is particularly important in the area of 'equal opportunities' to avoid the danger that a discussion about one dimension of inequality can become introspective, over-theoretical and disconnected from policy concerns. There are, however, stages when one source of disadvantage needs to be separated out so that it can be given due attention. But other inequalities always need to be borne in mind, and in the implementation of 'equal opportunities' within organizations it is essential to have policies which are comprehensive and coherent across the social divisions of gender, 'race' and disability.

Also, while it is important to state that women, ethnic minorities and disabled people are not homogeneous groups in their own right, because their experiences of disadvantage are tempered and altered by other social divisions, they do have considerable shared experience within their groups. Deem (1996) raised this as a note of caution in the area of gender. Although

recent feminist theories have urged us not to examine gender differences *per se* but to explore the different positions and identities taken by women, this omits the possibility that there are still systematic modes of discrimination experienced by social categories and distinct patternings which relate to gender as well as to other dimensions of social equality. Thus whilst it is important to be aware of diversity in the positive sense, particularly in relation to membership of ethnic minority groups, sexual orientation and identity, age, life style and so on, we should beware of losing sight of the concept of equality in a more general sense (p. 100).

Thus Deem (1996) argued that: 'It is important that we do not let the current fashion for focusing on difference and identity distract our attention from the possibility that the economic, the political and the cultural have a systematic influence on inequalities than might be supposed from an analysis which concentrates only on the politics of the differential identities of women' (p. 85). Following this line of argument this book explores 'equal opportunities' for women, ethnic minorities and disabled people as groups while also attempting to be sensitive to and acknowledge difference and diversity within these groups.

This book is divided into three parts. The first part looks at the relevance of 'equal opportunities' for social policy in Britain today, the theory behind 'equal opportunities', its political and legislative base, and influences on its current position. Chapter 1 examines evidence of disadvantage in Britain today for women, ethnic minorities and disabled people to answer the questions: Why do we need 'equal opportunities'?; and why is 'equal opportunities' important to social policy? It demonstrates the continuing inequality experienced first by women, then ethnic minority groups and finally disabled people by presenting some of the pertinent and relevant statistics available. For women, it considers inequality in education, employment, occupational segregation, earnings, unemployment and unpaid work. For ethnic minorities, it examines population figures, education, employment, occupational segregation, earnings, unemployment, and finally racial attacks and harassment. For disabled people, it highlights population figures, employment, income, and finally extra expenditure caused by disability. The fundamental argument promoted in this chapter is that we need 'equal opportunities' policies in Britain today to attempt to overcome inequality which still exists for the particular groups concentrated on in this book: women, ethnic minorities and disabled people.

Chapter 2 considers the theoretical background to 'equal opportunities'. It addresses the questions: What is 'equal opportunities'? And what do we mean by 'equal opportunities'? It analyses the often contentious and contested theoretical concepts involved in the area of 'equal opportunities'. The theories are examined on a societal level, looking at the concepts of discrimination and prejudice, types of equality, positive action and justice. At an organizational level it examines 'equal opportunities' in practice and the theory of 'equal opportunities' in organizations. Finally, it investigates the definitions and theoretical underpinnings of the concepts of disability, 'race' and gender.

Chapter 3 looks at the ideological and historical background to 'equal opportunities'. The first half highlights the politics of 'equal opportunities' by charting and exploring its development in Britain through four distinct eras: the 1940s–1950s, the 1960s–1970s, the 1980s and the 1990s. This analysis of the historical development is set in the context of the major driving forces and catalysts for 'equal opportunities' in the different decades, which have changed in dominance over time. The major forces are categorized as moral, legislative, political, economic and professional interests. The second half of the chapter examines the legislation that has been passed in this field. It looks at the most significant Acts in the areas of disability, gender and 'race'. These include: in the field of disability, the Disabled Persons (Employment) Acts 1944 and 1958, the Chronically Sick and Disabled Persons Act 1970, the Companies Act 1985, and the Disability Discrimination Act 1995; in the field of 'race' and religion, the Commonwealth Immigrants Act 1962, the Local Government Act 1966, the Immigration Act 1971, the Race Relations Act 1976, the British Nationality Act 1981, and the Fair Employment Protection Act, Northern Ireland 1989; and in the field of gender, the Equal Pay Act 1970 (amended 1984), the Sex Discrimination Act 1975 (amended 1986), and the Employment Rights Act 1996.

Finally, Chapter 4 appraises the influence of the European Union on 'equal opportunities' and examines the current state of national legislation. The first half of the chapter considers the past influence of the European Union (EU) on 'equal opportunities' legislation and policies in Britain in the areas of gender, 'race' and disability, and its potential for influence in the future. It shows that the EU has been both active and effective in making changes in the area of gender. However, in the areas of both 'race' and disability, the EU has been much less proactive. In fact, the lack of or even negative activity in the area of 'race' is shown to be in stark contrast to the area of gender. The second half of the chapter contains a criticism of national 'equal opportunities' legislation. It is shown to take an 'individualistic' approach with very little recall to 'group justice', to be 'protective' rather than proactive, and legally complex, leading to many unsuccessful cases in industrial tribunals. The recommendations for strengthening the law put forward by both the Equal Opportunities Commission and the Commission for Racial Equality and the criticisms of the Disability Discrimination Act by the disabled people's movement are considered. The final conclusion is that once strengthened, the law does have an important part to play in achieving 'equal opportunities' providing it is supported by the will of legislators and the judiciary.

Part Two of the book examines the key areas of social policy for 'equal opportunities' issues and developments from the perspectives of gender, 'race' and disability. These key areas are identified as education, employment, income maintenance, social services, health and housing. Chapter 5 examines employment and education. In the area of education, the issues shared by women, ethnic minorities and disabled people are under-achievement, differential access and discrimination. However, for women and ethnic minorities the previous patterns of under-achievement are altering substantially. There is evidence of a reversal in the differential educational success of girls and boys, which is beginning in the school system. Nevertheless, it is predicted that this will take many years to work through the higher levels of the educational system and into the labour market. There has also been a narrowing of the gap in the levels of educational attainment between Whites and ethnic minorities generally, and differential achievement occurring between ethnic minority groups. A policy area of particular significance for disabled people is the issue of 'segregated' education, and the detrimental and excluding effect this has for them. This still persists, and appears to be reproduced in the right to exclude disabled children from the National Curriculum.

The second half of the chapter shows that although women have entered the labour market in ever increasing numbers, they remain disadvantaged largely because of persistent occupational segregation. Sexual harassment has been shown to be widespread and prevalent across all types of work and little has been introduced in terms of 'family friendly' policies. Finally, ethnic minority women are shown to be in an even worse position than White women in the labour market. In general terms, ethnic minorities experience significant inequalities in the employment field in the types of jobs they obtain, earnings levels and vulnerability to unemployment. Patterns of employment have shifted and greater diversity has appeared between ethnic minority groups, although the employment patterns of ethnic minorities have still not converged with Whites. Disabled people are far less likely to be in paid employment than non-disabled people and, if in employment, they are disproportionately represented in lower status and paid jobs. Most employers have reservations about disabled people's ability to do certain jobs and their level of productivity. To combat this, the social model of disability is supported in an attempt to move away from the concentration on the labour supply side of the equation, which tries to make disabled people suitable for employment rather than looking at barriers to their involvement.

Chapter 6 examines the social policy areas of income maintenance and social services. First, looking at income maintenance, the growth in poverty, unemployment and the emphasis on private caring and means-tested social security benefits has disproportionately hit women, ethnic minorities and disabled people. Women's entitlement and access to benefit is severely limited because of policies based on assumptions about their traditional role. The crux of the matter is the linking of benefit entitlement to paid work. This also impacts on ethnic minorities and disabled people who find themselves in the lowest paid, most insecure jobs if they are in paid work at all. The added dimension of disadvantage for ethnic minorities is the actual and feared use of immigration rules, which limit their right to draw on public funds. For disabled people the system of income maintenance has been mainly based on the 'medical model' of disability, not on supporting their access to the labour market, which has discriminatory implications.

The second half of the chapter considers the area of social service provision. Despite women predominating as the users and service providers of social services, their needs are not being appropriately met. The development and emphasis on community care has disproportionately and detrimentally affected them, and they are to be found concentrated in lower level jobs with least power in decision making and little influence on the way services are provided. There is a low take-up of social service provision by ethnic minority communities generally. Explanations for this phenomenon have concentrated on the cultural aspects of ethnic minority communities. This has led to the inadequate investigation of the inappropriateness of service provision, which is variable and uneven within and between different local authorities. Community care is a crucial area of policy, which has been questioned from the position of disabled people and their carers. The main problem is that, despite the stated aim of reducing professional dominance, this has not happened in any meaningful way. In fact, professionals have consolidated their control. Fundamentally, it is argued that social work practice has been based on a too narrow individualistic perspective on disability which, by not recognizing that disability is a social phenomenon, has led to inadequate and ineffective policies for disabled people.

Chapter 7 examines the social policy areas of health and housing. In the area of health, women form the largest group of consumers and providers of health care. However, the NHS does not provide adequate or appropriate health care for women. It remains under the control of men and dominated by a male medical tradition. Although women are such a large majority of the NHS labour force, they are mainly in the lower levels of the hierarchy, with ethnic minority women even more disadvantaged than White women. Because of the 'medicalization of women's lives' women experience a lifetime of interventionist medicine often revolving around their fertility from male doctors who have been criticized for being patronizing and holding stereotypical views of women.

Ethnic minorities receive a qualitatively and quantitatively worse service from the NHS than White people. This situation continues despite its acknowledgement by the NHS and a substantial increase in research in this area. There has been an over emphasis on a cultural approach to this disadvantage that has resulted in a failure to examine structures both outside and inside the NHS, which determine the health of ethnic minority communities. Reforms in the control of the NHS have done little to improve the situation and there remains an under-representation of ethnic minorities at all levels of decision making. The health service stands accused of over-intervention in the area of disability, and taking over the control of decisions from disabled people by dictating the form of intervention in purely medical terms. Medical practitioners control and act as gatekeepers for disabled people's access not only to health services but also to other services and benefits. Medical intervention took the form of striving for 'normality' in behaviour and appearance for disabled people, and therefore a concentration on rehabilitation. Many changes are needed to ensure an equal service to disabled people, not least an increase in the numbers of disabled workers in the health service.

The second half of the chapter deals with housing. British housing policy has concentrated on promoting owner occupation above all other forms of tenure and reducing the resources that are available to 'social rented' housing. This meant that those with lower incomes, such as women, ethnic minorities and disabled people, were forced into private rented accommodation, which was generally of poorer quality. Women need public housing because they are likely to need their housing to accommodate their responsibility for children and the care of disabled, sick or elderly people, and their housing needs often arise out of an unexpected or sudden life event, pregnancy, relationship breakdown and physical violence. Women's homelessness is hidden and under-counted, because research in this area and policies to deal with it have concentrated on those sleeping rough who are more likely to be men. Women are also at a disadvantage in housing employment because they are less likely to be managers or represented in professional staff. Racial discrimination exists in all sectors of the housing market and all forms of tenure. Although housing tenure varies widely between different ethnic minority groups, overall they live in more overcrowded accommodation than Whites, are to be found concentrated in geographically racially segregated areas, and are disproportionately vulnerable to homelessness. Disabled people hold an inferior position to most other groups in terms of housing. The vast majority of owner-occupied housing is unsuitable for disabled people, and where disabled people are owner-occupiers they are concentrated in the properties with the poorest conditions because of their lack of income. Therefore, they are more reliant on the 'social rented' sector. However, substantial cuts in local government funding and insufficient funding for housing associations means that provision is inadequate and often provided on a segregated basis.

Chapter 8 concludes Part Two of the book. It argues that women, ethnic minorities and disabled people share a common position of marginalization and disadvantage in the key areas of social policy. Providers of services need to recognize and acknowledge the social divisions in society on the basis of 'race', gender and disability, because appropriate services cannot be provided on a 'colour, sex and disability blind approach'. It is also important not to simply take an approach to changing services, which concentrates on the service users themselves – either women, ethnic minorities or disabled people – because this diverts attention away from a critical examination of the service itself. It is argued that the dominance of a 'needs-based' approach to social policy provision must be changed to a 'rights-based' approach to effect 'equal opportunities'. Finally, there is an important relationship between the providers and the users of welfare provision. The representation of women, ethnic minorities and disabled people as workers in decision-making positions of power in welfare is essential to increase the likelihood that services will be appropriate, relevant and accessible for these groups. The determination of services for disabled people by non-disabled people, for women by men, and for ethnic minorities by White people, largely without their say or participation, needs to change.

Finally, in Part Three, Chapter 9 contains supporting documents which are relevant to the text of the book and of use for further student investigation. These documents are extracts from other books, articles or legislation, tables of statistics, or a summary of a particular topic drawn from various cited sources. They are suggested as complementary and additional information to the contents of the book and provide a catalyst for further discussion, study, and a useful source for seminar and tutorial work.

Glossary of Terms

Defining the following terms is both complex and controversial but also essential. Other writers will use different definitions and terms, but at least if their use within this book is clearly defined, it will allow the reader to contrast and compare the analysis with other work in the field. Therefore, some of the terms used in this book are explained below to try to help the reader to a clearer understanding.

'Equal opportunities'   is placed in inverted commas throughout the book because it is both a complex and contested concept. Although the term is widely used, there is often an assumed shared meaning, which may be seen to be somewhat superficial and at times erroneous when analysed further. The difficulty of definition is pursued in Chapter 2.

'Race'   is placed in inverted commas as it is now recognized as a social construction denoting a particular way in which communal differences come to be constructed, rather than a biological, genetic or physical concept (Rose *et al.*, 1984; Miles, 1989; Williams, 1989; Donald and Rattansi, 1992; Anthias and Yuval-Davis, 1993). However, it still has significant currency in both sociological analysis and official publications and classifications. The Labour Force Survey has classified its data by official definitions of 'race' since the mid-1980s, and from 1991, an 'ethnic' question was included in the Population Census, which asked for self-categorization of ethnic identity. 'Race' is used in British legislation to refer to such things as ethnic or national origins, nationality or citizenship and skin colour. In practice, visibly identifiable groups are focused upon, such as Asian, African and Black Caribbean communities, when references are made to 'race', but it is important to recognize that discrimination is also directed against White groups. For example, there is a long history of prejudice against Irish and Jewish people in Britain (Jackson, 1963).

Black   is used with a capital letter as is White because the terms refer to social-political identities rather than descriptive terms. Black has come to mean 'people affected by racism' (Williams, 1989, pp. ix–x; Cook and Watt, 1992; Mama, 1992, p. 80). In modern Britain, the term Black primarily refers to people of African, Asian and Caribbean descent. 'Black has been written with a capital letter as a means of signifying that it refers to more than a shade of skin. It refers to a group of people who wish to have their racial identity as encapsulating a total experience' (Pennie and Williams, 1987, p. 12).

Ethnic minorities   This term is broadly applied and widespread in official and academic publications, often with an implication of difference in colour. It is sometimes qualified by being linked with Black, i.e. Black and ethnic minority groups. The use of the term 'ethnic minorities' emphasizes the different ethnic groupings within the Black community, and may be used to avoid a false and imposed homogeneity of Black people when the heterogeneity in the different communities needs drawing out to differentiate forms and experiences of racism. We need to bear in mind that ethnic minority communities may not necessarily have much else in common than adverse treatment and experiences, and that both treatment and experiences may differ between groups. For example, although Black Caribbean children continue to under-achieve in schools and experience the highest exclusion rates, Indian children are now achieving better than Whites and have lower exclusion rates. Therefore, groups have to be disaggregated to provide a clearer understanding of the differentiation of experience and treatment within broader classifications. For instance ethnic minority communities may be differentiated by two broad groups: Asian and Black, or classified by country of origin, e.g. Indian, Pakistani or Bangladeshi, or even religion where this is relevant, e.g. Hindu, Muslim and Sikh. We need some reasonably understood and flexible ways of identifying and categorizing groups in the area of 'race', when discussing the differentiated experiences of certain groups.

Official categories are not without problems and contradictions. Although there is considerable overlap between them they are not consistent. The Labour Force Survey contains a category which specifically signifies a 'mixed-race' classification, which since 1992 has been further subdivided, whereas the Census only offers a Black/Other or Other category. This may pick up people from mixed descent but does not allow their quantification. This omission is important because as Nanton (1992) showed, this was the fastest growing community of all minority groups and they often experienced the same 'racial' prejudice and discrimination of other visible groups. Also, in both the Labour Force Survey and the Census the White category is not subdivided into ethnic or national categories. Looking at the categories on offer in the Census it is not clear where Black British-born people would put themselves. They may choose 'Black/Other', or their parental descent such as 'Indian' or 'Pakistani', or if they do not identify with the political classification of Black may choose 'Other'. All these official categories confuse social, national and political affiliations, ignore religion and do not differentiate between White groups who may experience discrimination (see Document 3 Chapter 9 for the official classifications used).

For consistency this book will use the Commission for Racial Equality's (CRE) classification in the area of 'race'. This is because it allows both the discussion and investigation of disadvantage and discrimination for ethnic minorities as a whole compared with the ethnic majority group (Whites), and also the opportunity to distinguish between ethnic minority groups. In other words it recognizes overall racial disadvantage within society, but also importantly acknowledges the complexity of the issue and its differential experience by different groups, and the heterogeneity of ethnic minority groups. The CRE classification is based on the origin of the different ethnic minority groups in Britain, and is as follows: Black Caribbean, Black African, Black Other, Indian, Pakistani, Bangladeshi, Chinese, Other Asian, and Other. They use the term 'ethnic minorities' to indicate that they are discussing all these groups together and excluding the ethnic majority (Whites). Also, when useful for analysis they use the terms Black groups to differentiate them from Asians, and South Asians (Indians, Pakistanis and Bangladeshis) to differentiate between the Asian groups.

Disability   The way that disability is defined is very important as it affects the way disabled people are viewed and the way they are treated. Definitions of disability have moved from ones based on a medicalized, individualistic approach to ones that emphasize the social dimensions of disability. The Disabled People's International definition is: 'The loss or limitation of opportunities to take part in the life of the community on an equal level with others due to physical and social barriers' (Oliver, 1991a).

Despite the recognition of the need to move to a social definition the World Health Organization offers definitions of **impairment, disability** and **handicap** which continue to concentrate on an individual's condition (Lonsdale, 1990; Oliver, 1990). **Impairment** is defined as any loss or abnormality of psychological, physiological or anatomical structure or function. **Disability** is seen as any restriction or lack (resulting from an impairment) of ability to perform an activity in the manner or within the range considered as normal for a human being. Finally, **handicap** is viewed as a disadvantage for a given individual resulting from an impairment or disability that limits the fulfilment of a role for that individual.

Disabled people This is the preferred term for people who are disabled which highlights the fact that they are 'disabled' by society.

People with learning difficulties This term is used to describe someone with an impairment of their intellectual abilities. It used to be called mental handicap.

Non-disabled people This term is preferred over 'able-bodied' to describe people without a disability because it does not imply a monopoly on ability.

Gender Sociology has for two decades made a clear distinction between sex and gender. It was argued that the fixed nature of sex based on biological determinants could be compared with the variability of gender as a cultural product that referred to the social classification into 'masculine' and 'feminine'. However, the clarity of the distinction between sex and gender has been challenged. The declared fact that sex is natural, biologically clear and divided into two groups is now being reappraised. The biological understanding of the determinant of sex difference is in fact still being investigated through medical research work in the area of chromosomal theory, and it is argued that this work is influenced by notions of gender (see Chapter 2 for a fuller discussion of this distinction).

Racism 'Racism is a process of systematic oppression directed towards people who are defined as inferior, usually in pseudo-biological terms such as skin colour' (Cook and Watt, 1987, p. 70).

Sexism 'Sexism is a process of systematic oppression directed towards women who are defined as inferior to men' (Cook and Watt, 1987, p. 70).

Disablism We can take a lead from Cook and Watt's (1987) definitions of racism and sexism and define 'disablism' as a process of systematic oppression directed towards disabled people who are defined as inferior to non-disabled people.

PART ONE

An introduction to equal opportunities

CHAPTER 1

The relevance of 'equal opportunities' for social policy in Britain today

Why do we need 'equal opportunities'? Why is 'equal opportunities' important to social policy?

The idea of 'equal opportunities' is at the core of social policy. Social policy as a discipline concerns itself with the relationship between opportunities to access welfare services provided and their outcome. It explores the ways in which the needs of different groups are constructed, the assumptions upon which policies are developed, differential access to employment and welfare services, and the different impacts on service users as a result.

Fundamentally, it can be argued that we need 'equal opportunities' policies in Britain today to attempt to overcome inequality which still exists for particular groups. In this book we are dealing with women, ethnic minority groups and disabled people. The book concentrates on the areas of gender, 'race' and disability, because women, ethnic minorities and disabled people have 'equal opportunities' legislation, which acknowledges their disadvantage and is in place presumably to do something about rectifying the situation. Despite this legislation, the social divisions of gender, 'race' and disability can be seen to continue to limit people's access to welfare services and employment.

For welfare services to be effective they need to be accessible, appropriate and relevant for all clients and potential clients. This calls for monitoring formal practices and the culture of the organization, which affect the accessibility and acceptability of services to all clients. Importantly, 'equal opportunities' in employment is closely linked to this fair provision of welfare services. An issue for all service providers dedicated to a quality, accessible and appropriate service for the whole community is that the employment of women, ethnic minority groups and disabled people should help sensitize the service to these groups. This is, of course, provided that they are not put in the lower paid non-decision-making posts, where they can have relatively little influence.

However, in employment, these groups in our society are severely disadvantaged. This disadvantage takes many forms. They are less likely to get jobs in the first place. When they are employed they are confined to particular types of jobs, which are generally among the most menial, the worst paid, and the least likely to carry promotion prospects. They may be subjected to harassment on the grounds of their gender, 'race' or disability, and suffer from institutional practices which discriminate against them either directly or indirectly. Obviously employers cannot be expected to tackle all the causes of this inequality, many of which are deeply embedded in the institutions and attitudes of society. However, employers can carry out 'equal opportunities' policies which seek to alleviate some of the worst effects and thereby allow the benefits of the employment of these groups to filter through to the welfare services they provide.

Evidence of disadvantage

The next section of this chapter will demonstrate the continuing inequality experienced first by women, then ethnic minority groups and finally disabled people by presenting some of the pertinent and relevant statistics available. However, it must be remembered that although we can obtain statistics concerning these particular groups, they are not homogeneous entities and different social factors can influence the level and form of disadvantage experienced by individuals and subgroups within these categories. Nevertheless, it can still be demonstrated that to talk of group structural disadvantage in the areas of gender, 'race' and disability still makes sense in Britain today.

Gender

Are we seeing significant signs of an increase in equality for women? Are women rapidly moving towards the position of economic independence? Some of the statistics available could suggest that the answer to these questions is yes, but other data would suggest that this is not the case.

Education

On the positive side, girls' and women's achievement has risen and their participation in post-compulsory education has increased. Over half of those now achieving grades A to C at GCSE, across all subjects, are young women. At the next stage, 23 per cent of women obtained two or more GCE A levels compared with 21 per cent of men (Equal Opportunities Commission, 1996a). Over the last decade the number of women students in post-compulsory education has risen by 49 per cent compared with 38 per cent for men. The rise in women's participation has been most dramatic in higher education where the number of full-time women students has doubled and part-time students trebled (Central Statistical Office, 1995). For the first time in the academic year 1994–95 half of the undergraduate students in higher education were women (EOC, 1996a).

However, when looking at the area of women's success in education, we need to be cautious. We have to acknowledge a serious caveat to these positive statistics, which places a severe constraint on women's equality. There is still clearly defined horizontal discipline segregation between women and men. For example, at GCSE level, while 57 per cent of those obtaining grades A to C in English are young women, they only make up 32 per cent of those gaining similar grades in physics. At higher education level, whereas women make up 70 per cent of English undergraduate students, they only make up 17 per cent of those in physics (EOC, 1996a).

Employment

One of the most outstanding changes in the labour market has been the dramatic increase in the number of women working. Over the last two decades women have made up an increasing proportion of the workforce, from 37 per cent in 1971 to 44 per cent in 1994 and still rising. The most marked increase has been in the group of women aged 25 to 34, from 45.5 per cent in 1971 to 71 per cent in 1994. This was occurring while the economic activity rate for all men fell to 73 per cent in 1994, and continues to fall (Central Statistical Office, 1995). While women's workforce participation is still affected by the age of their children, just over half of women whose youngest child is under five years are economically active. This rises to 70 per cent for those whose youngest child is aged five to ten and 78 per cent whose child is aged 11 to 15 (Central Statistical Office, 1995). As a result in over half of married couples with dependent children both partners are in paid employment.

However, most of the growth in women working identified above has been in part-time work where there are lower rates of pay and worse conditions than in full-time work, and the trend to more casualized labour has disproportionately impacted on women. Ethnic minority women tend to work in full-time jobs more than White women – 70 per cent compared with 56 per cent – but are still lower paid (EOC, 1994). However, overall in 1994, 45 per cent of women were working part-time, more than five times as many as men (Central Statistical Office, 1995). The government consistently blocked moves from the European Union to improve conditions for part-time workers, but has finally had to concede following court decisions against them.

Occupational segregation

Increased participation rates for women in the labour market have not reduced segregation. We still see both horizontal and vertical segregation of the workforce along gender lines. The issue is not the quantity of women in the labour force, but in which occupations and grades they are found. Horizontal segregation is where women and men have different types of occupation. Vertical segregation is where women and men are employed in the same occupation, but women are most commonly found in the lower grades. Also, although more women are returning to work after child bearing, they still experience a drop in occupational status returning to jobs at a lower level of remuneration and responsibility than before their career break (Central Statistical Office, 1995).

Looking at horizontal segregation, women and men tend to be employed in different occupations, and women are concentrated in a much smaller number of occupations than men. Four occupational groups together account for three-quarters of women's employment: professional and related work in education, welfare and health (teachers, social workers, nurses), clerical and related (secretaries), selling (shop assistants), and catering and cleaning (cooks and cleaners). Most women are employed in occupations where women predominate. For example, three-quarters of people working in clerical and secretarial work are women, two-thirds in personal service occupations and over 60 per cent in sales. Conversely, only one in ten workers in craft occupations and two in ten plant and machine operators are women. Women outnumber men by four to one in the health sector and two to one in education, but are outnumbered by men by nine to one in the construction industry (Central Statistical Office, 1995). This is not just a British phenomenon: in six EC Member States (Britain, Denmark, Germany, France, Spain and Belgium) over half of all employed women in 1990 were to be found in just six out of 58 subsectors of the labour market: retailing; health services; education; public administration; social and cultural services; banking, finance and insurance (Commission of the EC, 1992, p. 139).

Another area where women are segregated is in homeworking, that is working at home. The estimates of these often 'invisible workers' vary considerably from two million to about 450 000 in the UK (Central Statistical Office, 1995). However, this way of combining home responsibilities and paid work often condemns women to very low wages and poor conditions. Bagilhole (1986) found women working for as little as 9 pence an hour. They received 26 pence per 100 for stripping the plastic off wire ends, tying them in a knot and bundling them up. They had to pay for their own heating and lighting, and received no holiday, sick or maternity pay.

Vertical segregation exists because women are concentrated in the lower grades of all occupations, even in occupations where they predominate. Ethnic minority women tend to be in even lower status jobs than White women: for example, they make up a higher proportion of nursing auxiliaries than nurses (EOC, 1994). In school teaching, while women make up 81 per cent of all teachers in nursery and primary schools, they make up 90 per cent of those at the lowest level, but only 57 per cent of heads and deputy heads. In secondary schools, they make up 49 per cent of all teachers, 61 per cent at the lowest level and only 30 per cent of heads and deputy heads (Central Statistical Office, 1995). In higher education, one area of teaching where women do not dominate numerically, a similar pattern also emerges. They make up only 20 per cent of lecturers, 12 per cent of senior lecturers and only 5 per cent of professors (Deem, 1996).

Women have traditionally been under-represented in the police force. Only 16 per cent of constables are women, and only 6 per cent of sergeants (Central Statistical Office, 1995). Also, nine out of ten policewomen reported that they had experienced verbal sexual harassment, six out of ten had offensive comments made about their appearance, and three out of ten were subject to unwanted touching (Brown and Campbell, 1993).

According to a report by the Hansard Society (McRae, 1996), women represent only 9 per cent of Members of Parliament, 6 per cent of the House of Lords, and 15 per cent of senior civil servants. In contrast, if all things were equal, they would hold 339 of the seats in the House of Commons, not 60 as at present. While nearly half of lay magistrates are women, they make up only 5 per cent of professional judges (Central Statistical Office, 1995). Despite the Business in the Community, Opportunity 2000 campaign launched in 1991 to encourage women high-flyers, women accounted for only 1 per cent of executive directors. The Hansard Society (McRae, 1996) blames this on 'unthinking or overtly sexist attitudes' that continue to bar a woman's way. It concluded that women in management 'remain hampered by glass ceilings and hemmed in by glass walls'. This allows them to see where they might go but restricts their progress and earnings.

Earnings

Women are concentrated at the lower end of the distribution of earnings. Although there has been a narrowing of the wage differential between women and men, it is still present in all occupational sectors. On average women still earn only 72 per cent of men's wages per week and in some sectors it is as low as 60 per cent (New Earnings Survey, 1996). A third of women earn £190 per week or less compared with 13 per cent of men (Central Statistical Office, 1995). Also, ethnic minority women receive approximately three-quarters of White women's pay (EOC, 1994). A survey in Leicester found 55 per cent of White women, but 86 per cent of Asian women earning less than £150 per week (Duffy and Lincoln, 1990). The overall reasons for women's low pay are that they are concentrated in a small number of generally poorly paid occupations and industries, they have less access to additional payments on top of the basic wage such as overtime, bonus payments or shift allowances, and they are concentrated in part-time work which is particularly badly paid.

Unemployment

Official figures for unemployment put women's rates at about half that of men's. However, it is recognized as notoriously difficult to measure women's unemployment. Official statistics on unemployment are based on claimant count and therefore exclude many unemployed women who are not eligible to claim. Also, whereas part-time jobs count in official employment statistics, unemployed people seeking part-time work (who are more likely to be women) are not counted in the unemployment statistics. Ethnic minority women as a whole are more than twice as likely as White women to be unemployed. This rises to five times as likely for Pakistani women and nearly six times for Bangladeshi women (Owen, 1994). Even using the official count, women's unemployment rose faster than men's between 1979 and 1986, then declined faster from 1987 to 1990, but has accelerated again since 1991.

Unpaid work

One of the other major areas where women experience inequality is in the provision of unpaid work, and this has a major effect on their capacity to take paid work. They still carry the major responsibility for family and home in the private domain. In 1994, designated International Year of the Family, British men were found to work the longest hours in Europe, one in three working more than 48 hours per week. Whereas women shoulder the main responsibility for domestic work in 75 per cent of families (67 per cent in families even where both women and men are working full-time), local authorities provide daycare facilities for just 1 per cent of children under five and just 1 per cent of all workers are in a job-share scheme (Opportunity 2000, 1994).

In terms of housework, Bagilhole (1994a) found that even in households where both the woman and the man are in full-time paid work, women continue to undertake a disproportionate share. In the households in her survey, over 60 per cent of the women took prime responsibility for washing, changing sheets, ironing, cleaning the toilet, cooker, bath and kitchen floor, cooking, making the beds, dusting and putting clothes away. The men took the same level of responsibility only for car maintenance, cleaning the car and DIY (see Document 8 in Chapter 9 for details of the percentage of women and men taking responsibility for these household tasks).

Women are directly responsible for most of the care of children. It has been estimated that basic childcare tasks take at least 50 hours a week (Piachaud, 1985). Mothers in Britain on average earnings with two children are estimated to lose over £200 000 over their working lives because of time spent out of the labour market (Joshi and Davies, 1993). Britain provides minimal public day-care facilities. Compared with 12 other European Community countries, Britain ranks eleventh in provision for three to five year-olds, only Portugal provides less (Belgium, France, Denmark and Italy provide the most). Britain provides daycare for only 25 per cent of three-year-olds (Commission of the EC, 1992).

According to the General Household Survey, married women are more likely to be carers of dependent adults than either men or non-married women, and when men are carers it is often at the less demanding end of the scale. Overall nearly a fifth of women care for an elderly, sick or disabled person on a regular basis. This rises to 27 per cent in the age group 45 to 64. Various forms of care were given from practical support such as personal services, shopping and housework, to providing company and generally keeping an eye on relatives, neighbours and friends. This can be a substantial commitment for some women, with 12 per cent spending 50 hours or more a week on caring activities (Central Statistical Office, 1995). From this we can see that the government's development of and emphasis on 'community care' has in reality meant 'woman care'.

'Race'

Britain has always had ethnic minority populations with immigration mostly linked with a demand for labour. The Irish were the first to arrive in large numbers during the Industrial Revolution. Many people from the Caribbean, South Asia and Africa were encouraged to come to Britain to alleviate a labour shortage after the Second World War, and Bangladeshis were one of the last groups to arrive.

Population figures

It is estimated, using the 1991 Census data (Commission for Racial Equality, 1995a), that just over three million (5.5 per cent) of the 55 million population in Britain are from ethnic minority groups. Using the Commission for Racial Equality (CRE) classification of the ethnic minority population (see Chapter 9, Document 3), nearly half are South Asian (Indian, Pakistani and Bangladeshi) and 30 per cent are Black (Black Caribbean, Black African and Black Other). Overall, nearly half of these communities (46.8 per cent) were born in Britain and some three-quarters are British citizens (Owen, 1993a). The vast majority (97 per cent) of the ethnic minority population live in England in large urban areas. Looking at the distribution of population, we find 58 per cent of Black Caribbeans, 79 per cent of Black Africans, 44 per cent of Black Others and 54 per cent of Bangladeshis live in Greater London; 16 per cent of Black Caribbeans, 21 per cent of Pakistanis and 12 per cent of Bangladeshis live in the West Midlands; 20 per cent of Pakistanis live in Yorkshire and Humberside; and of Indians who are more widely spread: 53 per cent live in the South East and 30 per cent in the Midlands (CRE, 1995a).

In contrast to the White population, all the ethnic minority communities have relatively young populations with nearly half under 25 years old. Only 14 per cent are over 50, and 3 per cent are pensioners compared with 17 per cent of the White population. South Asians usually live in larger households with an average household size of 4.2, compared with 2.6 for Black and 2.4 for White households. Black groups have the largest proportions of single adult households excluding pensioners, 24 per cent compared with 12 per cent of White and 7 per cent of South Asian households (CRE, 1995a).

Education

In education there is evidence of significant under-achievement among some ethnic minority groups. However, this is a complex phenomenon where it is difficult to identify and measure the nature and extent of discrimination. The general pattern, in the past, of Black Caribbean and South Asian people being less likely than Whites to have formal qualifications is gradually changing (Jones, 1993). Not surprisingly, this is most marked in the younger age groups, particularly in the case of women. Alongside this phenomenon, a gap is opening up within the ethnic minority communities, particularly between relatively well-qualified African Asians and Indians, and poorly qualified Pakistanis and Bangladeshis.

This picture is even more complex if we look at different levels and types of educational provision. Generally, young ethnic minority people of 16–19 years are substantially more likely to continue in education than Whites. However, although at the point of leaving school Black Caribbeans have a similar profile to Whites, the proportion with higher education qualifications is lower among Black Caribbean men than among Whites, African Asians and Indians. Whereas, Black Caribbeans are more likely to have completed trade apprenticeships than other groups. It is argued that this partly reflects the education system in the Caribbean with a well-developed apprenticeship system, but little higher education in the British sense. In the Indian system, the higher education system is more developed, and trade apprenticeships are rare or nonexistent. Also, as education was seen as far more important for men than women, a high proportion of older women originating from the Indian subcontinent have never received any education. This is particularly marked for Pakistani and Bangladeshi women.

However, when we look further up the education system we see an even more complex picture, with higher proportions of certain ethnic minority 16–24 year olds studying full-time than the White population. For example, Black African young people born in Britain are two or three times more likely to be full-time students than the White population. This is a very mixed picture with Black Africans (17 per cent) and Indians (15 per cent) more likely to have further and higher education qualifications than White people (13 per cent), and Pakistanis, Black Caribbeans (7 per cent) and Bangladeshis (3 per cent) less likely (CRE, 1995a). However, overall this supports previous research findings that educational aspirations among ethnic minority groups were high (Singh, 1990; Tanna, 1990).

Employment

Levels of racial discrimination are still high in society and this is particularly true in the area of employment. Brown (1984) stated that, 'Britain's well established black population is still occupying the precarious and unattractive position of the earlier immigrants.' Overall in 1991 (CRE, 1995a), ethnic minority men and women were less likely to be economically active than the White population (that is in paid work, or unemployed but actively seeking work). An exception to this pattern is Black Caribbean women, 76 per cent of whom were economically active, which is a higher rate than for White women. Rates for Pakistani (29 per cent) and Bangladeshi (22 per cent) women are much lower. However, it is important to note that these figures are most likely to be under-estimates as they exclude home working and working in family businesses.

Overall the pattern of part-time work among ethnic minority workers is similar to the White population: most part-time jobs are held by women. However, if we look further into the statistics we find a more complex phenomenon: White women are more likely to be working part-time (37.1 per cent) than ethnic minority women (21.7 per cent), but ethnic minority men (4.6 per cent) are more likely to be working part-time than White men (3.5 per cent) (CRE, 1995c).

Occupational segregation

There are still differences between the ethnic minority population and the White population in the sectors and positions in the labour market in which they are found, demonstrating both horizontal and vertical segregation as in the case for women and men shown above. This is particularly so for the South Asian population. They were more likely to be self-employed than the White population, 17 per cent compared with 12 per cent of those in paid work. About one-quarter of all South Asians worked in skilled manual jobs compared with a third of White people. Only 11 per cent of Bangladeshis worked in managerial and technical occupations compared with 29 per cent of the White population. However, Indian men (5 per cent) are much more likely to be health professionals, mainly doctors, than White men (0.7 per cent), although it is important to note that they tend to be concentrated in unpopular specialisms like psychiatry and geriatrics (CRE, 1995c). Whereas only 1 per cent of White people work in the textile and clothing sector, the figure for Indian women and all Pakistanis is 12 per cent. The main areas where there is a difference between the Black and the White population is in the transport and communications sector which employs 18 per cent of Black Caribbean men compared with 9 per cent of White men. Also, only one in five Black Caribbeans worked as a managerial, professional or technical level compared with one in three White people (CRE, 1995a).

In 1994, Britain had only six ethnic minority Members of Parliament, whereas if all things were equal this should be six times higher at 36. Only 1 per cent of solicitors in England are from ethnic minority groups (CRE, 1995c) and there is only one ethnic minority judge at circuit level or above. Ethnic minorities make up only 1.6 per cent of the police force, with all but one officer below the rank of chief superintendent (CRE, 1995a). Studies have shown evidence of racial discrimination in the police force. A recent Home Office Report (1993) found evidence of 'unchallenged racist banter and a general scepticism about senior officers' commitment to equal opportunities'. A major case of racial discrimination was proved in the Singh v. The Chief Constable of The Nottinghamshire Constabulary. Constable Singh had been turned down for promotion to the CID which contained all White officers. The notion of 'fitting in' had been an important component of the selection criteria for promotion to the CID, and the tribunal upheld this as evidence of direct discrimination. With Court of Appeal backing, tribunals now commonly recognize that an excuse such as 'we wanted someone who would fit in' is often a danger signal that the choice was influenced not by the qualifications but by the 'race' of the successful candidate.

However, there has been an important change in the distribution of ethnic minorities between job levels (Jones, 1993). The proportion of Chinese, African Asian, and Indian men is now as high as White men in the top category (professional, managerial, employer). Despite this, Indian men's jobs are still polarized with a higher proportion of Indian men in semi-skilled and unskilled manual jobs than White men. Black Caribbean men still tend to be concentrated in skilled manual jobs. Pakistani and Bangladeshi men are generally still at much lower levels than White men. For women the differences between ethnic groups remains fairly small as in 1982.

In 1982, White men with A levels held distinctly better jobs than their South Asian equivalents. This is no longer the case: men with A levels and above from all ethnic minority groups except Black Caribbeans are more likely to be in professional jobs than Whites. However, if we look at those men with lower or no qualifications, we find that Whites are in higher jobs than ethnic minorities. Therefore, the main change since 1982 has been that highly qualified ethnic minority groups have started to percolate into professional work (Jones, 1993).

Earnings

Overall hourly rates of pay for ethnic minority workers are 10 per cent lower than for White workers (Labour Force Survey, 1995). This is accounted for by the fact that White men earn 17 per cent more than ethnic minority men. If we look at women, the picture is different: ethnic minority women earn slightly more overall than White women because, as shown above, more White women work part-time with the accompanying lower rates of pay than full-time work. Therefore, the low rates of pay for ethnic minority men mean that, unlike a comparison between White men and women, their average earnings per hour are only slightly higher than those of ethnic minority women.

Unemployment

Overall the ethnic minority population is twice as likely to be unemployed as Whites, irrespective of qualifications or job levels. In 1991 (CRE, 1995a) the unemployment rate for people from all ethnic minorities was 18 per cent compared with 9 per cent for the White population.

Among young people the rates were much higher. Figures from the 1991 Census reveal that in London the figure for 16–24 year old ethnic minority men is 40 per cent. Even people from ethnic minority groups with qualifications above A level are less likely than their White counterparts to be employed. A CRE study (1987a) showed that less than half ethnic minority graduates were in full-time jobs 12 months after graduation, compared with 70 per cent of White graduates. More recent figures show that 14 per cent of highly qualified ethnic minority men and 9 per cent of women were unable to get a job, compared with 5 per cent of White men and 4 per cent of women (CRE, 1995c).

Unemployment in 1982 was higher among Black Caribbeans and South Asians than Whites, and they were more vulnerable to rising unemployment, but also more susceptible to lowering unemployment. The gap between Whites and ethnic minorities in terms of unemployment was always there, but widened at times of high unemployment. Since 1982, even though overall rates of unemployment have fallen, the relatively high rates of unemployment among Black Caribbeans, Pakistanis and Bangladeshis have continued. In the mid-1980s, when unemployment was reaching its peak before beginning to fall, the gap between the rate for Whites and certain ethnic minorities was wider than at the end of the decade. The male unemployment rate for Black Caribbeans (26 per cent) was more than double that for Whites (11 per cent). Rates for Pakistani and Bangladeshi men were almost three times as high as Whites. As unemployment fell, the gap became smaller.

In the 1990s, the disparity between the unemployment rates for Whites and ethnic minorities is less, but there is still substantial divergence between ethnic minority groups. While African Asians and Indians have unemployment rates close to Whites, the rates for Black Caribbeans, Pakistanis and Bangladeshis is still much higher. Black groups (23 per cent), Pakistanis (29 per cent) and Bangladeshis (32 per cent) had the highest rates of unemployment within the ethnic minority population. While Black Caribbean men in non-manual occupations experience double the unemployment rate of White men, for Pakistanis the rate was four times (Jones, 1993, pp. 113–14). These differences between specific ethnic minority groups cannot be explained in terms of immigration as they are most marked among young people (16–24 years) who have spent most of their formative years in Britain. This shows that the differences in vulnerability to unemployment between specific ethnic minority groups is likely to persist.

Racial harassment and attacks

The CRE (1995b) defines racial harassment as 'verbal or physical aggression towards individuals or groups because of their colour, race, nationality, or ethnic or national origin' including 'attacks on property as well as on people' (p. 1). Racial harassment is a serious and widespread phenomenon in Britain. The Home Affairs Committee report (1986) stated that 'the most shameful and dispiriting aspect of "race" relations in Britain is the incidence of racial attacks and harassment'. In 1981, the Home Office report 'Racial Attacks' contained the first official estimates of racially motivated offences. It showed that Asians were 50 times more likely than Whites to be victims, and Black Caribbeans 36 times more likely. The British Crime Survey in 1992 estimated that there were 130 000 racially motivated crimes, 89 000 against South Asians and 41 000 against Black Caribbeans. While there is no overall evidence to show that racial attacks and harassment are increasing, we do see an increase in the number reported to the police. From 1988 to 1993 the total for England and Wales more than doubled in the London area. Also, it is estimated that only just over half of all racial incidents are reported to the police, and not all racial incidents are recorded as such (CRE, 1997a).

This disturbing phenomenon is spread throughout Europe. The 1990 Report of the Inquiry into Racism and Xenophobia to the European Parliament has shown Britain as a place where:

Within the four year period under review, there have been year after year reports of systematic and increasingly widespread racial violence which point to increasing ethnic tension . . . Racist attacks have taken the form of hooliganism and terrorising ethnic minority groups: their children have to put up with all sorts of racial harassment and violence and at home, they receive threatening phone calls, excreta and racist literature are pushed through their letter boxes, as well as petrol which is then ignited . . . There was the case of an Asian mother who used to see her two children spat on and stoned as they left home. Excrement was smeared on her door repeatedly. She did not seek help until her children had knives thrown at them, mainly because she thought that this was normal behaviour and expected nothing different (Ford, 1992).

Disability

Statistical data on disabled people are much more sparse than those available in the areas of gender and 'race'. Fewer nationally gathered statistics are broken down into the categories of disabled and non-disabled. The Office of Population and Censuses and Surveys (OPCS) carried out the only major national surveys of disability in Britain between 1985 and 1988. They have been criticized, primarily for using the medical model of disability based on an individual pathological approach rather than the social model of disability advocated by disabled people themselves (Oliver, 1996) (for a fuller discussion see Chapter 2 of this book). In the surveys, the authors focused on disability as 'a restriction or lack of ability to perform normal activities, which has resulted from the impairment of a structure or function of the body or mind' (Martin *et al.*, 1988, p. xi). From this definition, OPCS constructed a continuum of severity of disability based on 13 medical categories. Despite their faults, these surveys are the only ones that are relatively recent and extensive and provide us with the most comprehensive current statistics on disabled people.

Population figures

OPCS estimated that there are just over six million adults with one or more disabilities in Great Britain. The overall rate of disability rises with age, increasing significantly after 50 years and rising even more sharply after 70. The vast majority of disabled people (93 per cent) live in private households. This means that almost 14 per cent of all adults living in private households have at least one disability. Not surprisingly, the survey found that the proportion of disabled people living in private households diminished as one ascended their severity scale of disability. Whereas almost all of the one million adults in the lowest category of disability were living in private households, only half of the 200 000 adults in the highest category did so.

From the OPCS survey, we can see that there are considerably more disabled women than men at all except the lowest severity levels. In total there are over three-and-a-half million disabled women compared with about two-and-a-half million disabled men in Britain as a whole. This is partly because women live longer than men, therefore they experience more age-related disability. However, among those in the age group 75 or over, the rate of disability is higher for women, even after controlling for the greater proportion of elderly women. Therefore, we can say that elderly women are more likely to be disabled than elderly men. There are also geographical differences in the rates of disability. After standardizing for age distributions, the North, Wales and Yorkshire and Humberside had the highest rates of disability, while the southern regions had lower than average rates.

Employment

Martin and White (1988) used the data collected by OPCS to examine the financial circumstances of the disabled people living in private households. They set out 'to examine the extent to which disability affects people's income; to establish whether extra expenditure is incurred as a result of disability and to estimate the magnitude of that expenditure; [and] to evaluate the overall impact of disability on the standard of living and financial circumstances of disabled adults and their families' (p. xv). They show that disabled people of working age are much less likely to be employed than non-disabled people, even when the figures are controlled for age, sex and marital status. Only a minority of disabled people of working age are in paid employment (31 per cent), which means that 69 per cent have to rely on social security benefits for all or part of their income. Disability clearly affects the chances of being in paid work. The proportion of employed disabled people decreased with the increase in the severity of disability, from 48 per cent in the least severe category, down to only 2 per cent in the most severe category. Interestingly, unmarried disabled people were less likely to be working than those who were married.

Income

If we look at disabled people's income generated from earnings, benefits and other sources, we find that disabled people are among the
poorest in our society. On average, disabled working-age families had
only 72 per cent of the equivalent income of non-disabled working-age
families, and 34 per cent of disabled adults of working age had incomes
below the average for the general population, compared with 23 per
cent of equivalent non-disabled adults. One of the main reasons for this,
as mentioned above, is that most disabled people have to rely on social
security benefits for all or part of their income. Altogether 75 per cent
of disabled adults rely on state benefits (including retirement pension)
for their main source of income. The survey found that 35 per cent of
working-age families received a disability-related income maintenance
benefit, and 23 per cent were receiving supplementary benefit (now
called job-seekers allowance). More than half of all disabled house-
holders were in receipt of housing benefit.

It is also true that families of disabled adults with one or more
earners still had lower average incomes than non-disabled families with
the same number of earners. Both male and female disabled full-time
workers earn less than non-disabled workers, and this difference is not
accounted for by their hours of working. They are to be found in lower
paid jobs, both manual and non-manual. On average, full-time male
disabled workers earned only 81 per cent of equivalent non-disabled
male workers, and disabled women earned 88 per cent of equivalent
non-disabled women. Among disabled people there was also a decrease
in earnings as the severity of their disability increased.

Extra expenditure

In addition to the problem of lower incomes generally, disabled people
often incur extra expenditure because of their disability. On average,
disabled people were found to spend 8 per cent of their income on
disability-related expenditure. This includes two types of expenditure:
special expenditure on items specific to disabled people, such as equipment, furniture, medical and care costs; but also additional expenditure
on items required by non-disabled people, on which disabled people
need to spend more, such as fuel, clothing, bedding, travel, food and
laundry. The survey found that altogether 60 per cent of disabled adults
incurred regular expenditure on specific items for their disability, and 71
per cent spent more on items required by non-disabled people because
of their disability.

As would be expected, both of these types of expenditure rose
with the increasing severity of disability. Those in the severest category
of disability were spending on average 15 per cent of their income on
disability-related expenses. However, expenditure on disability was also
found to rise with level of income. This implies that many disabled
people are unable to spend the amount they need on their disability

because of low income levels. Altogether 24 per cent of disabled adults stated that they needed to spend more, but their incomes prevented them. The combination of generally lower incomes and extra expenditure on disability-related items means that disabled adults of working age have much less to spend on other items than equivalent non-disabled adults. On average, they have only 67 per cent of the remaining income of non-disabled adults.

We can see from this government-sponsored survey of disability that despite the well-justified criticisms of its methodology, it demonstrates that on average disabled people have lower incomes than non-disabled people. They are less likely to be in paid work, but if they are they earn less than non-disabled workers in general. They are therefore heavily reliant on state benefits with the resultant effect of low incomes. The majority incur extra expenditure of one sort or another because of their disability, and many cannot spend what they need. 'Overall, disabled adults are likely to experience some financial problems and to have lower standards of living than the population as a whole as a result of having lower average incomes' (Martin and White, 1988, p. xviii).

Summary

This chapter has explained the relevance of 'equal opportunities' for social policy in Britain today and answered the questions: Why do we need 'equal opportunities'? And why is 'equal opportunities' important to social policy? It is argued that the idea of 'equal opportunities' is at the core of social policy because social policy as a discipline concerns itself with the relationship between opportunities to access welfare services and the outcome of particular services on different groups within society. The fundamental argument promoted in this chapter is that we need 'equal opportunities' policies in Britain today to attempt to overcome inequality which still exists for the particular groups concentrated on in this book: women, ethnic minorities and disabled people.

The second part of the chapter examines the continuing inequality experienced first by women, then ethnic minority groups and finally disabled people by presenting some of the pertinent and relevant statistics available. From these we can see that gender, 'race' and disability continue to create economic and social divisions in Britain today. We find that although girls' and women's achievements are continuing to increase in the education system at all levels, there is still clearly defined segregation of women and men in different disciplines. More women now participate in the labour market, but equal pay has not been achieved or even moved towards in any meaningful way, and segregation of jobs by gender still remains. Also, women still carry the major burden of unpaid work because of their responsibility for family and home in the private domain.

In the area of 'race', examination of the education system provides a complex picture. Although there is still evidence of considerable underachievement by some groups, differential achievement patterns are emerging between different ethnic minority communities. However, racial discrimination covered by the Race Relations Act 1976 has certainly not decreased as fast as expected in the subsequent decades. In the labour market there are still high levels of racial discrimination, a pattern of segregation of jobs with ethnic minorities generally in lower paid, less secure positions and with higher levels of unemployment. Also, they have to contend with the widespread phenomenon of criminal racial harassment and violence.

The latest government survey acknowledges the scale of disadvantage linked to disability. Disabled people of working age are much less likely to be employed than non-disabled people. Only a minority of disabled people of working age are in paid employment, but if they are they earn less than non-disabled workers in general. Therefore, the majority have to rely on social security benefits for all or part of their income. In addition, the majority of disabled people incur extra expenditure of one sort or another because of their disability, and many cannot afford to spend what they need. This means that disabled people are among the poorest in Britain today.

CHAPTER 2

What is 'equal opportunities'? What do we mean by 'equal opportunities'?

To answer these questions this chapter will consider the area of theory in 'equal opportunities'. This will be examined on a societal level, on an organizational level, and from the perspective of the specific areas covered in the book: disability, 'race' and gender.

'Equal opportunities' as a concept is complex, contentious and controversial. It is linked to other important values such as social justice, which some would argue is a fundamental underpinning to liberal democratic societies. However, it is important to acknowledge that in highly stratified, modern industrial societies any move towards 'equal opportunities' would involve a fundamental change in power and reward in 'race', gender and disability relations, and the implications these have for people's life chances and social and economic positions. Even at an institutional level 'equal opportunities' can stoke up conflicts and expose difficulties within organizations that were previously dormant. It means different things to different people, and those members of society and particular organizations who have already benefited from inequality – usually White, non-disabled men – may resist 'equal opportunities' policies if they feel that their opportunities and prospects are threatened.

Everyone has an opinion and often a deeply held and emotional viewpoint on 'equal opportunities', and are often keen to share it! Some people are passionately in favour and some passionately against. When I worked as an Equal Opportunities Officer in local government, I soon learned not to admit to it at social gatherings to avoid either confrontation or lectures on how to do it better. 'Many people have still not disentangled equal opportunities from its specific political history' (Cheung-Judge and Henley, 1994, p. 3). The historical, ideological and political background to 'equal opportunities' still influences people's perception of it and their attitude towards it (see Chapter 3 for a discussion of this background to 'equal opportunities'). It still creates confusion, apprehension and suspicion in many people's minds, and is still associated by some with what they picture as the political extremism of the hard left. Some people, who were committed to 'equal opportunities' and have been early champions of its introduction into their own organizations, have also become disillusioned by the lack of success or slowness of achieving rewards, and their realization of the complexity, intricacy and long-term nature of the animal.

'Equal opportunities' has certainly spawned and attracted many myths that can camouflage the facts. These are a few suggestions taken from a Mencap leaflet: 'It's for Black people only. It's anti-White. It helps minorities at the expense of majorities. It means not employing the best people so standards drop. It's left-wing propaganda. It leads to conflict. It doesn't work' (Cheung-Judge and Henley, 1994). I am sure we can all add many more! They can all be countered with more dispassionate and logical statements. 'It aims for equality for all. It upholds social justice. It says no to discrimination. It makes the best use of human resources. It wants services to be accessible to everyone. It makes services appropriate to need. It gives people a fair chance in getting jobs. It is a legal obligation' (Cheung-Judge and Henley, 1994).

Research suggests that the debates around what 'equal opportunities' really mean at a societal and an organizational level raise many questions. Fundamental examples are: do we mean 'equality of opportunity' or 'equality of outcome'? (Jewson and Mason, 1986); and how much inequality or reward differential should there be in total in society or in an organization? (Cockburn, 1991). (These concepts and ideas are discussed later in this chapter.) This confusion points to the need for a rounded educational approach to 'equal opportunities', rather than a more narrow 'implementation of procedures' approach. In other words, these issues need to be discussed and be part of an awareness-training programme within organizations to assist in the effective implementation of formal policies and procedures.

Because of this complexity, 'equal opportunities' has to have a 'long agenda' not a 'short' one (Cockburn, 1991). Several reasons account for this imperative. As some 'equal opportunities' issues are dealt with others arise; there are often no easy solutions and in some cases no 'right' answers; one standard model set of policies cannot suit the needs of all organizations. In addition, 'equal opportunities' policies require organizations to commit resources to ensure their acceptance and implementation: for example, providing awareness training, altering buildings to make them accessible and user-friendly for disabled people, providing nurseries, personal leave schemes for staff at all levels, and workloads that recognize that staff may have caring responsibilities. 'Equal opportunities' is not just about conforming to procedures but also about how organizations function on a formal and informal level and the outcomes of this for employment and service delivery.

Despite all this controversy, many people would agree that, at least in theory, at both a societal and organizational level, 'equal opportunities' is desirable. It can be seen as conjuring up and being built on the commendable cornerstones of fairness, justice, morality, impartiality and accountability. 'This commitment to fairness and justice has helped many people stick with equal opportunities despite real problems caused largely by the way it has been handled' (Cheung-Judge and Henley, 1994, p. 4).

Definitions of 'equal opportunities'

Jenkins and Solomos (1989) showed that 'terms such as "equality of opportunity", "equality of access", "anti-discrimination policies", etc., have gained a wide currency over the last few years. So much so that there is much confusion and unease about what each of these terms means and, perhaps more fundamentally, what kind of objectives they are supposed to fulfil' (p. 3). However, both supporters and opponents of 'equal opportunities' can at least agree that it is not a simple concept with a shared understanding in society. Despite the difficulties of definition, we do need at this stage a reasonably clear and agreed idea of what the term 'equal opportunities' means: that is, a working definition to carry the discussion further. Perhaps we can begin by using one of the simplest and most common definitions of 'equal opportunities' which rests on the premise of not acting or treating anyone in a blatantly discriminatory manner. Collins (1992) offers us just such a definition: 'Basically equal opportunities is about treating everybody fairly and equally regardless of background or lifestyle' (p. 3).

However, this definition of 'equal opportunities' is based on the now disputed premise of treating everyone the same. It is important to note that different treatment can be meted out, not only in an unjust way, but also as part of the furtherance of 'equal opportunities'. The concepts behind unequal treatment and arguments for its use in the name of 'equal opportunities' are examined in the next section.

Theory at the societal level: should we treat everyone the same?

Discrimination and prejudice

Discrimination and prejudice are fundamental concepts which underpin unequal treatment of both individuals and groups within society. Discrimination leads to differential treatment of people ascribed to particular social categories. 'To establish that an action is discriminatory it is necessary to show that someone is treated differently because s/he is thought to belong to such a category; it therefore entails a comparison of a particular action with others' (Marshall, 1994). Different judgements and distinctions are not necessarily unfair or unjustifiable discrimination, but they may be. To decide whether discriminatory behaviour is just or unjust we need to know the grounds used for it, i.e. whether there is an objective or reasonable justification. British 'equal opportunities' legislation penalizes discriminatory behaviour based on sex, marital status, colour, 'race', ethnicity, national origins and disability.

Prejudice often informs unjust discrimination. Although it must be acknowledged that there can be prejudice towards a particular group, it is more frequently defined as holding hostile or negative attitudes towards individuals 'solely on the basis of their group membership, rather than their own merits' (Hilgard *et al.*, 1979). People often generalize about both individuals and groups. As Hilgard *et al.* (1979) explained, this is a necessary part of life. 'Generalizing from a set of experiences and treating individuals as members of a group are common and necessary practices. It is simply not possible to deal with every new person as if he or she were unique' (p. 548). However, when generalizations concern groups they are often called stereotypes, especially when beliefs about a group are over-generalized, if not misinformed or false, and applied too broadly to each member of the group.

In trying to explain negative prejudice, the first theories looked at personality types. It was felt that the more dogmatic, conservative, closed-minded personality would be more prejudiced (Adorno *et al.*, 1950). Then came theories which emphasized social variables. A relationship was found between a person's dissatisfaction with their financial position and the general political state of their country, and prejudice against certain groups. As part of this process 'scapegoating' was recognized as a substitution of targets for aggression and hostility (Hilgard *et al.*, 1979). Prejudice can be reduced through contact between different groups, but contact is not enough on its own as many studies concerned with White people's prejudice to ethnic minorities have shown (Cook, 1978). Certain conditions need to be present to reduce prejudice; the contact must be between those of equal status and individuals that counter our stereotypes, there must be potential for personal acquaintance, support for intergroup contact and pursuit of common goals (Cook, 1978).

Types of equality

If we take 'equal opportunities' just to mean avoiding unjust discrimination and prejudice – or in other words rationally and impartially treating everyone the same – this is a very simple and rather superficial conceptualization, which does not expose the complexity of the social, political and economic issues contained in the concept. Marshall (1994) takes us further in our attempt to unpack the concept of 'equal opportunities'. He recognized three main types of equality, which may help us in our search for a fuller understanding by enabling more penetrating examination of the complex concept of 'equal opportunities'. The definitions get deeper and more radical as we progress through them. First there is **'equality of opportunity'**, which is 'the provision of equality of access to institutions and social positions among relevant social groups'. An example of this would be that there are no formal rules that prohibit women's entry to university education. However, despite this, it is only very recently that women have entered higher education in the same numbers as men, and still they are concentrated in certain disciplines and only make up 20 per cent of the academic staff.

Second, Marshall (1994) offers us the concept of **'equality of condition'**. That is, equality not only of access but also in the circumstances of life for different social groups. It is possible to maximize 'equality of opportunity' without attending to 'equality of condition', as we have seen in the example of university education: merely allowing equal access does not resolve the unequal chances of achievement. Proponents of 'equality of opportunity' who relish the differential benefits obtained by persons with different resources ignore the basis of the material and cultural advantages, which some groups in society possess and others lack. Inequalities of 'condition' can be said to obstruct real 'equality of opportunity' because all those who are competing do not start from the same point.

Finally, we are offered the definition of **'equality of result or outcome'** (Marshall, 1994). This offers a **radical approach** to 'equal opportunities', which is the application of different policies or processes to different social groups in order to transform inequalities of condition at the beginning into equalities at the end (this is discussed more fully in the later section of this chapter dealing with the theory of 'equal opportunities' in organizations). An example here would be positive action in favour of women entering higher education in offering them access courses to disciplines where they are severely under-represented, such as science and engineering, to compensate for inequalities of 'condition', such as the lack of relevant qualifications due to inappropriate choices at earlier levels of education, which it can be argued restrict their 'equality of opportunity'. Jencks (1988) described this approach as the favourable treatment of those who have been disadvantaged by previous and historical discrimination and disadvantage, which leads us to the important and challenging idea that 'past disadvantages require us to treat people unequally' (p. 48).

Parekh (1992a) is one writer who has advocated the idea of preferential treatment for disadvantaged groups, because 'in spite of its limitations it is one of the few policy tools capable of breaking through the self-perpetuating cycle of deeply entrenched inequalities' (p. 278). On the other hand, Cunningham (1992) argued against this position. He takes a fundamental view that, because the source of many inequalities of 'condition' start early in life and are personal, it 'would require considerable intrusion on individual liberty and the family, and this is both unrealistic and impossible to enforce' (p. 178). As we see again 'equal opportunities' remains a contested concept often determined by one's political commitments and general fundamental outlook on society and life.

Positive action

Unequal treatment in the name of 'equal opportunities' is allowed in British 'equal opportunities' legislation in the areas of gender and 'race'. It thereby acknowledges the need for and condones different treatment to counteract past discrimination and disadvantages experienced by groups. However, this is only possible in very restricted ways as positive action in the areas of training and advertising. As Gregory (1987) argued, most of the legislation rests on ideas of individual disadvantage and redress, and therefore not on substantial change to structures within society (Chapter 3 has a full discussion of the legislation).

Legal positive action can be distinguished quite clearly from illegal positive or reverse discrimination. 'Although positive action focuses on group outcomes (for instance, representative proportions of men and women), the emphasis is still upon individual merit or capabilities'

(Blakemore and Drake, 1996, p. 11). Positive action is about bringing individuals up to a point, for example through training or the acquisition of qualifications, where they can compete equally with other individuals. Despite popular myth, it does not constitute preferential treatment which gives people jobs purely because they are women or ethnic minorities. However, although legitimate positive action has not actually been fully utilized (Pitt, 1992) due to lack of understanding, those who are perceived to have gained from it are more likely to have negative evaluations made of them by their peers (Heilman, 1994).

It is a commonly held view that preferential treatment for disadvantaged groups is based on the aim of 'proportionality, that is, to ensuring that disadvantaged groups are represented in all, most or even major institutions in proportion to their number in the population at large' (Parekh, 1992a, p. 270). While the concept of proportionality is linked to the idea of moving towards 'equality of outcome' by increasing the numbers of under-represented groups to somewhere near their representation elsewhere, this might be tempered and circumscribed in various ways, for example, by proportions of ethnic minorities in the local area, or by the proportion of suitably qualified women in the recruitment catchment area of an organization. Therefore, if the principle of proportionality is accepted, flexible approaches can be dealt with on an administrative and practical level. In fact the British 'equal opportunities' legislation legitimizes positive action for particular groups on the basis that they are disproportionately under-represented in certain positions or levels within an organization.

Morris and Nott (1991) advocated the radical approach of different treatment in the area of gender, which acknowledges previous and present inequality of condition. Their argument ran along the lines that:

Eliminating discrimination and outlawing different treatment between men and women does not represent 'equality of opportunity' because it does not and cannot address the fundamental disadvantages that women experience throughout their lives. To aim simply to eliminate discrimination and ensure equal treatment, as opposed to 'equality of opportunity', is tantamount to asserting that the Ritz is open to all – the availability of a facility does not mean that everyone has the wherewithal to take advantage of it. Thus, an employer who espouses an 'equal opportunities' policy and advertises jobs accordingly is doubtless to be commended, but the policy is meaningless if no woman is in a position to apply because of the age limits imposed or the qualifications demanded or if the hours required rule out those with domestic commitments (p. 193). [As they acknowledged] ... special treatment for women in the form of additional rights, positive action or positive discrimination might be said to advance the cause of equality of opportunity, but this is at the cost of equal treatment ... the argument that according special treatment to women implies discrimination against men ... has to be faced. (p. 194)

Justice

More backing for the radical approach can be drawn from philosophical debates that have addressed the concept of 'justice'. Rawls (1971) claimed that the principles of 'justice' were those that would be chosen by persons located behind a veil of ignorance that rendered them ignorant of their own future position in the world: that is, how rational and impartial individuals would reason. Deprived of any knowledge of their own economic interests, rational people would favour the difference principle, according to which inequalities are only just if they work to the advantage of the least well off. Therefore, 'justice' is concerned with ensuring that every person receives what is due to them (Cohen, 1986) on the basis of their particular characteristics and circumstances (Buchanan and Mathieu, 1986) even if this means unequal treatment. As Buchanan and Mathieu (1986) put it: 'People should be treated as equals in the proportion that they are equals . . . [and] . . . people should be treated as unequals only to the extent that they are unequal' (p. 18).

In other words, people should be treated in ways that enable them to enjoy the same level of well-being or quality of life as everyone else. 'In this way, the principle of equality does not prescribe positively that all human beings be treated alike . . . To act justly, then, is to treat all men [*sic*] alike except where there are relevant differences between them' (Benn and Peters, 1959, p. 111). Where relevant differences between cases are identified, Frankena (1962) argued that it was not unjust to treat different cases in different ways.

If the most general definition of justice is that each person should have what they are entitled to according to personal characteristics and circumstances, how do we decide on that entitlement? Miller (1976) put forward three main principles of distributive justice, '**rights, deserts, and needs**', none of which dictated an 'equal treatment' approach to 'equal opportunities'. The first principle of '**rights**' was relatively straightforward: an individual receives justice according to the rules and regulations within their society. Second, in terms of '**deserts**', individuals are rewarded in terms of such things as their moral virtues, productive efforts, capacities and merit. As shown above, the principle of selecting people on merit is enshrined in the 'equal opportunities' legislation where, even when legitimate positive action is taken either in the form of advertising or training, final selection for posts must be made on what is generally termed the principle of 'the best person for the job'. As Pitt (1992) argued 'positive action is not committed to the preference of a less-qualified candidate' (p. 282).

However, despite popular impressions this approach is not unproblematic. There is the assumption that 'merit's claim to reward is morally self-evident and needs no justification', whereas in reality '. . . what constitutes merit is a social decision and a matter of social policy' (Parekh, 1992a, p. 276). We have to question what traditional definitions of merit actually expound. The accepted criteria for merit are maintained by the established and the powerful, which may yield them a false veneer of objectivity. Also, Parekh (1992a) asked us to consider whether holding traditionally defined merit, such as the highest qualifications, does always by itself confer rights to employment. 'It views merit as the sole basis of desert, which it is not . . . it is an important source of the claim, but not the only one' (p. 275). We need to accept that 'equal opportunities' based on the concept of 'deserts' is complex. For example, some disabled people and women may have lower productive capabilities in certain areas of paid work, but contribute different qualities. In the case of women, a wider societal approach would lead to recognition of other contributions to society, such as caring for dependent children. Also, importantly, some groups in society, while not holding conventional qualifications, may have other skills, such as language or an empathy with particular cultures that mean that they are 'the best person for the job'.

Finally, in the area of '**needs**', individuals are entitled to the things they lack or are necessary to them. This needs-based approach would appear the most rational and to favour the more radical '**equality of outcome**' approach to 'equal opportunities' by treating people differently where it is warranted. However, the great difficulties in defining need should not be under-estimated (Jencks, 1988). Blakemore and Drake (1996) argued that what they coin as this 'humane justice' approach to equality 'despite its great potential, is beset with unresolved questions' (p. 46). This can be illustrated in the area of disability. Oliver (1996) argues strongly against a needs-based approach because the power relations between disabled people and professionals, either medical practitioners or social workers, determine that they interpret and define needs, not the disabled people themselves.

'Equal opportunities' in practice

As was argued earlier, the various different views and theories of 'equal opportunities' make it a complex and difficult concept. Although it is important to look at the concepts and ideas behind it to further our understanding, if we get too bogged down in the theory we may lose sight of the practicalities and demands of application to different groups in different societies and times. It is therefore useful to measure the relative merits of these different approaches on a more practical and applied level. The justifications for these approaches must be set in a social, political and economic and even organizational context. This may lead to the ironing out of what appear to be contradictions and philosophical flaws. An example of this was Glazer's (1987) opinion that while affirmative action has had an highly unfavourable influence on American society, it is at the same time totally acceptable and even desirable to alleviate and improve the position of the lower castes in India. Also, different approaches and justifications may be used for different groups within the same society. Certain measures may be accepted in the area of disability, which are not appropriate for gender because of different historical and present-day situations of different groups. As Blakemore and Drake (1996) pointed out, 'although there are important philosophical arguments to consider in relation to different concepts of equal opportunity, they cannot be applied as absolute principle' (p. 75). 'Equal opportunities' is a matter of social policy. As such it is affected by political, economic and practical considerations, it is open to debate, different priority setting and, ultimately, decisions on the desirability of outcomes. The next section considers theories around the more practical application of 'equal opportunities' at an organizational level.

Theory of 'equal opportunities' in organizations

There is relatively little theoretical underpinning of the area of 'equal opportunities' at an organizational level. Its imprecise conceptualization has led to a plethora of different understandings, assumptions and methods of policy implementation. The practice of 'equal opportunities' is linked most strongly to management theory – where it is linked to any theory at all – and it does not have a long history of research. There has been relatively little work done on trying to theorize 'equal opportunities' in Britain.

At an organizational level, the **'equality of treatment'** approach dictates that 'equal opportunities' means 'policies and practices [that] do not result in any individual or group receiving less favourable treatment on grounds that are not material' (Cheung-Judge and Henley, 1994, p. 4). Despite the detailed list of immaterial grounds offered by Cheung-Judge and Henley ('race, colour, ethnic or national origin, creed, gender, marital status, religious belief, class, disability or sexuality'), some of which exceed the British legislative base (such as religious belief, class and sexuality), other grounds can always be added: for example, the social division of age is growing in significance and recognition. Action on these issues usually takes the form of the introduction of regulations on procedures and practices that are designed to eradicate discriminatory practice and ensure equal treatment. While this is certainly an important aspect of reducing disadvantage, it can be argued not sufficient, in that it does not recognize or acknowledge the ideas of 'different needs and the different capabilities of different people' (Clarke, 1990).

We can move on from this approach to differentiate institutional policies and practices based more on issues of outcomes and results, the **'equality of outcome'** approach. The CRE (1989a) undertook research to assess the impact of its Code of Practice (CRE, 1984a), which was designed to eliminate racial discrimination and promote equality of opportunity in employment. The survey of 899 employers revealed a high level of awareness of the Code, but only at a basic level. About two-thirds of employers had formal written policies. However, very few of these policies were comprehensive with effective monitoring in place. The CRE identified the differentiation between procedures and outcomes. Many employers mistakenly assumed that 'once the processes and procedures were put right the organisation would be an equal opportunity employer, irrespective of the end result' (p. 37).

This essential difference between procedures and outcomes was taken up by Jewson and Mason (1986) when they conceptualized 'equal opportunities' into two basic approaches, the **'liberal'** and **'radical'** perspectives.

They later extended these to identify three distinct positions on 'equal opportunities': the '**minimalist**' position, '**liberal**' perspective and '**radical**' perspective (Jewson and Mason, 1993). The '**minimalist**' perspective, commonly encountered in private industry and among politicians of the right, assumed that market decisions will maximize fairness, and only individual irrationality and prejudice introduce distortions.

The '**liberal**' perspective went a stage further, starting from the premise that 'equality of opportunity exists when all individuals are enabled freely and equally to compete for social rewards . . . policy makers are required to ensure that the rules of competition are not discriminatory' (Jewson and Mason, 1986). It took on the '**equality of treatment**' approach assuming that a 'level playing ground' will ensure 'equal opportunities', and recognizing that institutional discrimination may exist in the form of unfair procedures and practices. The task of 'equal opportunities' was seen as the elimination of barriers to free competition between individuals. It emphasized the development of fair, bureaucratic and formal procedures and rules for recruitment and selection, and training in these procedures. 'For liberals the aim of the policy is to ensure that procedural justice is done and seen to be done' (Jewson *et al.*, 1995). This approach was favoured by private businesses that recognized that these policies produced insurance against potential future legal problems and difficulties, and preserved a reputation for good employment practice or paternalism, which was good for public relations and thus gave a commercial advantage.

Finally, they identified the '**radical**' perspective, which took 'equal opportunities' on to another plane by adopting the '**equality of outcome**' approach. This was most often encountered in local authorities and on the political left. In contrast to the other two approaches it 'seeks to intervene directly in workplace practices in order to achieve a fair distribution of rewards among employees . . . [it is] primarily concerned with the outcome of the contest rather than the rules of the game'. It rejected individualistic conceptions of fairness and placed it at the level of the group. This was seen as a far more politicized approach and training programmes were directed 'to raise the consciousness of the oppressed and the oppressors' (Jewson *et al.*, 1995).

In practice, Jewson and Mason acknowledged that the approaches they identified were 'ideal types' not seen in a pure form in reality. They argued that in fact those engaged in forming 'equal opportunities' policies were 'rarely theoretically or logically consistent' and 'practical political pressures as well as confused thinking' often led to a mixing of the 'liberal' and 'radical' approaches (Jewson *et al.*, 1995). Cockburn (1989) examined their conceptualization and argued that their dichotomy of the '**liberal**' and '**radical**' approaches is not an adequate interpretation of what was really happening. She built on their theory by suggesting and adding the idea that organizations in pursuit of 'equal opportunities' for women adopted either a '**short**' or a '**long agenda**'. The '**short agenda**' was broadly akin to the liberal approach and introduced new measures to minimize bias in recruitment and promotion. The '**long**

agenda' instead 'has to be recognised as a project of transformation for organisations . . . it brings into view the nature and purpose of institutions and the processes by which the power of some groups over others in institutions is built and renewed'. So it favoured the radical approach, but went further because it 'looks for change in the nature of power, in the melting away of the white male monoculture'.

Cockburn's (1989) 'long agenda' approach has not been widely recognized or adopted in the 1990s. Within organizations the original push to get 'equal opportunities' on the agenda was often a **'radical'** one, but when accepted by management it can and does become institutionalized as a matter of procedures. There is an emphasis now on considering 'equal opportunities' as part of general organizational change theory. Opportunity 2000, the government-backed campaign to increase women's participation in management, both in terms of numbers and their position, is heavily based on this approach, stressing the rationale for 'equal opportunities' as good business practice. So too is much of the work done on women in management, which often concentrates on the stresses placed on women in the workplace, but largely suggests methods of adaptation and assimilation for them to use (Davidson and Cooper, 1992), rather than suggesting that cultural change of the organization is appropriate.

Another new approach along these lines that had its origins in the USA is the idea of 'managing diversity' (Kandola *et al.*, 1995). Having acknowledged that the workforce consists of a diverse population of people, this approach argues that the way forward is to 'harness' these differences to 'create a productive environment in which each person feels valued, where their talents are being fully utilised, and in which organisational goals are met'. Kandola *et al.* (1995) argue that this approach differs from traditional 'equal opportunities' practice in a number of ways: it goes beyond the minimalist approach of compliance with anti-discrimination legislation; it embraces all individuals, not simply targeted groups and so avoids resistance from groups outside the focus of 'equal opportunities' policies; and it aims to challenge the culture of organizations. However, this approach has been criticized primarily for being individualistic and therefore not addressing the issue of group inequality within an organization.

The next section in this chapter considers the groups that 'equal opportunities' legislation has identified for attention: women, ethnic minorities, and disabled people, and examines the theoretical underpinnings of disability, 'race' and gender.

Which groups is 'equal opportunities' concerned about? Definitions and theoretical underpinnings of disability, 'race' and gender from an 'equal opportunities' perspective

'Equal opportunities' is concerned with all the groups in society who experience disadvantage and discriminatory treatment. This can include treatment based on the grounds of gender, 'race', disability, sexuality, social class and age. However, as mentioned in Chapter 1, this book concentrates on the areas of gender, 'race' and disability because these are the areas covered by legislation in Britain. Disability was the first area to come under the law – albeit in a very limited way – just after the Second World War. Then in the 1960s and 1970s came legislation on 'race' and gender. The Acts on gender were amended in the 1980s because of pressure from the European Union, as it is now called, and for the first time anti-discrimination legislation came on to the statute book for disabled people in the 1990s (see Chapter 3 for a fuller discussion of the legislation).

Before discussing the theories about and background to the disadvantage experienced by women, ethnic minorities and disabled people it is important to acknowledge that these are not exclusive categories or homogenous groups. An illustration of this is the way in which Morris (1991a, 1992a) took issue with feminist analysis that viewed the care of disabled people as an oppression for women as disadvantaged workers. This approach was taken to its limit by Finch's (1984) statement that: 'On balance it seems to me that the residential route is the only one which ultimately will offer us a way out of the impasse of caring' (p. 16). Morris saw this as based on the assumption that women were all non-disabled and as totally denying the existence and numerical dominance of women among disabled people. 'Such definitions ignore, and thus perpetuate the oppression of, impaired people, the majority of whom, in Britain today at least, are women' (p. 73).

Like all social divisions in society they can be manifested in an individual in different ways and with a different impact at different times and in different circumstances. When we look at the relationships between gender, 'race' and disability, we must see them as dynamic and interactive. It is not enough to add mixed categories such as ethnic minority women or disabled women into existing frameworks. At first terms like 'double' then 'triple' oppression were used to try to conceptualize the complexity of people's experiences and disadvantage. More sophisticated analyses referred to the way that 'race', like other social divisions, altogether reconstituted the way in which oppressions were manifest and experienced rather than just adding an extra layer (Williams, 1989; Anthias and Yuval-Davis, 1993). As Begum (1994) pointed out: 'Potentially the list [of oppressions] is endless, but simply counting the different types of oppression will not tell us anything. Notions of "double disadvantage" or "triple jeopardy" do nothing to facilitate understanding of multiple and simultaneous oppression' (p. 17). Brah (1992a) in her examination of the issues facing Asian women in Britain set a model for considering the complex interaction of gender and 'race' instead of the old model of multiple disadvantages piled on top of one another. She analysed 'the social processes through which gender divisions have been constructed and reproduced against the background of colonialisation and imperialism' (p. 64). She argued that: 'Capitalism, patriarchy and imperialism are *not* independent albeit interlocking systems – they are part of the same structure. Capitalist social relations are themselves patriarchal and imperialist in form' (p. 64).

What we have to deal with are multiple layers of identity and intersection of factors. For example, an ethnic minority woman may encounter either sexism or racism at different times and in different circumstances or she may experience one or the other oppression tempered and changed by the other. Joseph and Lewis (1981) offer a fairytale analogy to explain this phenomenon. Three ethnic minority women assume the role of Snow White, rather than the Black Queen! They each in turn respond to the question: 'Mirror, mirror on the wall, what is the greatest oppressor of us all?' The first woman argues that, being Black, racism is the main cause of her oppression. The second explains that her life is dominated and controlled by men, therefore sexism is her greatest oppressor. The third woman says that it is not possible to respond because her gender, 'race' and class were all causes of her oppression.

If we take the oppressions of racism, sexism and disablism, a person can be pictured as a sponge floating on a societal pool of social divisions. The liquid contains a mixture of sexism, racism and disablism both in individual portions and in different mixes. At certain times the sponge will encounter and soak up various disadvantages, and in different combinations and proportions. This imagery is not meant to suggest passivity on the part of the oppressed individual but rather that what the oppression demands is a pragmatic reaction. An ethnic minority woman might need to fight racism at one point and sexism at another time, and at other times the sexism she is fighting is tainted and influenced by racism. Her allies may change in these different fights and so might her strategy. The dynamic mix of sexism, racism and disablism demands different reactions at different times and in different contexts.

Having established the complexity and dynamic nature of the social divisions of disability, 'race' and gender, this section concentrates on the issues and theories that have grown up around the issue of 'equal opportunities' for these groups. The aim here is to set the scene by looking at some of the key concepts and theoretical ideas surrounding these groups which are relevant to 'equal opportunities'.

Disability

Towards a social definition

The recent and more politicized disability movement has rejected the image of disabled people as deviants from an 'able-bodied' norm and have emphasized the differing capacities and abilities of disabled people (Morris, 1991a). Definitions of disability are undergoing changes to a social rather than a medical model. Previously, because of the dominant position of the medical profession, disability was defined in terms of clinical conditions such as arthritis, multiple sclerosis, stroke, epilepsy, and spinal injury, and seen as a 'personal tragedy' arising from disease or an accident. If we consider the traditional terms used to categorize disabled people they often stemmed from their particular clinical condition, for example, the 'blind' and the 'deaf'. These terms did not recognize the shared experience of stigma, exclusion, discrimination and dependency of disabled people (Lonsdale, 1990). Now, because they do not take account of the social dimensions of disability the limitations of such definitions have been recognized.

'In redefining the nature of disability, disabled people are asserting that they are a disadvantaged or oppressed minority group whose unequal economic and social position stems from discrimination and lack of access to power' (Leach, 1989, p. 66). The distinction between the two terms 'impairment' and 'disability' adds to an understanding of the social dimension of disabled people's inequality. Impairment refers to the functional limitations which affect a person's body, whereas disability refers to the loss or limitation of opportunities owing to social, physical and attitudinal barriers. Examples are: an inability to walk is an impairment, whereas an inability to enter a building because the entrance is up a flight of steps is a disability; an inability to speak is an impairment but an inability to communicate because appropriate technical aids are not made available is a disability; an inability to move one's body is an impairment but an inability to get out of bed because appropriate physical help is not available is a disability (Martin and White, 1988).

The Disabled People's International challenged the World Health Organization's definitions of impairment, disability and handicap which continued to concentrate on an individual's condition (Lonsdale, 1990; Oliver, 1990) (the distinction between impairment and disability is explained further in the glossary in the introduction to this book). They offered their own alternative definition as 'the loss or limitation of opportunities to take part in the life of the community on an equal level with others due to physical and social barriers' (Oliver, 1991a). The Union of Physically Impaired Against Segregation suggested its definition of disability as 'the disadvantage or restriction of activity caused by a contemporary social organisation which takes no or little account of people who have physical impairments and thus excludes them from the mainstream of social activities' (Oliver, 1991a). These definitions see disability as a social restriction rather than an individual limitation. Disability therefore refers to the oppression which people with physical, sensory or intellectual impairments, or those who are mentally ill, experience as a result of prejudicial attitudes and discriminatory actions. People are disabled by society's reaction to impairment. 'This is not to deny that the degree of social restriction may differ depending upon clinical condition or functional limitation, but to assert that these differences are less important than the commonalities imposed on the experience of disability by social restriction' (Oliver, 1991a).

This shift in definition has led a move away from the idea of the 'rehabilitation' of individual disabled people to a concern instead to restructure society and the environment to accommodate and empower all citizens (Oliver, 1989, 1996). Disability can now be seen for what it is: a product of the built environment which is reinforced by social values and beliefs (Finkelstein, 1980; Abberley, 1987; Swain *et al.*, 1993). Also, the move to a social definition of disability has raised and encouraged a debate on the issue of the acceptable terms for referring to disabled people. Language is important for many reasons. First, disabled people have the right to decide what terms they wish to use to describe themselves. Second, challenging previously accepted language can encourage people to examine the often stereotyped attitudes and images that have become linked with disabled people, which enhances the appreciation of disabled people's disadvantage.

This is not to suggest that the use of language is simply agreed upon even among disabled people themselves. While Lonsdale (1990) sought to emphasize the importance of the social foundation of disability by using the term 'people with disabilities', which puts people first, an alternative view was put forward by Oliver (1990). He argued that by putting the person first it 'flies in the face of reality as it is experienced by disabled people themselves who argue that far from being an appendage, disability is an essential part of the self, in this view it is nonsensical to talk about the person and the disability separately and consequently disabled people are demanding acceptance as they are, as disabled people' (p. xii). The term 'disabled people' was seen as politically more powerful by placing the emphasis on how society actively oppressed people with a whole range of impairments.

Disablism

'Disablism is the operation of attitudinal, environmental and institutional barriers to deny disabled people full human and civil rights' (Begum, 1994). Only disabled people can voice its true experience as the following example illustrates.

This leg, not me you understand, had polio when I was one year old and it is not normal. If I cover it up perhaps they won't realize for a while, at least until I get up. This leg was my passport to being bullied in school, to being called names like 'spastic' and 'cripple', to being both hated and feared as well as over-protected to shield me from both. (Finger, 1992)

Disablism means that disabled people are in an inferior position to other groups. They are disadvantaged in terms of housing (Borsay, 1986), employment (Lonsdale, 1986), finance (Martin and White, 1988), transport (Hoad, 1986) and education (Anderson, 1979). Disabled people have also been denied access to key political, educational and cultural institutions which could enable them to participate fully in society (Oliver, 1990). Oliver (1991a) argued that this exclusion of disabled people has had profound effects on social relations, resulting not only in the marginalization of disabled people within labour markets, but from society as a whole.

Finkelstein (1980, 1981) argued that the reason for this was not because of disabled people's perceived or real physical limitations, but because changes in the work system have excluded them from the work process. He developed an evolutionary model linked to the history of disability as follows. Historical changes in the work process, through the rise of capitalism from feudalism, have led to the changing needs of the labour market. In Britain, before the industrial revolution, feudal society's economic base was agriculture or small-scale industry, which did not preclude the great majority of disabled people from participating in the production process or making at least a contribution. Disabled people were regarded as individually unfortunate but not segregated from society. However, the process of industrialization shifted the place of work from the home to the factory. Under capitalism, many more disabled people were excluded from the production process because speed, enforced discipline, and time-keeping became production imperatives, alongside a growth in formal educational requirements. As a result disabled people came to be regarded as a social and educational problem and more and more were segregated in workhouses, asylums and special schools out of the mainstream.

Is this explanation an over-simplification? It highlighted the role of the mode of production in significantly influencing perceptions and experiences of disability. It certainly implied that Britain before capitalism was some kind of idealized society where minority groups were treated more benignly, which is questionable. It does not explore negative attitudes towards disability, such as fear or hostility, or ideas commonly held in society that disabled people are incapable of running their own lives. Within institutional settings and outside in the community, disabled people's lives are often controlled by professionals in power over them (see Chapter 5 for a discussion of social services and disabled people's issues). However, although a labour market explanation cannot adequately contain these elements, it can and does usefully move the analysis away from individual impairment and clinical conditions to structural explanations of disabled people's disadvantage.

'Race'

'Race' is a concept which is widely acknowledged to have no substance as it has been discredited biologically and as derived from scientific racism (Rose *et al.*, 1984; Miles, 1989). Carter *et al.* (1996) declared it to be 'a virtually vacuous concept . . . lacking a real world referent'. However, it does retain considerable currency, particularly in legislation. In immigration controls, Goldberg (1993) showed that it had been successfully used by states 'to naturalize differences and normalize exclusions'. In British race relations law, it is used to refer to such things as ethnic origin, nationality and skin colour. Also, from a sociological point of view, 'race' denotes a particular way in which communal differences come to be constructed. The fact that 'race' has no biological basis does not appear to undermine its usefulness as a social and political concept.

For these reasons Anthias and Yuval-Davis (1993) argued that it cannot be erased from the analytical map.

With the rise of the civil rights movement in the 1960s, activists preferred the use of the term Black in order to denote people from ethnic minorities to promote unity and symbolize the shared experience of discrimination, prejudice, inequality and racism. However, its use has been challenged. Modood (1988) argued that the term Black is only accepted by a minority of activists in the Asian community, and its positive concept of blackness was actually detrimental to Asians because it suggested a hierarchy, with those who were 'more black' because of their African origins being at the top. On the other hand, Mama (1989, 1992) favoured the term Black and pointed out that there are many Black communities in Europe and America whose identity is not linked with Africa. She cautioned us to be aware of some of the dangers of emphasizing different ethnicities and cultures. While accepting that it was important for different communities to recognize and maintain their particular cultural identities and histories, she pointed out that 'race and culture have been played off against each other in quite negative ways'. In fact, she argued that concentration on ethnicity can be a useful tool for hiding racism, 'the culturalization or ethnicization of race as a state-orchestrated process which, by focusing on the language, food, habits and clothing of black . . . people masks and denies the fact of discrimination' (Mama, 1992, p. 80). She maintained the importance of the term Black as denoting the shared experience – albeit in different forms and degrees – of class, gender and racial oppression (Mama, 1984).

Alongside this argument, while not wanting to deny the important issue of continuing racism, it is important to acknowledge that the ethnic minority community is heterogeneous, comprising a number of diverse groupings and individuals defined by religion, gender, class, language, historical roots, age, ability, sexuality, wealth and geographical origins, which can all have an impact on their opportunities. In this book, the reason for using the CRE terminology in the field of 'race', which differentiates between different ethnic minority groupings, is that the impact of racial disadvantage and discrimination in Britain is becoming more complex and differentiated between the groups. When considering the impact of social policy, it is no longer possible to use blanket terms such as the Black community. An example of this is in education where Asian children are now performing better than Whites, while Black Caribbeans are still underachieving (see Chapters 4 and 5 for a discussion of the key social policy areas and 'race').

Racism

For Black people racism is a day-to-day experience. 'The first time my son was called a nigger, he was about 16 months old. The insult, delivered by an old man in an overcoat, stomping through the park, was directed at Marcus in his pushchair but intended for me to hear' (Ware, 1985).

There is an enormous amount of literature on the issue of racism. Hesse *et al.* (1992) cited Gilroy as arguing that: 'The word racism has become too easy to say and too difficult to explain'. The term was introduced in the 1930s to refer to doctrines of racial superiority. In the 1960s, it was given wider connotation. Racism consists of structures within society, policies and procedures within institutions (institutional racism) and prejudice among individuals (individual racism), which maintain and encourage inequality and discrimination on the grounds of 'race', when certain racial categories are imbued with negative meaning (Benedict, 1968; Miles, 1989). The CRE (1990a) warned us that 'the pervasiveness and deep rootedness of racism requires us to be continually vigilant and to understand that, simply because it no longer finds the same expression, it has not been erased' (p. 7).

Throughout the 1980s the approach of 'multiculturalism' was adopted particularly in schools where it emphasized the need to understand, accept and respect the cultural aspects of other groups within society to facilitate 'good race relations'. This has been labelled somewhat derogatorily as the 'three Ss approach' – saris, samosas and steel drums. The approach has been criticized for its lack of analysis of power which, it was argued, obscured and obfuscated racism. It was felt important for 'Black' people to unite against this common front. It was also argued that the term 'race relations' was inadequate because racism had to be located within economic, political and ideological relations rather than relations between 'races' (Miles, 1982).

More recent work on 'race' has suggested that the shift to an emphasis on racism as a uniting oppression of Black people can limit thinking by ignoring difference and diversity within ethnic minority communities (Rattansi, 1992; Gilroy, 1993). However, Anthias and Yuval-Davis (1993) argued for the retention of the concept of racism, maintaining that power and racist effects were central to its definition: 'racism is a set of postulates, images and . . . practices which serve to differentiate and dominate . . . serving to deny full participation in economic, social, political and cultural life' (p. 15). They in fact used the concept of 'racisms' to acknowledge difference and diversity. 'These are all differently experienced by different class, ethnic and gender categories' (p. 2). They argued that there was neither a 'unitary system' of racism, nor a 'unitary perpetrator or victim' (p. 2). They understood 'racisms' as modes of exclusion, inferiorization, subordination and exploitation, in different social and historical contexts. Extreme examples were given as extermination, slavery and segregation.

There has been a long-standing historical link between Europe and Asia, Africa and the Americas characterized by 'economic exploitation, gross inhumanity and political subjugation, which relied on the use of military force and racist ideology to legitimise and perpetuate "white" supremacy' (Lester and Bindman, 1972). Hartmann and Husbands (1974) stated that the

main ideas about race and colour that have been current in Britain developed as a result of colonial expansion from the late sixteenth century onwards. Since that time the essential character of relations between the British and the indigenous inhabitants of other continents has been the domination of the non-white by the white . . . As the colonial period progressed, these ideas became elaborated and more and more widely diffused, until by the end of the nineteenth century the idea of white superiority held central place in British national culture. (p. 20)

However, as Hall *et al.* (1978) pointed out, racism today is its own animal. Even though the new form builds upon the old, it is also importantly connected to present-day social, economic and political factors.

If we look at post-1945 Black immigration, we find that it is 'littered with periodic short-term crises over immigration', and Saggar (1991), in pointing this out, asked us 'to remember that this was the backdrop to the genesis of race-related public policy-making in British central and local government' (p. 27). The Indian Workers Association stated that: 'the so called "integration" policy of the Government is both ludicrous and hypocritical. It preaches the equality of the races and yet at the same time restricted coloured immigration under the racialist Commonwealth Immigrants Act' (John, 1969, p. 161). Current social policy towards ethnic minorities has been shaped and determined by the tenor of the series of immigration and race relations Acts over the last three decades, serving to reinforce, legitimize and perpetuate racist assumptions and stereotypes. 'Given the perceptions of post-war "Black" immigration to Britain, "Black" people are not only blamed [by some people] for present economic ills, but are given no credit for – nor are believed to have made any positive, useful or productive contributions to Britain whatsoever' (GLC, 1986, p. 4). This is demonstrated by the little-known fact that 57 per cent of all immigrants who arrived in Britain between 1945 and 1984 were White (Labour Force Survey, 1984).

All political parties agreed on discriminatory controls at the point of entry in the name of racial harmony. In 1978, Margaret Thatcher stated that her party in power would see an end to immigration for the sake of 'race relations' to preserve the 'British way of life' (Brandt, 1986). As Crewe (1983) pointed out, 'there are votes for the picking in fanning the flames of racial resentment' (p. 263). 'Despite all the laws banning racial discrimination and violence, the government and the police treat Black people as second-class citizens. Thus are individual racists encouraged to feel that they have a free hand. Without official racism, racial attacks would not and could not take place in Britain on the scale or with the severity that they do' (Thompson, 1988, p. 88). Certain events have proved very worrying in this area, such as the victory of a British National Party candidate in the Tower Hamlet local by-election in autumn 1993, the threat of far right political groups in Europe, and the ever-present and widespread incidence of racist attacks.

Gender

For two decades sociology has made a clear distinction between sex and gender. This distinction was introduced into Britain by the work of Oakley (1972) who emphasized the fixed nature of sex based on biological determinants compared to the variability of gender as a cultural product. 'Sex is a word that refers to the biological differences between male and female: the visible difference in genitalia, the related difference in procreative function. "Gender", however, is a matter of culture: it refers to the social classification into "masculine" and "feminine"' (Oakley, 1972, p. 16). The central issue was whether gender, the social construction of sex, was in any way biologically determined.

There had been a strong tradition that argued for biological difference and inferiority to explain women's subordination to men. In the nineteenth century, women were viewed as totally controlled by their ovaries and menstrual cycle. For example, women were seen as genetically programmed to be passive and men as aggressive. Therefore, drawing a clear distinction between sex, as natural and biologically given, and gender, as malleable and culturally produced, 'made a profound contribution to feminist thinking' (Hoods-Williams, 1996). It encouraged numerous studies that looked at the importance of socialization and gender-role stereotyping as alternative ways of understanding the difference between women's and men's positions in various arenas, such as the labour market and education.

However, the clarity of the distinction between sex and gender is beginning to be challenged, particularly by post-structuralist thinkers (Barrett and Phillips, 1992). One side of this challenge comes about because the declared fact that sex is natural, biologically clear and divided into two groups is now being reappraised. Hoods-Williams (1996) showed that the biological understanding of the determinant of sex difference is in fact inadequate and still being investigated. He argued that medical research work in the area of chromosomal theory can be seen as tautological because conventional external evidence of a person being a woman or a man is used before testing their chromosomes to find the determinant of that sex. In this way: 'Gender is always already implicated within the attempts to define sex – whether as difference or similarity' (Hoods-Williams, 1996, p. 13). It is interesting to note that Oakley (1972) put inverted commas around gender. It may be that in the future we shall see the use of inverted commas around sex in the same way as we do for 'race' because that concept will also be recognized as having no clear biological determinant. However, what this also means is that a reanalysis of the concept of gender is also on the cards (Lorber, 1994).

Sexism and feminism

Women can explain the influence of sexism on their lives.

Five years in the Civil Service have changed me from a career woman. I think, like most other women, I have realised that unless I am prepared to make quite disproportionate sacrifices, I will not succeed in the Civil Service. Having accepted that, you can either seek satisfaction elsewhere, in the home, or in your family, or seek to change the existing structures. Unless you are extraordinarily ambitious, the sexism and sexual harassment soon puts you in your place (Bagilhole, 1994a).

As we have seen with racism, sexism consists of structures within society, policies and procedures within institutions (institutional sexism) and prejudice among individuals (individual sexism) which maintain and encourage inequality and discrimination, this time on the grounds of sex. 'Sexism occurs at different levels from the individual to the institutionalized, but all forms combine to preserve inequality' (Marshall, 1994). Cook and Watt (1987) define it as 'a process of systematic oppression directed towards women who are defined as inferior to men' (p. 70). The recognition and identification of the sexist nature of society and women's subordination compared with men, and the desire to change this, has led to the feminist movement. 'Contemporary feminism argues that sexist social beliefs and practices not only limit the activities of women, but are an impertinent way of making distinctions between the sexes, because they are not founded on evidence' (Humm, 1995).

Offen (1992) asked the questions: 'What is feminism? Who is a feminist?' (p. 68). She answered herself in the following way: 'Everyone seems to have different answers, and every answer is infused with a political and emotional charge. The word "feminism" continues to inspire controversy – indeed, even to evoke fear among a sizeable portion of the general public' (Offen, 1992, p. 69). Part of the explanation for this is that feminist analysis draws on different traditions, different feminisms. Dale and Foster (1986) identified liberal feminism, radical feminism and socialist feminism, whereas others have expanded the list. For example, Williams (1989) included libertarian feminism, welfare feminism and Black feminism. Stacey (1993) sounded a warning note to these ever-expanding categorizations: attempts to categorize feminists can in fact work to over-simplify and at worst exclude some feminist thinking. Certainly all types of feminism share an awareness of the disadvantage and inequality that women experience and that 'women's subordination must be questioned and challenged' (Abbott and Wallace, 1990, p. 10).

Historically the main planks of feminist thinking have been liberal feminism, socialist feminism and radical feminism. These approaches differ in their identification of the causes of women's disadvantage and therefore in their proposed solutions. For example, liberal feminism has a concern with individualistic and reforming 'equal opportunities': that is, equal rights, equal treatment and equal access in education, employment and politics, associated with the 'equal opportunities' legislation in the 1970s. Socialist and radical feminists see the cause as stemming from the social structure of society and social relations within it, either predominantly and centrally capitalism for the former, or patriarchy for the latter.

Walby (1990) argued as a socialist feminist that 'class relations and the economic exploitation of one class by another are the central features of social structure and these determine the nature of gender relations' (p. 4). These relations are seen as important both in determining material conditions for women and creating an ideological explanation for them. George and Wilding (1994) explained these relations from the material position of women's traditional role as mother and wife as 'unpaid labour in the home is a subsidy to capitalism because it reduces the cost of reproducing the next generation of workers and servicing male breadwinners' (p. 132).

Radical feminists look to patriarchy as an explanation for women's oppression within society. Patriarchy has been defined as male domination and the power of men to control women. It is 'a system of social structures and practices in which men dominate, oppress and exploit women. The use of the term social structure is important here, since it clearly implies rejection both of biological determinism, and the notion that every individual man is in a dominant position and every woman in a subordinate one' (Walby, 1990, p. 20). Male social power is seen as located in and derived from two separate arenas: 'private' relations within the household or family and 'public' relations of economic, ideological and political power. In the household, women's labour is expropriated by their partners. In the labour market women are excluded from the better forms of paid work and segregated into the worse jobs, which are classified as less skilled and therefore less paid.

These different strands of feminism shared the common theme of the search for universal explanations of women's subordination, the emphasis on the universalism and commonality of the women's cause. Now this has been challenged and there is a growing recognition of difference and diversity within the category 'women', and the way their oppression is experienced. Initially this challenge came mainly from Black feminists (Hooks, 1981; Amos and Parmar, 1984; Jarrett-Macauley, 1996), but it has been reiterated by working-class women, lesbians, disabled women and older women.

These challenges have led to radical changes in feminism, an acknowledgement of difference among women and, some would argue, more relevant, inclusive and comprehensive feminist thinking. However, dangers in following the diversity argument too far have been highlighted. It would, ultimately, logically lead to the fragmentation of feminism into so many small parts and causes that would make it untenable, if not as a theory then certainly as a political force for change. As Soper (1994) argued:

One is bound to feel that feminism as theory has pulled the rug from under feminism as politics. For politics is essentially a group affair, based on the ideas of making "common cause", and feminism, like any other politics, has always implied a banding together, a movement based on the solidarity sisterhood of women, who are linked by perhaps very little else than their sameness and "common cause" as women. (pp. 14–15)

Despite the fact that feminism has changed, society has not. As Evans (1994) continued to point out, this means that the position of women remains, in some senses, common.

The second sex is still precisely that: throughout the West women have a lower level of higher and professional education than men, they are paid less, have less social power and are still assumed to have the primary, if not exclusive, responsibility for the care of children and dependent relatives ... Women in some Western societies may have made some inroads in some portions of junior/middle management, but to all effects and purposes the public world, of institutional power, remains dominated by men. (Evans, 1994, p. 1)

Soper (1994) also argued that there are 'some concrete and universal dimensions of women's lives' (p. 19). She cited the example of the reality of men's violence and the threat of men's violence against women, describing the way in which 'women live in a kind of alertness to the possibility of attack and must to some degree organize their lives in order to minimize its threat' (p. 19). An example of this might be not walking on the streets alone after dark. Therefore, there are 'conditions that are differently experienced simply by virtue of which sex you happen to be, and in that sense they are universally differentiated between the sexes: *all* men and *all* women are subject to them *differently*' (Soper, 1994, p. 20). Finally, then, we see a call for feminist thinking to move forward in two ways at the same time, always recognizing and acknowledging the importance and value both of diversity and difference, but also of gender-specific issues and at times the universal category of women (Offen, 1992; Soper, 1994).

Summary

This chapter considers the relatively neglected area of theory in 'equal opportunities'. It addresses the difficult questions: what is 'equal opportunities'? and what do we mean by 'equal opportunities'?

The first part of the chapter examines these questions on a societal level and an organizational level. It explores different definitions of 'equal opportunities', moving from a simple definition based on 'equal treatment' to the more complex and deeper definitions based on unequal or preferential treatment and 'equality of outcome'. It investigates and discusses the different and often complex concepts associated with 'equal opportunities' at a societal level: discrimination, prejudice, different perspectives on equality ('equality of opportunity', 'equality of condition' and 'equality of outcome'), positive action and justice. The chapter then looks at 'equal opportunities' at organizational level and highlights some of the major perspectives and approaches to 'equal opportunities' identified by writers in this field.

The second part of the chapter explores concepts relevant to the theory of 'equal opportunities' which emanate specifically from the areas of disability, 'race' and gender. It is divided into these three areas, but for each area it begins by interrogating the concepts of disability, 'race' and gender themselves. For disability it explores the debate about the appropriateness of the 'medical model' of disability versus the 'social model'. For 'race' it explains the recognition that the term is no longer substantiated by biology, but still retains a social and political cogency. In the area of gender, it highlights the questioning and challenging of the previously accepted clear distinction between the biological and fixed nature of sex and the variable cultural product of gender. Finally, it investigates the concepts of disablism, racism and sexism.

CHAPTER 3

'Equal opportunities':
the politics and the legislation

The ideological and historical background to 'equal opportunities'

'Equal opportunities' is a political phenomenon even though it impacts on most people only as organizational or bureaucratic procedures, and there are many factors which create a motivation for its introduction and development. 'Equal opportunities' policies did not simply arise because governments decided to legislate or employers decided to improve their personnel policies. The radical heritage of 'equal opportunities' should not be forgotten. 'Equal opportunities', like any other rights in society and in the workplace, were not given on a plate, but came about because people campaigned and struggled for them. The civil rights and women's movements have played an important part in its recognition and the growing disability rights movement is now also making an important contribution. Sivanandan (1976) demonstrates this political action in the area of 'race': 'The fact of the matter was that *laissez-faire* immigration and *laissez-faire* discrimination had thrown up social problems which after the riots of 1958 and the growing militancy of a Black underclass, were taking on political proportions that the government – irrespective of party – could not ignore' (p. 352).

This section charts and explores the development of 'equal opportunities' in Britain through what can be seen as four distinct eras of 'equal opportunities': the1940s–1950s, the 1960s–1970s, the 1980s and the 1990s. This analysis of the historical development will be set in the context of the major driving forces and catalysts for 'equal opportunities' in the different decades, which have changed in dominance over time. The major forces can be categorized as moral, legislative, political, economic and professional interests. Although we can see that there is often a combination of forces acting on the development of 'equal opportunities' in the different eras identified, on the whole it is possible to speculate about the dominant force.

The Four Eras of 'Equal Opportunities': 1940s–1950s, 1960s–1970s, 1980s, 1990s

1940s–50s: Emphasis on disability – the 'moral era'?

Because of lack of action, this can hardly be described as an 'equal opportunities' era at all. Nevertheless, thinking at this time on 'equal opportunities' was based on morality and on ideas of equality and just-ice. After much lobbying, during the 1940s and 1950s the earliest 'equal opportunities' legislation came into being. This was designed to assist soldiers returning from the Second World War, who had become disabled fighting for their country, to obtain work. The Disabled Persons (Employment) Act (DPEA) was passed in 1944 and amended in 1958. One of the things it set down was a quota system of a requirement of 3 per cent for disabled workers in workforces of more than 20 (the details of the Act are discussed later in this chapter). As Oliver (1990) says, the DPEA was influenced by the 'collective guilt of seeing ex-servicemen disabled while fighting for their country' (p. 89).

1960s–1970s: Gender, 'race' and gay men's issues – the legislative era?

It is argued that, 'The term equal opportunities had its beginnings in British legal history' (Cheung-Judge and Henley, 1994, p. 2). During the 1960s and 1970s, the major legislation to outlaw 'race' and sex discrimination was laid down. Also, while there has never been any legislation on same-sex relations between women, in 1967, during this mood of legislative change and liberalization, the Sexual Offences Act was passed which for the first time sanctioned sexual relations between consenting adult men (21 years and over) in private. Importantly for social policy, provision was made in the Sex Discrimination Act and Race Relations Act to enable welfare organizations to recruit workers from specific sexes and racial groups to deliver appropriate personal services to members of their own group (Genuine Occupational Quali-fications). The caring professions, such as social work, health author-ities, youth and community services, made use of this provision. There was also provision for positive action in advertising and training for women and ethnic minorities. (The different provisions of the legisla-tion are discussed in more detail later in this chapter.)

Patterns of labour-market segregation and disadvantage experienced by women and ethnic minorities were an important part of the context in which this anti-discrimination legislation developed in this period. There was an increasing return of women to the labour market, but they were highly concentrated in certain industrial sectors through ver-tical segregation and at the bottom of organizations through horizontal segregation (Bagilhole, 1994a). Also, large-scale immigration of people from the New Commonwealth and Pakistan had been encouraged and they were highly concentrated geographically, industrially and occupa-tionally (Brown, 1984).

For women the initiative for 'equal opportunities' legislation came from a combination of pressures, ranging from the newly emergent and growing women's movement to more long-standing and traditional forms of women's organizations, such as trade unions. These pressures con-verged institutionally in campaigns for equal pay and anti-discrimination legislation, culminating in the Equal Pay Act 1970 and the Sex Dis-crimination Act 1975. For ethnic minorities, the successful passing of the 1976 Race Relations Act owed much to the momentum in the 'equal opportunities' field established by the legislation on sex discrimination. This Act built on and strengthened the previous Acts of 1965 and 1968, which had sought to give ethnic minorities the same rights of access to housing, public places and services as the White majority.

However, all the Race Relations Acts were presented as part of a double-edged package. The promotion of 'good race relations' through legal prohibitions on discrimination was held to need balancing by the increasingly restrictive regulation of ethnic minority immigration. At this time came Enoch Powell's famous 'rivers of blood' speech in Birmingham in 1968, which even went beyond the advocacy of strengthening immigration controls to introduce the idea of sending ethnic minority immigrants settled in Britain back to their country of origin. 'As I look ahead, I am filled with foreboding. Like the Romans, I seem to see "the River Tiber foaming with much blood". The tragic and intractable phenomenon which we watch with horror on the other side of the Atlantic, but which there is interwoven with the history and existence of the States itself, is coming upon us here by our own volition and our neglect' (*Observer*, 1968). In this process the issue of immigration came to mean Black immigration (Layton-Henry, 1984), and as Solomos (1992) argues this speech was the catalyst which 'established repatriation as part of the political agenda' (p. 18). (For a full discussion of the politics of immigration see Solomos, 1989 and 1992.)

The underlying philosophy behind 'equal opportunities' in the area of 'race' was based on what has been called a 'colour-blind approach': policies and practices which gave equal access and equal treatment, but failed to recognize the historical and contemporary reality of ethnic minority group's experiences and to acknowledge their different needs. This approach rested on the premise that the 'problem', identified as resting in ethnic minorities themselves, would disappear over time. The focus of attention for academics was the internal make-up of ethnic minority groups, such as culture, social lifestyles and means of adaptation (Patterson, 1965; Rex and Moore, 1967). Parmar (1981) describes how pathological perspectives informed such investigations. The purpose of such research was 'to explain Black cultures to white people so that white people could learn to become more tolerant, and secondly, the "objective" "race" expert and sociologist sought to inform policy-makers about the ways in which state policies could be implemented in order to aid the task of integration' (p. 22).

Some of the remnants of the moral force driving 'equal opportunities' in the 1940s and 1950s remained as an influence. When White people behaved in a racist manner there were perceived to be two sets of victims, both ethnic minorities and the White people themselves who were also seen as victims of their own inhumanity. Clifton Robinson, Chair of Commission for Racial Equality, wrote at this time: 'We should see more clearly that racism is a problem created by whites with more direct and dire consequences for Blacks but in a more general sense also affecting whites. Prejudice, discrimination, the denial of opportunities, injustice and hate not only affect the victims, but also the perpetrators. It lessens the humanity of both, Black and white' (Beauchamp, 1979, p. 3). This created the approach of 'Racism Awareness Training' in the 1980s, which had the aim of exposing Whites to the racist nature of their own behaviour with the assumption that they would reform in the light of this revelation. It has been argued that this form of training was both questionable in its effectiveness and counterproductive in that it took up the energies of activists and diverted resources away from ethnic minority groups themselves (Sivanandan, 1985).

'Equal opportunities' policy at the workplace was in its infancy and consisted of *ad hoc* responses to special needs rather than systematic reviews of the recruitment and selection process as a whole. As an example in the area of 'race', if any provisions were made they were isolated and specific for ethnic minority employees who were perceived, as a result of culture or migration, to require and be entitled to exceptional arrangements. There was an emphasis on extended leave, interpreters and time off for religious observance (Department of Employment, 1972). Discrimination was predominantly seen as a product of prejudiced individuals and there was little appreciation of the existence of systematic structural disadvantage and discrimination.

1980s: Markets and individuals: Threats to gender and 'race', no hope for disability – the political era?

Even during the legislative era of the 1960s and 1970s, 'equal opportunities' developments were a political response to campaigning and political pressure both nationally and locally. However, in the late 1970s and early 1980s, there was a sea change in political outlooks, policy objectives and economic organization. The election of Margaret Thatcher in 1979 heralded a decisive turning away from Keynsianism and 'welfare statism'. This led to a polarization of political philosophies that had direct implications for 'equal opportunities'. As Cheung-Judge and Henley (1994) argue: 'Within a decade the idea of equal opportunities changed from a sleepy ideological abstraction to a controversial and high-profile fact of life' (p. 3).

The urban disorders of 1980, 1981 and 1985 effectively signalled to both sides of the political spectrum the deficiencies of the previous notion of the 'colour-blind approach' to 'race' issues. On the political left, the 'riots' were seen as evidence of the revolutionary potential of 'racialized' minorities (Jewson, 1990). Traditionally their political action had taken the form of promoting solidarity within horizontally defined strata, predominantly the working class. Now alternative sources of collective identities and interest groups were recognized as important. These included women, ethnic minorities and disabled people. This recognition was reflected in policies adopted by a number of Labour-controlled local authorities, particularly in the London boroughs, but also in the provinces (Bagilhole, 1992, 1993a, 1994b). A prime example of this approach was the Greater London Council (GLC), responsible at that time for running many public services for the whole of the Greater London area. In 1980, a Labour majority came to power with a major priority to further equality for all oppressed groups in terms of employment and service delivery. They introduced many radical policies in this area and became a left-wing beacon of the 'equal opportunities' movement. Debates within local authorities over 'equal opportunities' had a pivotal role in changing local authority structures and cultures, and attacks on their power by central government were fuelled in part by hostility to the prominence they gave to these issues.

In contrast, the political right asserted the primacy of the self-reliant individual, pursuit of individual interest, personal gratification and the releasing of the enterprise of individuals by freeing them from collective controls. From this point of view, although the constraints of racial and sexual discrimination were seen as intolerable, equally unacceptable was to reward collective interests or recognize collective rights (Hall, 1983). In pursuing 'equal opportunities' for individuals, the market was seen as the best guarantor of fairness. Enoch Powell claimed that 'the market economy . . . is the most effective enemy of discrimination between individuals, classes and races' (Foot, 1969, p. 129). At the same time, on the right, there was a renewed emphasis on British nationalism, building on Powell's philosophy in the 1960s by attempting to draw and define the boundaries of the nation and 'Britishness'. There was a heightened emphasis on the idea of a unified and unitary British national culture. As part of this ideology, the 1981 Nationality Act was used to redefine British citizenship and, in the process, excluded large numbers of people in Commonwealth countries.

At the same time, there were accusations that ethnic minorities were 'swamping' Britain with 'alien cultures'. In 1986, a Conservative Education Minister in a speech to Her Majesty's Inspectors of Schools declared: 'I believe that in areas where there are few or no members of ethnic minority groups, there is a genuine and not dishonourable fear that British values and traditions – the very stuff of school education – are likely to be put at risk if too much allowance is made for cultural backgrounds and attitudes of ethnic minorities' (Tomlinson, 1990, p. 27). Norman Tebbit also came up with his infamous 'cricket test' to gauge a person's 'Britishness'. If any Asian or Black Caribbean gave their support to India, Pakistan or the West Indies cricket teams while they were playing England, they had failed.

One of the major policy thrusts of the government was to reduce public expenditure through cuts in state welfare services, such as nurseries and elderly day care. This had a disproportionate effect on women as the major carers in society. The predominant political climate during the 1980s meant there was no likelihood that the government would strengthen or develop the 'equal opportunities' legislation. In 1991, the Commission for Racial Equality (CRE), the body set up by the government of the day in 1976 to oversee, monitor and make recommendations for the improvement in 'race' legislation, noted that it had yet to receive a formal government response to its 1985 proposals for reform of the

Race Relations Act (CRE, 1991). In fact, the necessity of organizations such as the CRE and Equal Opportunities Commission (EOC) (the equivalent body for the Sex Discrimination Act 1975) was questioned by the political right. Also, at this time the government resisted 'equal value' amendments to the Equal Pay Act 1970, which were emanating from the European Community. Given this climate the campaigns by disabled people's organizations fell on deaf ears, and attempts to introduce a private member's anti-discrimination bill for disabled people were actively blocked by the government.

1990s: Acceptance of 'equal opportunities' by the establishment and hopes for disability through the growing militancy of disabled people's groups – the economic, public relations and professional era?

Increasingly in the 1990s, a business case has been argued for 'equal opportunities'. This essentially rests on two premises. First, that both private and public sectors of the economy are underutilizing the full range of skills and talents in the population because of continuing unequal opportunities for some groups in society. Second, that it should be possible for organizations to increase their efficiency and effectiveness by projecting a more pluralistic self-image and thereby widening its pool of potential customers. Joanna Foster, Chair of the EOC, stated, 'equal opportunities in the nineties is about economic efficiency and social justice' (Ross and Schneider, 1992, p. xxi). Virginia Bottomley, the then Minister of State for Health, when launching a nationwide 'equal opportunities' programme for ethnic minority staff in the National Health Service, stated, 'I want to stress that taking action to promote equality in employment is not just a matter of moral justice, or of fairness to people from minority ethnic groups, it is good, sound common sense, and it makes business sense, too. Otherwise the NHS will lose the benefit of their skills' (*India Mail*, 14–20 December 1993).

As part of this change in outlook, a 'managing diversity' approach has been advocated, which claimed to harness 'equal opportunities' strategies to business competitiveness (Kandola *et al.*, 1995). They argued that diversity and difference between people can be managed to add value to the organization. The primary aims were said to be to improve the skills of all staff through personal development, and to create a workforce which was representative of the organization's customer or client base. However, how new this approach was must be tempered by their acknowledgement that 'although the breadth of focus is quite different' it does have 'many initiatives in common' with old approaches to 'equal opportunities' (1995, 34).

Dickens (1994) argues the business case justification for 'equal opportunities' is not sufficient on its own, because private and public sector employers will have different views on economic realities and organizational objectives. The CRE (1995e) acknowledges this by distinguishing a 'business case' for 'equal opportunities' in the private sector and a 'quality case' in the public sector. However, 'equal opportunities' can be viewed as a chance for organizations to portray themselves as good and fair for customers or clients. In the 1980s, this was already beginning to become a priority even for organizations in the public sector such as local authorities who were major service providers. 'The centrepiece of the GLC's anti-racist strategy was the declaration of London as an "anti-racist zone" and the announcement that 1984 was to be an anti-racist year in which the struggle against racism would be a continual and primary focus of the council's work. These commitments took the council into the realm of popular politics, and relied on public awareness campaigning marshalled through billboards and press advertisements' (Gilroy, 1987, p. 138).

'Equal opportunities' has become a buzzword and an integral part of the jargon of professional white-collar workers, especially those with responsibility over personnel and human resource matters in organizations. It thus enhances the careers of certain professionals: 'the successful promotion of an equal opportunities policy may well be seen as a means of increasing the role of personnel at the expense of line management. Resistance to the policy on the part of line management may then be a manifestation of a disagreement over policy but it may equally be motivated by considerations of power unrelated to the policy in question' (Mason, 1990, p. 58). It is argued that this managerial adoption of 'equal opportunities' has contributed to its depoliticization. As we saw in Chapter 2, the term 'equal opportunities', in its adopted form of equal treatment, has come to represent administrative procedures rather than ideological and political issues. 'Equal opportunity policy development seems plausibly linked to bureaucratisation, and possibly appeals to bureaucratic organisations or branches of organisations because of its formalising qualities . . . The promotion of equality of outcome, by contrast, requires the suspension or sidelining of bureaucratic norms and procedures within an organisation and (at least temporarily) the elevation of politics to a position of command' (Gibbon, 1993, p. 248).

Through this system of sanatization and incorporation into bureaucratic procedures, the true and original objectives of 'equal opportunities' have become diverted and subverted. Young (1990) argues that policies that emphasize procedural routines and operations are 'regulatory rather than redistributive. They give prominence to those who will play a role in achieving greater systematisation of procedures: personnel managers and "race" relations staff . . . The criteria for the success of such a policy are generally implicit and the activity seen as self-justifying' (pp. 32–3). In the area of 'race', Law (1996) identifies this process as 'a move from the politics of "race" to the management of "race"'. He argues that 'liberal equal opportunities management has flowered and become entwined with the "new managerialism" to form a dominant policy ideology which may be termed, ethnic managerialism' (p. x).

While equality and group justice was the concern of the political left in the 1980s, the emphasis is now on quality. Citizen's and customer's charters have been advocated by the government in many service-delivery areas, and local government is now using phrases such as 'total quality management' and asking departments and voluntary organizations who receive funding to come up with measurable 'quality standards' (Bagilhole, 1996a; 1996b). As Gilroy (1993) points out, 'The "e" has been dropped and there is now a new buzz word: "quality" ' (p. ix). However, she argues that the emphasis on quality should reassert equality as a fundamental underpinning because the service must be delivered to and meet the needs of the whole community, including women, ethnic minorities and disabled people.

We have seen a possible change of heart during the 1990s. Although the conventional thinking from the 'New Right' Conservatives has been to celebrate inequality (Forbes, 1991), both Valerie Amos and Herman Ouseley (1994), the then heads of the EOC and CRE respectively, argued that the 1990s have been 'characterised as the decade of equal opportunities in Britain' (p. xi). Michael Howard, as the Conservative Minister of Employment, vigorously endorsed the principles and practice of 'equal opportunities' policy, when giving a speech to a national conference jointly hosted by the EOC and CRE in 1991, where he launched the Employment Department's 'Ten Point Plan for Equal Opportunities'. These included specific recommendations that had previously been regarded as controversial, and were certainly beyond the legally required minimum action, including systematic ethnic monitoring of employees and the setting of equality targets. Also in 1991, John Major, the Prime Minister, made a supportive speech at the launch of Opportunity 2000, a business-led campaign 'to increase the quantity and quality of women's participation in the workforce' (*Equal Opportunities Review*, 1992). It would seem that in the 1990s, some 'equal opportunities' policies in the areas of gender and 'race' were not only compatible with political thinking on the right, but also encouraged. We can see from this that 'equal opportunities' as equal treatment can coexist with the idea of individualistic competition; 'equal opportunity is not rejected, just redefined into a vision of a perfectly competitive society' (Forbes, 1991, p. 27).

However, it is important to note that we are still confronted with tangible evidence that inequality continues despite the existence of race relations and sex discrimination legislation for 20 years or more (see Chapter 1). We have seen an increasing number of women participating in the labour market, albeit on a part-time basis, but there have been few and diminishing resources allocated to this field of policy. European Union proposals for women have been resisted, the Social Chapter was blocked and structural changes in the public sector as a result of compulsory competitive tendering have disproportionately and detrimentally affected women's work within the context of very inadequate childcare provision. The labour market has been increasingly casualized and fragmented, and has maintained a high level of unemployment within some ethnic minority communities. We have seen no strengthening of 'equal opportunity' legislation on gender or 'race' or extension of help to individuals taking cases (despite calls from both the CRE and the EOC), and although codes of practice have been accepted they are not mandatory.

We have also seen proposals designed to restrict the entry of refugees and those wishing to claim asylum, including the restriction of their right to social security benefits.

In the area of homosexuality, discriminatory laws still exist despite other European countries introducing the same age of consent for opposite and same-sex relationships. While lesbians and their relationships remain virtually invisible in the law, gay men, to stay within the law (despite the lowering of the age of consent from 21), must still be over 18 and confine their sexual relationships to the private sphere. Also, Clause 28 of the Local Government Act 1988 forbids local authorities from 'promoting' homosexuality as an acceptable family relationship. Further, despite growing concern over the difficulties and discrimination faced by older workers in the job market, the Conservative government refused to introduce legislation in this area.

In contradiction to all these negative trends, we have seen the Conservative government's final submission to pressure to introduce an anti-discrimination Act for disabled people. This was after growing militancy, including direct action and civil disobedience, by disabled people and an increase in public support (Barnes, 1991; Bynoe *et al.*, 1991; Shakespeare, 1993). This was a long-fought battle. Since 1979, opposition parties have attempted to introduce more than a dozen Private Members' Bills on this issue. Also, despite the important recognition the Act gave to the operation of discrimination against disabled people, it is much weaker in many respects than the equivalent Acts in the areas of 'race' and sex discrimination. It did not meet the demands of disabled people's organizations.

Amos and Ouseley (1994) argued that 'in many ways there has been a failure at national level to keep equality as a central feature of public policy debate and development' and that what was needed was 'a strategic approach at different levels of society' (p. xi). Perhaps this is too gentle an assertion and what we have seen in effect are obstacles and barriers to equality not only maintained but increased. We see a continued 'backlash' against 'equal opportunities'. One subtle form that this takes is to highlight the increasing stresses and strains that women now face maintaining paid work alongside their continuing responsibility for most of the unpaid work involved in family situations, and then to blame these on feminism. Faludi (1991) exposed this as 'the big lie, it stands the truth boldly on its head and proclaims that the very steps that have elevated women's position have actually led to their downfall'. She shows that, according to surveys in the USA, 75 to 95 per cent of women think that feminism has improved their lives. As Baird (1992a) argued, the problem for women is 'hardly the product of too much equality: rather the universal outcome of universal inequality' (p. 6). Faludi (1991) reported the psychiatrist Dr Baker Miller who maintained that the backlash was strategic by occurring well in advance of women achieving equality because 'Backlashes occur when advances have been too small, before changes are sufficient to help many people. It is almost as if the leaders of the backlash use the fear of change as a threat before major change has occurred'. In Britain a backlash has occurred in the form of accusations of 'political correctness' against 'equal opportunities' initiatives. This is often seen as sufficient criticism to ensure that policies and practices are viewed as loony-left, illiberal, repressive, extreme and based on totally fallacious premises. This has mirrored the increasing opposition to 'affirmative action' led by the Republican Party in the USA in the areas of 'race' and gender, which has produced some important court cases that have overturned previous practices in 'equal opportunities'.

Despite a confused picture during the 1990s, we can identify some change in approach to 'equal opportunities', which involved less overt opposition from the Conservative government. Several reasons have been proposed for this phenomenon: a search for electoral advantage through women's, ethnic minorities' and disabled people's votes; fears of further urban disorders, particularly in the light of the increasingly vocal and effective organization on the part of sections of the Islamic community; and concern about the 'demographic time bomb' of fewer numbers of young people and anticipated shortages of labour which would need to be replaced by women and ethnic minorities. While 'in 1986 almost one in four of the labour force was under 25, by 2001 this will have fallen to less than one in six before increasing slightly by 2006' (Central Statistical Office, 1994, p. 56). Although this threat has been mitigated by the continuing high levels of unemployment, there is still concern over skill shortages. Industrial sectors, keen to maximize the range of talents and abilities available to them from the whole of society and to retain skilled and trained staff, have recognized 'equal opportunities' policies as cost effective. As one Halifax Building Society manager put it, 'having the right people with the right skills in the right job justifies any expense of an equal opportunities policy. When you get the wrong people it is very expensive. If equal opportunities are inherent then it saves you a lot of money' (*Independent*, 1992). The last suggestion, to add to this list, comes from Jewson and Mason (1993). They argued that the demise of local authorities' power and therefore their advocacy of 'radical equal opportunities' has reduced antagonism and thereby encouraged 'liberal approaches' by private firms.

'Equal opportunities' appears to have become respectable, and to some extent has been colonized by the establishment. However, as the evidence in Chapter 1 demonstrates, it still continues to remain an unobtained goal for women, ethnic minorities and disabled people in Britain. Chapters 5, 6 and 7 of this book will look more specifically at the major different areas of concern for social policy to see what has been achieved through the various approaches that have been adopted to 'equal opportunities'.

The 'equal opportunities' legislation

The carrot or the stick?

The idea of legislation setting down how people can behave is fundamental to British law. 'Equal opportunities' legislation is no exception.

Many people mistakenly believe that such legislation is aimed at their personal attitudes and that it attempts to govern how they think or feel about certain aspects of their life. This is far from the truth, although the Members of Parliament who drafted the original Bills probably expected them to change society eventually. Some people believe that eliminating discrimination requires the use of strong enforcement powers: the 'stick' approach. Others believe that over time education, persuasion and voluntary measures will be sufficient and that 'you catch more flies with jam than with vinegar': the 'carrot' approach. Whichever route is taken the law has an essential part to play in the provision of 'equal opportunities' and the elimination of discrimination by providing a fundamental underpinning of society's belief in fairness and justice. However, it must be borne in mind that legislation, by eliminating overt discrimination, may encourage covert and more subtle forms of discrimination which are harder to uncover and eliminate.

The most significant Acts in the areas of disability, gender and race, in chronological order

- Disabled Persons (Employment) Acts (DPEA) 1944 and 1958
- Commonwealth Immigrants Act 1962
- Local Government Act 1966
- Chronically Sick and Disabled Persons Act 1970
- Equal Pay Act (EPA) 1970 (amended 1984)
- Immigration Act 1971
- Sex Discrimination Act (SDA) 1975 (amended 1986)
- Race Relations Act (RRA) 1976
- British Nationality Act 1981
- Companies Act 1985
- Fair Employment Protection Act, Northern Ireland 1989
- Disability Discrimination Act (DDA) 1995
- Employment Rights Act 1996

We now look at the various legislation in more detail categorized by its area of concern. First we consider the area of disability, then 'race' and religion, and finally gender.

Legislation in the area of disability

Disabled Persons (Employment) Acts 1944 and 1958

Until 1995, these two Acts were the key pieces of legislation governing the employment of disabled people. Provoked by returning disabled soldiers from the Second World War, the Disabled Persons (Employment) Act 1944, as amended by the 1958 Act, concentrated on the individual disabled person rather than on their physical and social environment. The 1944 Act defined a disabled person as 'a person who, on account of injury, disease, or congenital deformity, is substantially handicapped in obtaining or keeping employment'. It was based on the belief that disabled people could not be expected to compete for work with the non-disabled because of their medical condition. Therefore they were perceived to need compensation for their misfortune and access to lower status occupations, often in segregated settings.

These Acts set up the disabled persons' register. Registration was voluntary and open to both employed and unemployed disabled people who conformed to certain regulations. The legislation placed certain duties on employers with 20 or more employees in relation to the employment of registered disabled people. The 1944 Act established the quota system under which an employer of more than 20 workers had a duty to employ a 3 per cent quota of disabled workers who were registered under the Act. It was not an offence to be below the quota, but in this situation an employer had a duty to employ suitable registered disabled people – if any were available when vacancies arose – until the quota was reached. They could not engage or offer to engage anyone other than a registered disabled person without first obtaining a permit from the Disablement Resettlement Officer (DRO) to do so, and they could not discharge a disabled worker without reasonable cause. Two occupations were designated under the Act as especially suitable for disabled people: passenger electric lift attendant and car park attendant. An employer was not allowed to engage or transfer into these occupations anyone other than a registered disabled person unless a permit to do so had been obtained from the DRO, and these employees were not included in the quota. Importantly, employers could apply for overall exemption from the quota each year, if there were not enough suitable applicants. Therefore, despite the quota being set as low as 3 per cent, it was not adhered to by the majority of employers, with exemption permits being allowed as a matter of course (Gooding, 1994). Employers were required to keep records relating to the employment of disabled people for two years from the time to which they relate, which had to be open to inspection.

Companies Act 1985

A section of the Companies Act 1985 requires companies with on average more than 250 employees to state the policy they have operated towards the recruitment of disabled people, the continuing employment of those workers who become disabled, and for the training, career development and promotion of disabled workers in the previous financial year. This statement must be published in their Annual Report. These requirements relate to all disabled workers, not just those who are registered disabled, as do the 1944 and 1958 Acts.

Chronically Sick and Disabled Persons Act 1970

The Chronically Sick and Disabled Persons Act (CSDPA) 1970 was and still is recognized as a milestone in the establishment of the right of access to services for disabled people, which made significant improvements to the level and type of benefits and services available (Birkett and Worman, 1988). The Act placed a new obligation on local authorities to know how many disabled people are in their catchment area and to make arrangements to meet their needs. This has led to social services departments in local authorities keeping registers of disabled people and Birkett and Worman (1988) argue that their access to services has improved. The Act is wide ranging and includes welfare and housing (such as home helps, aids and adaptations); access to and facilities at public premises and educational establishments; the setting up of advisory committees; and co-options to local authority committees. The Act also introduced the 'Orange Badge Scheme' issued by local authorities 'for motor vehicles driven by or used for the carriage of disabled people'. This has increased access by allowing more lenient parking rules for disabled people.

However, the funding for the majority of these services and provisions in the Act come out of hard-pressed local authority budgets and therefore 'tend to be uneven and many are vulnerable to economic pressures' (Birkett and Worman, 1988, p. 33). There is also confusion about how far these rights can be enforced. The clause 'in so far as it is in the circumstances both practicable and reasonable' that appears in various sections can be used to cancel out the intentions of the Act.

Disability Discrimination Act 1995

The 1944 and 1958 Acts, including the 3 per cent quota, have proved to be a dismal failure. Schools and colleges, public places, transport systems, even health and welfare services continue to exclude and segregate disabled people, often forcing them into poverty and dependence. Therefore, there has been a concerted campaign for an anti-discrimination law for disabled people. Disabled people want self-determination, not charity, and individual enforceable rights to set boundaries between acceptable and non-acceptable behaviour to encourage a change of attitude so that disabled people are seen as equal citizens, not as objects of pity and charity. We can trace their politics to the USA civil rights movement and the USA disability lobby, which persuaded Congress to pass the 'Americans with Disabilities Act'. This and other USA laws make detailed provision for individual rights in employment, public services, transport and housing. Parallels can be drawn with anti-racist and feminist politics, but disability takes many forms and can happen to anyone. An extra dimension also needs to be considered when equal rights legislation is designed for disabled people: that is, the discriminatory effect of 'unequal burdens'. These are extra expenses directly related to a person's disability; examples include a special diet or transport costs.

Laws in the USA and Australia place an obligation on employers, education institutions, transport systems and services to take reasonable steps so that disabled people can live as equal citizens. For employers this would mean making the workplace accessible, restructuring jobs or modifying equipment. As a result of individual suits brought under the American law, the Washington Metro system has been overhauled, lift buttons are marked with raised printing and Braille, lights on platforms warn deaf people of approaching trains, and discounted fares help those who need a travelling companion. By contrast, London's Underground currently makes no accommodation for disabled people. Wheelchair users still have to ride in the guard's van of some British Rail trains, along with carrier pigeons and bicycles. It remains a common experience among blind people in Britain to call a minicab, only to be told by the driver that he does not take dogs. In Australia, in comparison, it is a criminal offence for an employer to require a blind person to part company with a guide dog.

From 1982 to 1995 there were a total of seven attempts to introduce anti-discrimination legislation for disabled people along the lines of the Sex Discrimination Act (SDA) and Race Relations Act (RRA) in the areas of gender and 'race' (Barnes, 1991). Each attempt failed, sometimes by the government 'talking out' the bill so that no time remained for a vote in Parliament. The government based its major reason for opposition on the cost implications. To counter this, both moral and economic arguments were advanced. First, that all citizens had an equal right to participate in society. Second, that if disabled people were given the means to make use of their skills, this would save money that would otherwise be spent on social security and special programmes. The 'Rights Now' campaign heavily criticized and disputed the government's cost analysis. They argued that it did not take into account any gains that might accrue from savings in benefits and increased taxation gathered if disabled people are given jobs. Also, it was an overestimation of cost because many buildings had already been made at least partly accessible for disabled people (Gooding *et al.*, 1994). Those who opposed the legislation also argued that the laws against sex and 'race' discrimination have not worked well, and therefore there was no point in having any more legislation of this kind. An answer given to this was that for all their shortcomings, the laws have had a positive impact on many individuals' lives and played a role in creating a climate favourable to change. Another very contentious argument was put forward by some government ministers that disabled people would not be able to handle legislation in their area. In this vein, Hugh Rossi, a Conservative MP, argued, 'I wonder whether we should be doing disabled people, who have enough to contend with in life, a wrong if we were to invite them into such seas of uncharted and uncertain litigation' (Hansard, 1991). Nicholas Scott, when he was the Minister responsible for disabled people, said progress was being made and that 'rather than legislating, the most constructive and productive way forward is through raising awareness in the community as a whole' (Hansard, 1991).

The Americans with Disabilities Act 1990 was seen as an example for Britain, and each attempt to introduce legislation received more support. Finally, the government succumbed to pressure and Royal Assent was given to the Disability Discrimination Act (DDA) on 8 November

1995. As Barnes (1991) has consistently advocated the arguments were eventually recognized that 'the denial of equal rights for disabled people cannot be morally justified when other disadvantaged groups have protection under the law, no matter how inadequate that protection may be'. William Hague, the Minister for Disabled in 1995, stated in a press release that, 'Taken together, the measures will play an important role in changing attitudes towards people with disabilities.' But, perhaps ominously, he also stated that, 'They will also give disabled people greater opportunities without imposing undue burdens on business or employers.' In fact the legislation has been described as 'a minimalist stance in which potential rights are hedged about with qualifications, limitations, and "escape clauses" for employers and others, and in which exhortation replaces compulsion as the main tool of implementation' (Blakemore and Drake, 1996).

Despite this criticism, disability was predicted as being one of the key 'equal opportunities' issues in the late 1990s, and the DDA was heralded as 'the most important discrimination legislation in a generation' and as being 'in some respects the most radical of discrimination laws' (EOR, 1996a, p. 31). The Act:

- deems people to have a disability if they have 'a physical or mental impairment which has a substantial and long-term adverse effect on their ability to carry out normal day-to-day activities' (long-term is defined by the fact that the disability must last or be expected to last for 12 months)
- makes it unlawful for employers to discriminate on the grounds of disability
- places a new duty on employers of 20 or more employees to reasonably accommodate the needs of a disabled person by at least considering making changes or additional provisions to enable them to work
- contains a right of access to goods, facilities, services and premises; further and higher education; and public transport including taxis, public service vehicles and railways
- establishes a National Disability Council to advise the government on the elimination of discrimination against disabled people
- gives disabled people the right to take complaints of discrimination to industrial tribunals with no upper limit placed on compensation awards
- amends and repeals some provisions of the Disabled Persons (Employment) Act 1944, including importantly the 'quota system'

Legislation in the area of 'race'

Local Government Act 1966

The Local Government Act 1966 contained the provision for government money to be provided to help subsidize posts, which were named after the relevant section of the Act (Section XI), set up by local authorities to deal with what was considered to be the 'problem' of 'disproportionate' numbers of immigrants from the New Commonwealth and Pakistan in their service delivery areas. This was seen very much as compensation to local authorities having to deal with the 'problems' such as non-English-speaking children in schools and immigrants with extra social difficulties. The posts funded were mostly teaching and social worker posts. 'Section XI' funding was always a contentious and contested issue. Criticism came from the Black community that it was not used in the right way: either the posts were seen as not relevant or the appointees to the posts were seen as not appropriate. For example, too many White people were recruited without suitable bilingual skills and cultural awareness. Also, even if Black people were appointed to the posts they were often insecure and dead-end specialist posts; funding from government was always under threat; and they were never seen as permanent. In fact, the level of subsidy to local authorities has gradually been withdrawn despite protests.

Race Relations Act 1976

The first anti-discrimination legislation in Britain was the Race Relations Act 1965, with a subsequent Act in 1968. These were limited in scope. The 1965 Act outlawed direct discrimination in public places where previously 'Whites only' admittance procedures were legal. The 1968 Act included employment and housing, therefore eliminating overt signs such as 'No coloureds, Irish or Dogs' outside accommodation for rent. However, as Blakemore and Drake (1996) pointed out the 'deeper and more pervasive effects of racism continued to be felt' (p. 121). These Acts, which were extremely cautious (Gregory, 1987; Jenkins and Solomos, 1989), were replaced by the last and most far-reaching 'race' legislation, the Race Relations Act (RRA) 1976, whose main provisions came into force on 13 June 1977. It mirrored the Sex Discrimination Act passed the previous year. The RRA repealed the previous Acts and established the Commission for Racial Equality (CRE) to oversee the Act for the government and to make recommendations to enhance its effectiveness.

The Commission for Racial Equality has both duties and powers. Its duties are:

- to work towards the elimination of discrimination
- to promote equality of opportunity and good 'race' relations between people of different racial groups
- to keep the workings of the Act under review and propose amendments, (amendments have been proposed since 1985, but no formal response has been forthcoming from the government)
- to make grants to organizations, promoting their aims, and also allocate money to research and educational activities – with the approval of the Home Secretary.

Its powers are:

- to carry out formal investigations, on its own initiative or as required by the Secretary of State, where there is suspicion of racial discrimination (these have been limited by a lack of expertise in the CRE itself (McCrudden *et al.*, 1991, p. 113)
- to serve non-discrimination notices where there is found to be discriminatory practices

- to help, advise and represent individuals taking cases under the legislation (people who have this support are more successful than others, but this support is limited by budget restraints)
- to produce and publish a code of practice. This is not legally binding but it is admissible in evidence to tribunals.

One of the major recognized problems with the powers of the CRE is that it does not have recourse to sufficient sanctions to make reluctant employers change bad and discriminatory practices. Also, as Blakemore and Drake (1996) pointed out, there has always been confusion about its role between the 'carrot or the stick'. The question of 'how far it should be a regulatory agency as opposed to a public awareness body, has dogged its history and weakened its impact in the employment field' (p. 128).

The Act makes racial discrimination unlawful in employment, training and related matters, education, the provision of goods, facilities and services, and the disposal and management of premises. The conditions of the Act are expressed in terms of 'racial grounds' and 'racial groups'. These terms are defined as relating to 'colour, race, nationality (including citizenship) or other ethnic or national origins'. A group can be defined by reference to its ethnic origins if it constitutes a separate and distinct community. However, the Act only gives individuals a right of direct access to industrial tribunals. 'Class actions' cannot be taken under the legislation.

The jurisdiction of the Act does not cover Northern Ireland and, importantly, it does not cover religious discrimination. This is only covered in Northern Ireland under the Fair Employment Act which is discussed later. Despite CRE calls to extend the Act to outlaw religious discrimination, it is still possible to discriminate on these grounds unless religious affiliation counts as membership of an ethnic group, such as the Jewish community. Or, in another example, indirect discrimination might be deemed to have occurred if an employer does not recruit Muslims because this would disproportionately discriminate against people from Pakistan and Bangladesh, many of whom are Muslims (Employment Department, 1995). Also, incitement to racial hatred, since 1986 included in the Public Order Act, is the only area classified as a criminal offence and therefore open to stronger penalties.

McCrudden *et al.* (1991, pp. 154–5) showed that ethnic minorities have utilized the RRA more than women have used the SDA, and three-quarters of all cases were heard within six months. Between 1992–93 and 1993–94, the total of race discrimination cases showed a 20 per cent increase to 1304. However, a substantial majority were withdrawn or settled and a very small minority of these were successful at tribunal. Problems were identified as the lack of expertise and specialist knowledge on 'race' discrimination on behalf of tribunal members and the lack of processes to ensure compensation awarded is actually paid (Gregory, 1987, p. 81).

The Act recognizes three kinds of discrimination: direct, indirect and victimization. Direct discrimination arises where a person treats another person less favourably on racial grounds than they treat, or would treat, someone else. An example of direct discrimination would be not considering a job applicant from a particular racial group because it was felt that they might be unreliable (Employment Department, 1995). Indirect discrimination is an important aspect of 'equal opportunities' law. It consists of treatment which can be described as equal in a formal sense between racial groups, but discriminatory in its effect on one particular racial group. To establish indirect discrimination it must be shown that:

- the requirement/condition was applied equally to persons of any racial group
- a considerably smaller proportion of a particular racial group can comply with it
- it is to the person's detriment because they suffer as a result
- it cannot be shown to be justifiable for a particular employment

Examples of indirect discrimination include recruiting by word of mouth from friends or relatives of employees if this excludes certain racial groups; and requiring women to wear skirts as this would rule out Asian women who have to wear trousers for religious or cultural reasons (Employment Department, 1995). In practice, there has been very little use made of the category of indirect discrimination. 'The vast majority of cases heard by industrial tribunals were concerned only with direct discrimination, hence the tribunals were articulating concepts only in that area' (McCrudden *et al.*, 1991, p. 271). Finally, victimization counts as discrimination under the Act when a person who has asserted their rights under the Act, either by bringing proceedings or giving evidence, is treated less favourably.

Discrimination is not unlawful where a person's 'race' is a 'Genuine Occupational Qualification' (GOQ) for a job. GOQs apply for reasons of authenticity or where the job holder provides individuals with personal services promoting their welfare or education or similar personal services, and those services can most effectively be provided by an individual of a particular 'race'. The Act also permits employers to take positive action to overcome the effects of past discrimination in a very limited way:

- where there is an imbalance in the numbers of particular racial groups doing particular work for an employer in the preceeding 12 months the employer may provide training for a particular racial group for that work
- and/or encourage members of the minority racial group to apply through advertising

Positive action is not to be confused with positive discrimination. Discrimination at the point of selection for work because of under-representation of a particular racial group is not permissible. Section 71 of the RRA is a unique and very important enabling and positive part of the Act. It places a specific duty on local authorities to:

- make appropriate arrangements with a view to ensuring that their various functions are carried out with due regard to the need to eliminate unlawful racial discrimination

- to promote equality of opportunities and good 'race' relations between people of different racial groups

There is no specific offence of racial harassment in either civil or criminal law. However, assaults of any kind are covered by criminal law, and a number of existing laws, both civil and criminal, can be used against perpetrators of racial incidents. These include: the Local Government Act 1972; the Race Relations Act 1976; the Public Order Act 1986; the Malicious Communications Act 1988; and the Criminal Justice Act 1991 (CRE, 1995b). The Criminal Justice and Public Order Act 1994 also makes it an offence to cause intentional harassment. There has been a strong campaign to try to persuade the government to give legal recognition to racial motivation in incidents of harassment and violence. The CRE has campaigned for racial harassment and attacks to be made a specific offence.

Immigration legislation and controls

Assumptions have been made that we can only have good 'race relations' by restricting the numbers of ethnic minority immigrants into Britain. There has always been immigration into and emigration from Britain, but after the Second World War immigration began to be given 'racial' connotations. Immigrant became synonymous with Black ethnic minorities. When people talked about immigrants they meant only Black immigrants, and all ethnic minorities were considered immigrants even though increasing numbers were born in Britain. The issue of the immigration of ethnic minorities became transfixed on the 'numbers game' and around such questions as: How many can Britain take? Will they take White people's jobs or houses? How many will change British culture?

This view was voiced through the notions of a 'fear of swamping' of our national culture and a rather crude call to nationalism. Typical of this approach was the following extract from a speech by Margaret Thatcher: 'the British character has done so much for democracy, for law, and done so much throughout the world, that if there is any fear that it might be swamped, people are going to react and be rather hostile to those coming in. So, if you want good race relations, you've got to allay people's fears on numbers' (Thatcher, 1978). The most articulate expression of this 'two-pronged attack' approach of 'keep them out, treat them fair' came from a former Labour MP: 'without integration, limitation is inexcusable; without limitation, integration is impossible' (Hattersley, 1965). Brah (1992a) described this process as 'a case study in how common-sense racism was appropriated into the mainstream of British parliamentary politics with the result that patriarchal racism is now institutionalized within the state apparatus' (p. 70).

Immigration controls have also always discriminated on the grounds of gender, seeing men as workers and women as dependants. As Brah (1992a) argued the arranged marriage system in some Asian communities was seen as a license for immigration which might override rules no matter how tightly drawn. Therefore, immigration controls determining the entry of foreign husbands and fiancés were tightened up for ethnic minority immigrants five times from 1969 to 1983. In 1985, the European Commission of Human Rights pronounced that British immigration controls discriminated against women. The government's response has been to equalize the issue by making it as difficult for Black ethnic minority men as it was for women to bring their husband or fiancé into the country. Where a partner is brought into the country, admission is subject to the 'primary purpose rule'. The immigrant has to prove the prime reason for entering is to marry rather than any other social or economic reason. They have to prove that their marriage is 'genuine'. There have been cases in the past of Asian women having to endure the humiliation of 'virginity tests' to gain entry.

Successive governments attempted to regulate, control and eventually stop the immigration of Black ethnic minorities into Britain (Sivanandan, 1982; MacDonald, 1983; Miles and Phizacklea, 1984). The first legislative measures controlling the immigration of citizens of Britain and the colonies were introduced in the Commonwealth Immigrants Act 1962, with its system of work vouchers which had to be obtained prior to entry. The 1968 Commonwealth Immigrants Act was passed in Parliament in three days withdrawing African Asians' right to enter, which had been given as part of independence settlements. It introduced immigration control for Commonwealth citizens who were non-patrials (that is, those who did not have a parent or grandparent born in Britain) and also put a limit on the number of work vouchers issued. This revealed the blatant racism underlying the law as White immigrants from such places as Australia, America and South Africa were far more likely to be patrials.

The 1969 Immigration Appeals Act extended the deportation powers of the Home Office. However, the 1971 Immigration Act was the most significant piece of legislation up to that date: it extended the deportation powers even further, but even more importantly it abolished the work-voucher system and therefore effectively stopped primary Black ethnic minority immigration. From this time the major form of immigration was restricted to secondary immigration: that is, wives and dependants. In addition, although men who entered Britain before the enactment date, 1 January 1973, were promised the automatic right to be joined by dependants, this was revoked by the 1988 Immigration Act.

The next significant piece of legislation came in the British Nationality Act 1981, which created three classes of citizenship and stated that citizenship could only be acquired by birth, descent or naturalization. Eligibility for citizenship is largely confined to people born of British parents or parents settled here. Many British citizens, for example those with dual nationality, such as Britain and a Caribbean country, had to register their desire to become a citizen under the new rules to retain their citizenship, which they had previously thought was theirs as of right.

The latest piece of legislation in this long saga of tightening and restricting the immigration of Black ethnic minorities to this country is based around the area of political asylum seekers. This is in the form of an Asylum and Immigration Act. The Act restricts the rights of refugees and asylum seekers, specifically their rights to social security benefits. It introduced a so-called 'white list' of countries which are considered safe and therefore automatically excluded asylum seekers from these countries who will be viewed as 'economic migrants' and turned away. There were originally seven designated 'white list' countries: India, Pakistan, Bulgaria, Cyprus, Ghana, Poland and Romania. Asylum claims from these countries are presumed to be unfounded and put through a procedure which would give claimants only ten days to produce the necessary documents (*Guardian*, 1996a). Provision within the Act removes asylum seekers to a so-called 'safe' third country if they have passed through such a designated country before arriving in Britain.

Because of these numerous immigration controls on ethnic minorities, many Asian families remain separated, and some women and children settled sometimes for many years in Britain have become liable for deportation caused by divorce or the death of their husband.

Legislation in the area of religion

Northern Ireland Fair Employment Act 1989

In Britain, the only law against religious discrimination is restricted to Northern Ireland. This legislation takes a firm, proactive and innovative approach to improve equality between the Catholic and Protestant communities in terms of employment. It outlaws direct and indirect discrimination on religious grounds. It requires private sector employers with more than ten employees and all public sector employers to register with the Fair Employment Commission (FEC) (similar to the EOC and the CRE, but with stronger powers over employers), and to monitor the religious composition of their workforces. The FEC can also enforce compulsory monitoring of recruitment and selection by employers with more than 250 employees. Also, all employers must review their employment practices every three years to make sure that they comply with the law. Failure to do so is a criminal offence. If the review reveals a problem, employers are required to take appropriate affirmative action and provide targets with a timetable. Both government contracts and grants may also be removed if employers refuse to comply with the legislation (Cooper, 1994; Sheehan, 1995).

However, Sheehan (1995) does identify limitations to this legislation. Because of the stipulation of the size of firms that are covered by the law, 30 per cent of the workforce are excluded from monitoring. These small firms are where women are disproportionately represented. The undefined concept of 'fair participation' in employment also underpins the legislation and powers of the FEC rather than anti-discrimination as in the SDA and RRA. As Sheehan (1995) explains, 'the Act has no remit to ensure equal treatment and just outcomes' (p. 75).

Legislation in the area of gender

Equal Pay Act 1970 (amended 1983)

There has been pressure for equal pay between men and women for a very long time. The Trade Union Congress passed a resolution in favour of this principle as far back as 1888, but it was not until 1970 that the first legislation in this area was passed in Britain. The legislation did not become fully operational until December 1975. The Equal Pay Act (EPA) allows women to claim equal pay with men if they are engaged on similar work or work of equal value on an individual case basis. As with the Sex Discrimination Act, this Act applies to both women and men, but the likelihood of a man making a claim for equal pay with a women is less likely, given the disparity in women's wages. This is in fact an indictment of the Act itself, which has not significantly narrowed the gap between the average earnings of men and women.

In July 1982, the European Court of Justice ruled that the Equal Pay Act did not fully comply with the 1975 EC Directive on Equal Pay. The British law was considered deficient because a woman could only obtain equal pay in respect of work which had an equal value to that of her male counterpart if a job evaluation scheme or study had been implemented. Although disagreeing with the judgement, the government finally changed the law on 1 January 1983. Therefore, as the Employment Department (1995) guide explained, even two different jobs can have 'equal value' if they place equal demands on workers in terms of effort, skill and decision-making. It is important, too, under the Act, that traditional male abilities, such as physical strength, are not given greater weighting than what are considered to be typical female skills, such as manual dexterity. The following example was cited:

A female cook was held by an industrial tribunal to be employed on work of equal value with that of male painters, thermal insulation engineers and joiners working for the same employer. The jobs were assessed under five headings: physical demands; environmental demands; planning and decision-making; skills and knowledge; and responsibility. The overall scores of the jobs were found to be equal. (p. 4)

Sex Discrimination Act 1975 (amended 1986)

The main provisions of the Sex Discrimination Act (SDA) came into force in 1975. It was amended in 1986 to bring it into line with the European Community Council's Equal Treatment Directive. The employment provisions of the Act were extended to include private households, firms with five or fewer employees, and collective agreements relating to pay, which had been previously excluded. The Act makes discrimination on the grounds of sex or marital status unlawful in employment, training and related matters, education, the provision of goods, facilities and services, and the disposal and management of premises. There is no protection under the Act for lesbian or gay men's rights. Although the

Act is drafted in terms of women being the object of discrimination, men can and have successfully brought claims under its provisions. For example, men have gained cheaper admission to swimming pools for retired people on an equal age basis to women by bringing a case to an industrial tribunal on the grounds of indirect discrimination. This was because although the conditions for cheaper entrance were equally applied to both women and men – they had to be retired – disproportionately fewer men could comply with the condition because of their later retirement age. The Act gives individuals a right of direct access to industrial tribunals.

There are, however, exceptions to the SDA where discrimination between the sexes is not unlawful. This includes:

- situations where discrimination is necessary in order to comply with a statute or regulation in force before the passing of the Act. For example, the provisions of the Factories Act 1961 in relation to the employment of women are still in force
- where female employees are given special treatment in connection with pregnancy or childbirth
- in respect of provisions relating to death or retirement

European law may have implications for the last general exception contained in the Act, and may limit its broad scope. There has been controversy over pension rights: a successful case was taken to the European Court where an employer was found to be discriminating against a woman by making her retire at 62 while her male colleagues could continue working until 65. The government has now decided to phase in equal retirement ages for men and women at 65 years of age.

Lawful discrimination in the form of 'Genuine Occupational Qualifications' (GOQ) is allowed in the same way as for the Race Relations Act. However, in respect of sex discrimination only, certain extra GOQs apply where:

- for reasons of decency or privacy it is desirable to employ men only or women only for a particular job (e.g. because the job-holder works with people who are in a state of undress or where physical contact is necessary)
- the job makes it necessary for the job-holder to live on the premises and the only available building provides sleeping and sanitary facilities for one sex (in these cases the employer may continue to employ people of one sex, providing that it is not reasonably practicable to alter the accommodation or provide other premises)
- the job is in a single-sex establishment for persons requiring special care; and where the job is a joint appointment to be held by a married couple

The SDA established the Equal Opportunities Commission (EOC) with the same duties and powers as the CRE, but obviously in the areas of gender, and the same positive action provisions were established in the areas of training and advertising, with the same conditions laid down. The Act also recognizes the same three categories of discrimination: direct, indirect and victimization. An example of direct discrimination would be not interviewing or appointing a woman because it was felt that, because of her sex, she would not fit into the organization (Employment Department, 1995). Examples of indirect discrimination include: insisting on an unnecessary height requirement; requiring a person to work evenings when this is not operationally necessary; and refusing training or promotion to part-timers, if most part-time jobs are held by women and most full-time ones by men (Employment Department, 1995).

Indirect discrimination against a married person is similar in concept to indirect sex and 'race' discrimination and may arise where a condition or requirement was applied equally to married and unmarried people of the same sex but which was discriminatory in its effect on married people. A requirement to be mobile for a job might be detrimental to more married than single people.

A fuller example of the way in which the courts decide whether indirect sex discrimination has taken place is illustrated by the following successful case of Home Office v. Holmes involving a woman employee returning to work following maternity leave. On returning, she asked if she could work on a part-time basis. The Home Office refused. Ms Holmes then took her case to an industrial tribunal on the grounds of indirect discrimination. The tribunal decided that the requirement to work full-time:

- disproportionately affected women. Proof of this was accepted by statistics which showed that there were fewer women of child-bearing age in employment because of domestic responsibilities, which put a greater burden on women
- was unjustifiable as it was convenient for management to impose a requirement of full-time working, but it was not strictly necessary.

However, the tribunal added that if as a result of their decision a greater demand for part-time work arose so as to substantially affect the organization's efficiency, it would be open to the Home Office to reimpose the condition of full-time working. It is important to note that this was an individual case and every case is heard on its own merits.

The Employment Rights Act 1996

The Employment Rights Act applies to all employees but it holds particular interest in 'equal opportunities' terms for women in relation to maternity provisions. These provide that a woman may claim maternity leave, maternity pay and the right to return to work providing certain conditions of employment are met and notification of her intentions to exercise her rights under the Act are given. The Act also provides that a woman cannot unreasonably be refused time off for ante-natal care and has the right to be paid for the time off.

Omissions from the legislation

None of the 'equal opportunities' legislation covers any protection of rights for lesbians and gay men. Another major area of disadvantage which stands out as being not addressed by anti-discrimination legislation is age. McEwen (1990) argues that age is 'the unrecognized discrimination'. The government adamantly refused to consider legislation in this area despite acknowledging the problem, arguing instead for persuasion and exhortation to employers. Age discrimination is legal in Britain providing it cannot be shown to contravene the SDA whereby women are less likely to be able to comply with lower age restrictions on posts because more women take time out of careers for child-bearing and rearing. An EOC survey of job advertisements showed that more than one-quarter stated an age preference and two-thirds asked for applicants aged under 35 (Laczko and Phillipson, 1990, p. 88).

Summary

This chapter has looked at both the politics and the legislation behind 'equal opportunities' in Britain. First, it investigated and analysed the ideological and historical background to 'equal opportunities' through its division into four different eras: the 'moral' era of the 1940s–1950s; the legislative era of the 1960s–1970s; the political era of the 1980s; and finally the economic, public relations and professional era of the 1990s. It is argued that these eras can be distinguished by the politics of the time which led to differing legislation and organizational approaches to 'equal opportunities'. The analysis is carried out in the light of the major driving forces and catalysts for change in the different decades.

In terms of developments, the first era was hardly an 'equal opportunities' era at all. Nevertheless, early thinking on 'equal opportunities' during the 1940s and 1950s was based on morality and ideas of equality and justice, and this era produced the first legislation in the area of disability. During the second era, the 1960s and the 1970s, the major legislation was laid down to outlaw 'race' and sex discrimination. The third era, the 1980s, brought a major change in political outlooks, policy objectives and economic organization with a shift to an emphasis on markets and individuals, and a sharp division between the political left and right. Finally, with the 1990s came a partial acceptance of 'equal opportunities' by the establishment and successful pressure from the growing militancy of disabled people's groups for their own anti-discrimination legislation.

The second half of the chapter detailed and discussed the most important and significant legislation in the field of 'equal opportunities'. This legislation has covered both employment and access to services in the areas of disability, 'race', religion and gender. These Acts include, in the area of disability, the Disabled Persons (Employment) Acts 1944 and 1958, the Chronically Sick and Disabled Persons Act 1970, the Companies Act 1985 and the Disability Discrimination Act 1995. In the area of 'race' and religion we see the Commonwealth Immigrants Act 1962, the Local Government Act 1966, the Immigration Act 1971, the Race Relations Act 1976, the British Nationality Act 1981, and the Fair

Employment Protection Act, Northern Ireland, 1989. Finally, in the area of gender are the Equal Pay Act 1970 (amended 1984), the Sex Discrimination Act 1975 (amended 1986), and the Employment Rights Act 1996. The main provisions of the Acts are set out and examined in the light of their potential limitations.

CHAPTER 4

'Equal opportunities' in Britain today: the influence of the European Union and an appraisal of the current state of national legislation

This chapter considers the influence of the European Union to date and its potential for influence in the future on 'equal opportunities' legislation and policies in Britain in the areas of gender, 'race' and disability. It then moves on to examine current national legislation and its potential impact on 'equal opportunities'.

The European Union

With the European Union's (EU) increasing significance and influence on national legislation, it is important that we look beyond national boundaries for influence on 'equal opportunities'. The preamble to the Treaty of Rome stated that its signatories were 'determined to lay the foundation of ever closer union among the peoples of Europe'. Its objectives were the establishment of a common market, the approximation of economic policies of the member states and the harmonious development of economic activities. To this end it aimed to achieve the 'approximation of the laws of the member states to the extent required for the proper functioning of the Common Market'.

The aims and principles of the EU dictate that its laws must be applied uniformly and have supremacy over any conflicting national legislation. To enable EU law to be enacted in Britain it was necessary for Parliament to introduce the European Communities Act 1972. This allows EU laws to have effect in Britain without any further British legislation, but the Act is subject to the doctrine of Parliamentary supremacy. In other words, it could in principle be repealed at any time. Moreover, in 1992, we saw further integration with the completion of the single European market, intended to give the freedom to EU citizens to work, to establish businesses and to trade in other EU countries.

Legislation from the EU takes several different forms. Roelofs (1995) offered us a useful distinction between two ways in which it is enacted, both of which have been used in the area of 'equal opportunities': 'regulatory policy' and 'soft law'. Regulatory policy takes the form of regulations and directives, both of which are binding on the Member States. However, whereas regulations are immediately binding and rigidly applied in the form that has been mutually agreed, directives require member states to achieve a specific end result within a certain period of time through national legislation. Directives have been favoured in the application of 'equal opportunities', particularly in the field of gender equality (as we will see later in this chapter). They are only effective against the state, but the European Court of Justice (ECJ) has a wide view of what constitutes the state, including a wide variety of formally autonomous bodies (a British example was the case of Foster v. British Gas, 1990). On the other hand, soft law takes the form of recommendations on policy goals. They attempt to influence member states, but have no sanctions attached. 'Equal opportunities' policy has tended to move more recently to this diluted form in the area of gender equality to attempt to ensure consensus.

European Union influence on British 'equal opportunities' policy

As illustrated above, accession into the EU has had a major impact on the British legal system. Even previously established legislation, such as the Equal Pay Act, had to be amended to meet EU requirements (see Chapter 3). The EU can be seen to be fundamentally grounded in the issue of 'equal opportunities'. Article 14 of the European Convention for the Protection of Human Rights required that the other rights and freedoms secured under the convention 'shall be secured without discrimination on any ground such as sex, race, colour, religion, or political affiliation'.

However, 'equal opportunities' has been seen by the EU largely in terms of gender (Spelling, 1995), and this is one of the few policy areas where EU policy has outstripped the policy of member states (Warner, 1984). Roelofs (1995) showed that if we look at the EU's social policy framework, there are only three areas in which it is clearly active. One is the equal treatment of women and men (the others are the co-ordination of social insurance schemes and health and safety). Blakemore and Drake (1996) argued that 'the teeth of European Community law are almost entirely felt in the area of equal opportunities for women' (p. 42). As Meehan (1993a) demonstrated gender equality has been given 'pride of place' in European legislation, while other areas, particularly 'race', have been relatively ignored. Two reasons were suggested for this. First, France insisted on the equal treatment of women and men being included in the original Treaty, because it had already made policy moves in the area of equal pay for equal or the same work and did not want unfair competition from other member states (Hantrais, 1993). Second, by concentrating on women's issues, the EU was reaching 50 per cent of its population, or more cynically convincing 50 per cent of its electorate that it was relevant and important (Roelofs, 1995). There are 165 million women in the EU, with over 53 million in employment (Crawley and Slowey, 1995). We will see this concentration on women's issues and the relative neglect of the issues of 'race' and disability more clearly in the following sections.

Gender

The European Commission (1994) claimed that 'it is now widely recognised that the legal framework reflecting social policy at European Union level has been a catalyst for major social change in the Member States' (p. 41). Crawley and Slowey (1995) also felt that EU influence has been a major benefit for women: 'Almost all the gains working women in the United Kingdom have made over the past decade can be traced to changes in legislation at the European level' (p. 8).

However, generally Britain has been characterized by a cautious, if not negative, approach to European legislation and the government has shown a repeated reluctance to bring Britain into line with other European states, even in the area of gender inequality where the EU has been most active. EU sex discrimination law has been evoked on more occasions in the British courts than in any other Member State and on occasions the EU has brought proceedings against Britain to force their compliance. This is because the Equal Opportunities Commission has been actively involved in invoking European Law to win sex discrimination cases against the government. Many of these cases brought about changes to British law (Meehan, 1993a). Any changes that have been introduced by the British government, because of EU pressure, appear to have been done so grudgingly, at the last possible moment, in the narrowest possible way and in a piecemeal fashion (Meehan, 1993b; Crawley and Slowey, 1995). Crawley and Slowey (1995) cited the example of the progress of the 1992 Directive on Pregnant Women at Work. Over two years Britain blocked it and attempted to water it down, and then finally implemented it in a minimalist way in the Trade Union and Employment Rights Bill 1993. Britain has also blocked and stalled Directives on Parental Leave and Protection for Part-time and Temporary Workers.

The legal framework of Community Law regarding equal treatment of the sexes consists of several directives, treaty terms, decisions of the European Court of Justice and the general principle of the removal of sex discrimination as a fundamental right. It originates in Article 119 of the Treaty of Rome 1957, which established the principle of equal treatment for women and men workers in terms of pay. It states:

Each member state shall during the first stage ensure and subsequently maintain the principle that men and women should receive equal pay for equal work. For purposes of this article, "pay" means the ordinary basic or minimum wage or salary and any other consideration whether in cash or in kind which the worker receives, directly or indirectly, in respect of his [sic] employment from his employer. Equal pay without discrimination based on sex means:

(a) that pay for the same work at piece rates shall be calculated on the basis of the same unit of measurement;

(b) that pay for the same work at time rates shall be the same for the same job (Roelofs, 1995, p. 131).

This principle achieved very little action until the 1970s, when there was a growth in the women's movement and a political climate more receptive to challenge. A series of five Directives followed on:

- The Equal Pay Directive (75/117) 1975
- The Equal Treatment Directive (76/207) 1976
- The Directive on Equality in Social Security (79/7) 1979
- The Directive on Equal Treatment in Occupational Social Security (86/378) 1986
- The Sex Discrimination (Self-Employed) Directive (86/613) 1986

The first, the Equal Pay Directive, developed the principle of equal pay for work of equal value. In 1979, the European Commission found that Britain's Equal Pay Act did not conform to this principle and subsequently forced its amendment (Maes, 1990, p. 55). The Equal Treatment Directive ruled out sex discrimination in access to employment, selection criteria, access to all jobs and all levels of the hierarchy, opportunities for training and vocational guidance, promotion procedures and other terms and conditions of employment (Myles, 1992). Exceptions were still possible where sex was a genuine occupational qualification for reasons of authenticity or the personal nature of the work, and for the protection of pregnant women and mothers (see Chapter 3 for how this corresponds to the Sex Discrimination Act). The Social Security Directive covered equal treatment in the area of statutory social security schemes to employed, self-employed, retired and invalided workers insured against sickness, redundancy, accidents at work, occupational diseases and non-contributory benefits. The fourth directive dealt with private occupational or non-statutory pension and insurance schemes, and the last covers the position of women who are self-employed, especially in family business and in agriculture. Subsequent directives have been relatively ineffectual and were often blocked by Britain. These included those covering parental leave, part-time work, the shifting of the burden of proof of discrimination from the complainant to the employer, and atypical work. A directive governing the protection of pregnant women at work did come into force in 1991. However, the objections raised by the British government meant that it was seriously neutralized to prescribe only the minimum norms, which the Member States are to satisfy, and to prohibit them from reducing their national legislation in this area. As Roelofs (1995) pointed out, this leaves about 60 per cent of women in Britain with no right to maternity leave.

In the area of 'soft law', the EU has made several recommendations in areas such as positive action (1984), 'equal opportunities' in education (1985) and vocational training (1987). A Recommendation on Child Care came into effect in 1992 intending to encourage more effective child care, leave of absence arrangements for both parents from work, and therefore, a more equal distribution of responsibility between women and men for child-rearing.

The deterioration in the economic climate in Europe and political moves against regulatory policies from the EU have led to the development of a series of action programmes on 'equal opportunities' for women from the 1980s. These programmes concentrate on persuasion and carry no sanctions. The first programme was for 1982 to 1985 and concentrated on consolidating and implementing existing legislation and attempting to promote positive action programmes. Despite many of these initiatives being limited and small-scale, a positive assessment was made by the European Commission and a similar consolidating second programme launched for 1986 to 1990 with the addition of the area of technological change. The third programme for 1991 to 1995, which again aimed to endorse existing legislation, also included issues such as the integration of women into the labour market and the improvement of the social position of women. The fourth action programme for 1996 to 2000 was only passed after considerable opposition, principally this time from Germany, which led to its budget being halved from 60 million ECU to 30 million (£51 million) (EOR, 1996b). This programme appeared to concentrate on promotion rather than action. It sought to promote the 'mainstreaming' of 'equal opportunities' through its integration into all policies, measures and activities in the Community and its Member States. It offered support for projects aimed at identifying and transferring good practice, conducting studies and research, implementation of any action to promote the exchange and dissemination of information on equal pay, equal treatment and 'equal opportunities', and monitoring, analysis and assessment of action taken under the programme (CEC, 1995).

European Union legislation has produced changes towards greater equality for women in Britain, mainly because of decisions made by the European Court of Justice (ECJ). The following are some examples. The European Equal Treatment Directive has been very influential in the area of pensions. Action programmes during the 1980s and later European Court of Justice decisions have made it unavoidable for Britain to equalize the retirement ages for women and men. Women and men have always been treated differently in Britain with regard to retirement and subsequent pension entitlement. One case was Marshall v. Southampton and South West Area Health Authority. Marshall's compulsory retirement at 62 was tested, within Britain, as less favourable treatment under the Sex Discrimination Act. This was rejected by the Industrial Tribunal on the grounds that the Act excluded retirement issues. Marshall then claimed that her forced retirement was contrary to the European Equal Treatment Directive and this was upheld by the ECJ. This decision was based on the concept that compulsory early retirement constituted unfair dismissal rather than differences in the pensionable age between men and women. A second case was Foster v. British Gas Plc 1990 where the ECJ decided that because of the European Equal Treatment Directive female employees forced to retire at the age of 60, where men could continue until they were 65, must be entitled to compensation for loss of earnings (Meehan, 1993b).

Another area of influence for the Equal Treatment Directive was the example of compensation awards given to women who were unlawfully dismissed from the armed forces because they became pregnant. The high compensation awards in these cases were also allowed because the limit of £11 000 was ruled by the ECJ as against European law in August 1993. In 1994, the first woman to have her case heard was awarded a record amount of £172,912 (EOR, 1994a). In the area of equal pay, the European Equal Pay Directive states that equal pay should be given to work of equal value in terms of effort, skill and decision making, whereas the Equal Pay Act 1970 only provided for similar and equivalent work. Enforcement proceedings were brought against the British government by the European Commission which led to the Equal Pay Act being amended to give the right to equal value claims (Callender, 1996).

Race

The ethnic minority population in the EU stands at 2.6 per cent or nine million people (Forbes and Mead, 1992). However, when we look to Europe we find that 'race' is an area 'from which the language of human or fundamental rights . . . has been noticeably absent' and EU law has not developed to protect people from racial discrimination (de Búrca, 1995). This is despite the fact that throughout the Member States there are not many comprehensive and effective measures to combat racial discrimination and in many states they are entirely absent (Forbes and Mead, 1992). This lack of activity on 'race' contrasts with the position of sex discrimination as 'pride of place' (Meehan, 1993a). 'European legislation on gender and race equality could . . . be seen as occupying the opposite ends of a spectrum from significant to minimal concern' (Blakemore and Drake, 1996, p. 41). Given its proposals on 'equal opportunities' for women, the EU appears to have legal competence to tackle racial discrimination, and the lack of action on this issue seems to represent a lack of political will and much less consensus among Member States.

The European Parliament has called for the 'review and amendment of national legislation against political extremism, racism and racial discrimination'. All this falls short of what is required: community legislation against racial discrimination. There is increasingly well-developed Community law against aspects of sex discrimination, so why not against racial discrimination? If the actual motivation for equal pay legislation was to ensure that no Member States' employers were at a competitive disadvantage by providing equal pay, then there is an equally forceful argument that no Member States' employers should be at a competitive disadvantage by taking measures to eliminate racial discrimination. Despite this, anti-discrimination law on the grounds of 'race' remains largely untouched by European Law. The European Convention of Human Rights does condemn racial discrimination, but, as Forbes and Mead (1992) argue;

- conventions are important only through the *pressure* they place on governments to introduce domestic legislation to prohibit discrimination in employment
- access to the provisions of conventions is very poor
- a prerequisite for effective protection from discrimination in employment is the *actual* introduction of such legislation. (p. ii).

In comparative terms Britain has a better framework for protection against racial discrimination than the other member states of the EU

(Forbes and Mead, 1992). 'Even as it stands, the Race Relations Act is in advance of specific race legislation elsewhere in the European Community' (CRE, 1991, p. 5). This means that ethnic minorities coming to Britain from Europe fall within the protection of British laws, whereas ethnic minorities going from Britain to Europe lose the protection of British laws, and are not so well protected elsewhere. There is the real danger that a process of harmonizaion of laws might lead not to an improvement in protection from racial discrimination across Europe, but to a reduction to the lowest common denominator. That could all be done in the name of free trade.

It has been observed that 'race' issues may be moving on to the EU agenda, although the EU still uses language such as 'immigrants' and 'migrants' in this area, a discourse which can be seen to be out-of-date and no longer relevant in Britain. However, in contrast to Britain where 'immigrants' have settled and are nationals, there are problems in Germany with the status of, for example, 'migrant' workers of Turkish origin who may have been born, educated, worked and paid taxes in Germany, but do not have German nationality. Rights to non-discrimination on grounds of nationality under Article 7 and to free movement under Article 48 relate only to EU nationals (EUNs) and do not have a role in countering 'race' discrimination for ethnic minorities who possess community nationality. In fact, it has been argued that this type of discourse has had a negative impact on ethnic minority EUNs.

To facilitate freedom of movement within the EU for EUNs, the EU's emergent immigration policy has developed into one of 'Fortress Europe', which, while providing 'freedom to move for those within the fortress', also provides 'insurmountable barriers excluding those who are not' (Hervey, 1995, p. 99). As part of this process, Brah (1992b) described how the EU has moved towards a common definition of European by a process of exclusion of what are labelled third country nationals (TCNs) whose 'otherness' is emphasized and became identified with 'race' and ethnic origin and inevitably colour of skin. This has led to the EU being labelled as a 'White Man's Club' (Dummett, 1991, p. 169). Sivanandan (1988) in his description of 'common market racism' showed how the 'negative list' of countries whose citizens need visas to enter the EU disproportionately contains countries in Africa, the Caribbean, the Indian subcontinent and the Middle East. At the EU level the same forums that discuss immigration issues also deal with drug trafficking and terrorism (Rex, 1992). Alongside this associated stigma, Hervey (1995) pointed out the language of racism in the EU's statements on immigration and asylum-seekers policies, using such phrases as 'migration pressure' and 'controlling migration flows' to solve a 'problem'. Hervey (1995) argued that these policies to control and limit the immigration of TCNs has an impact on Black EUNs. Because the dominant image of the EU is White European, emphasized through the promotion of commonality of European cultural heritage, other cultures in the EU are 'marginalised or silenced'. Black EUNs are also likely to be discriminated against by association with stereotyped 'problem' groups, such as TCNs and illegal immigrants (Paul, 1991; Webber, 1991). This has already led to reports of victimization and harassment of Black EUNs by immigration officials and the police.

There have been reports to the European Parliament in 1985 and 1990 which have documented the disturbing facts on the rise in racism and xenophobia in Europe (Ford, 1992). Their findings included anxiety about:

- the rise of extreme right-wing groups in Europe
- the fact that France and Germany have the largest number of extreme right-wing members of parliament
- Britain, Germany, France, Italy and Denmark have the worst examples of racist attacks
- in Ireland racism was directed against Gypsies

Recommendations for the preparation of a draft directive on race discrimination have been made following the Declaration on Racism and Xenophobia adopted in 1986. However, a 1992 resolution adopted by the EU placed primary responsibility for action with the individual member states (Bourne and Whitmore, 1993). The European Council in 1994 proposed a Consultative Commission to encourage tolerance and understanding of foreigners. However, so far there have only been various forms of 'soft law', such as declarations on racism and xenophobia (fear of strangers), but nothing is backed up by regulatory policies. These have been described as remaining at the level of rhetoric, as various declarations have not been followed up by 'hard law' (Hervey, 1995).

European action on 'race' issues was likely to be encouraged by developments in Central and Eastern Europe – and unemployment. The increase in the number of refugees and political asylum-seekers combined with the Europe-wide recession has led to the increased incidence of racist activities and attacks. There was also a mention of the growing pressure from the European Parliament on the Commission to take further 'concrete action to combat discrimination on the grounds of race, religion, age and disability', and its increasingly unjustifiable omittance from the European Treaties (European Commission, 1994). This led to an EU summit declaration in 1996 outlawing racism and xenophobia.

Disability

Similar to the position on 'race', despite recognizing that there are 30 million disabled people in Europe, 10 per cent of the population, there are no European Community regulations or directives dealing specifically with discrimination against disability (European Commission, 1994). 'The claims and interests of disabled people do not seem to have attained the same status of "fundamental rights" protected within Community law' (de Búrca, 1995). Instead there have been action programmes, recommendations and resolutions developed to promote the social and economic integration of disabled people. These include:

- Social Action Programme 1974
- Community Action Programme 1983
- Recommendation on Employment 1986
- Programme on Integration of Children in Schools 1987
- Second Community Programme – Special Emphasis on Independent Living 1988–1991
- Report on Equal Access to Vocational Training and Employment 1989
- Action Programme on Mobility and Provision of Transport 1990
- Resolution on Integration of Children and Young Adults into Education 1990
- Third Community Action Programme 1992–1996

The 1986 recommendation did endorse the elimination of discrimination and positive action in the area of disabled people's employment. But this can be seen again, as in the field of 'race', as only 'soft law', which has not been followed up with binding directives (Burca, 1995; Oliver, 1996). This was even though the first official report on the progress of the second action programme recognized that 'disabled people form one of the most disadvantaged groups in the population' (Daunt, 1991, p. 151). There was also recognition from the European Commission (1994) that there was a need for change: 'as a group, people with disabilities undoubtedly face a wide range of obstacles which prevent them from achieving full economic and social integration' (p. 51). Despite this, one judgement by the ECJ can be seen as detrimental to disabled people's rights. In the 1989 case of Bettray v. Staatssecretaris Van Justitie, the Court decided that disabled people who were in rehabilitative sheltered employment might not constitute 'workers' and would therefore not be eligible to protection given to workers under EU law (Burca, 1995).

Lunt and Thornton (1993) reported on the development of policies for the employment of disabled people in the member states of the EU. They found that generally there was an emphasis on the recruitment rather than retention or career development of disabled people, and mostly a commitment to compulsory employment measures stipulating targets for the open employment of disabled people. Exceptions to this pattern are Denmark and Britain. In Denmark, disabled people are entitled to financial, practical or social support on the basis of need, not disability itself, and not linked to the labour market. The idea of a 'quota system' has been ruled out because the categorization of people as disabled is seen as contradicting basic social rights and as discriminatory. Britain is the first Member State to introduce a Disability Discrimination Act and to remove its 'quota system'. Lunt and Thornton (1993) identified a move away from compensatory measures towards facilitating the right to work and a shift to an ideology of independence and responsibility. This was in the context of the growing influence of disabled people's organizations and pressures for deinstitutionalization.

Many Member States have developed proactive policies on employment opportunities for disabled people. Two examples of Germany and Italy, given below, are drawn from Lunt and Thornton's (1993) examination of employment policies for disabled people in 15 EU and non-EU countries. Germany's legislative approach to the employment of disabled people was underpinned by rehabilitation rather than by benefits and rooted in traditions of compulsory employment. In the old East Germany, when it was still a separate state, it guaranteed all disabled people a job. Employers had to meet a 10 per cent quota, but there were no sanctions. Now in unified Germany there is a 6 per cent quota of registered disabled employees for both public and private sector employers with at least 16 employees. Registration gives access to other benefits, including an extra week's holiday and travel concessions and does not appear to be an obstacle to the success of the legislation. The current Severely Disabled Persons Act, introduced in 1974 and amended in 1986, is strictly enforced. If employers are below their quota, they pay a monthly fine which goes towards the cost for other companies of adapting their premises for disabled workers. This provides money from industry through the state to disabled people. As well as the compensation levy, employers are required to examine every vacant position for its potential for a severely disabled person, and provide special protection and representation of disabled workers in the workplace. Another interesting example of an innovative project for the supported open employment for young people with severe learning difficulties comes from Genoa in Italy (Lunt and Thornton, 1993). Genoa has a completely integrated education system with no special schools. After compulsory schooling the project 'intercepts' young people and prepares, matches, places and gives continuous support for them in the workplace. The project relies on co-workers to teach job skills as opposed to professionals providing work skills, and believes it is sustained by demonstrating success to employers. During the initial training period the project pays the young person's salary and the employer provides the training and support of co-workers. After the training the employer takes on the full financial responsibility for the worker, but the project continues to give permanent support when needed.

'Equal opportunities' in Britain in the 1990s

Possible future influence of the EU

Further benefits may be expected for women in the future from the EU. It remains strongly committed to 'equal opportunities' for women as the following statement demonstrated:

This adaptability and creativity of women is a strength that should be harnessed to the drive for growth and competitiveness in the EU. Lower activity rates of women in the EU (66%) compared to women in the USA, Japan and non-EU countries (72%) is a factor which militates against achieving greater competitiveness, especially given the current predominance of women in second- and third-level education in the EU and their generally higher educational attainments. (European Commission, 1994, p. 41)

However, there has been criticism of European legislation in this area, as it was shaped on the principle of equal treatment for workers, which did little to break down 'stereotypes and to take account of the different, real experiences of men and women at work and in the family' (Meehan, 1993b, p. 200). Also, Britain remains opposed to any extension of Community control, especially in the field of social policy. As Roelofs (1995) argued: 'EU law has given women more legal instruments with which to insist on an improvement in their position. But the restricted scope of the equal opportunities policy is largely a result of the decisive role which the member states themselves play in the Union's decision-making process' (p. 139).

Britain has opted out of two notable developments of European legislation: the Social Charter (the Community Charter of the Fundamental Rights of Workers) approved by the European Council in December 1989, and the implementation of the Treaty of Maastricht's (1991) clauses on employees' rights and employer–employee relations. The European Social Charter was the social dimension of the single European Market, which was supported by all Member States in 1989, except the UK (Meehan, 1993b; Roelofs, 1995). Its formal title was 'The Community Charter of Fundamental Social Rights for Workers' and these included the right of men and women to equal treatment, and the social and professional integration of disabled people (see Chapter 9 for the actual wording of the relevant Articles from the Charter). Again, the issue of racial discrimination was almost totally ignored – only being mentioned in the preamble – and its elimination was not cited as a fundamental social right.

The Social Charter's subsequent action programme included provisions on the right of men and women to equal treatment, on health and safety at work, rights to retraining, freedom of movement and employment, social protection and social security, improvement of living and working conditions, rights to consultation and worker participation, and protection for workers excluded from the workforce such as older and disabled people. As Collins (1991) showed the reactions to the implementation of the Charter have been mixed in the other 11 Member States, but all except Britain have made some moves. The Treaty of Maastricht signified and confirmed the commitment of all but Britain to continue developments in the area of social legislation.

In 1996 at the European Women's Summit hosted by the Italian Presidency of the EU a 'Charter of Rome' was signed 'as a declaration of political will to promote the presence of women in decision-making' (*Women of Europe Newsletter*, 1996). The Member States that signed 'committed themselves to develop within their countries incentives, laws and regulatory measures to achieve a balanced participation of women and men in decision making' (*Women of Europe Newsletter*, 1996). There were only two Member States who did not sign up to the 'Charter': Spain because it was in the process of forming a new government, and the UK which refused to sign it for political reasons. What role European law will play in the future of 'equal opportunities' in Britain therefore remains unclear. Community law is unquestionably moving towards equality as a fundamental right, but at this stage it is difficult to say exactly how this will effect UK law. However, despite its resistance, Britain's 'equal opportunities' legislation, certainly in the area of gender, will continue to be influenced and affected by the ECJ, the court of appeal since the signing of the Treaty of Rome in 1957, which can and does amend or even override British court decisions and pre-Maastricht 'equal opportunities' legislation to which Britain is committed.

National Legislation

The official concept of 'equal opportunities' in Britain is very much influenced by the framework used in the legislation of the 1970s: the Equal Pay Act, Sex Discrimination Act and Race Relations Act, and subsequently the Disability Discrimination Act 1995. It can be argued that this has limited thinking about the subject in several ways: it takes an 'individualistic' approach with very little recall to 'group justice', it is 'protective' rather than proactive, and it is legally complex, leading to many unsuccessful cases in industrial tribunals.

The dominant feature of the legislation is that it is premised on individual justice. The approach is fundamentally 'individualistic' rather than 'collective', despite individuals having to belong to a particular group to be eligible to invoke the law. In other words, to use the Sex Discrimination Act one must be either a woman or a man who is being treated differently to the other sex, but recourse under the law is only as an individual. This arises from the traditional British legal convention that people appear before the courts as individuals. Therefore, individuals have to take cases on their own and where 'equal opportunities' remedies are applied by industrial tribunals these are restricted to individuals. Thus the Sex, Race and Disability Discrimination Acts require complainants to find someone who is a member of the legally defined 'other' group in an identical situation with which to compare themselves in order to prove that discrimination has taken place. This is regardless of the fact that most women, ethnic minorities and disabled people rarely find themselves in directly comparable situations with men, White people and non-disabled people. These groups have usually already been filtered into an occupational or skills-based ghetto where different standards prevail.

An example of this is the Equal Pay Act, where employers were given five years to prepare for its implementation. Most employers used this period to remove all women from jobs where they might have been able to claim comparability with men, making occupational segregation worse than it was before (Glucklich, 1984). Also, although the Equal Pay legislation allows women to claim equal pay for work of equal value, its effect remains limited by the fact that, in the final analysis, the judgement of what is the value of any given job remains a subjective one. Even the most impartial arbiter will inevitably be influenced by such factors as:

- the scarcity of the skills involved in a job
- the amount of formal training required to do it, which may merely be a reflection of the organizational strength of the people who negotiated the prevailing apprenticeship or training agreement rather than the intrinsic difficulty of the job
- the difficulty of recruitment in the area
- the 'going rate' for this type of work
- judgements about the level of responsibility involved which reflect prevailing views about the relative value of different types of work

These considerations will inevitably reproduce many of the ideas which have led to the present devaluing of the work done by women. An example of these difficulties was in a job-evaluation scheme in which I was involved, undertaken in a local authority for their manual workers. When some 'men's jobs', such as refuse collection, were scoring lower than some 'women's jobs', such as cooks, the trade unions asked for a reallocation of the points system. Skills which women are expected to carry out without payment in the home as part of their normal household duties, such as childcare, cleaning, cooking or communicating with 'difficult', sick or elderly people are unlikely to be valued as highly as those traditionally undertaken by men in the labour market.

Very few parts of the British 'equal opportunities' legislation are based on 'group justice'. There is, first, the work of the Equal Opportunities Commission, the Commission for Racial Equality and the National Disability Council which covers everyone who belongs to an appropriate group as defined by the legislation. Second, another area is the prohibition of indirect discrimination, which is rarely used by complainants. This consists of treatment which can be described as equal in a formal sense between groups, but discriminatory in its effect on one particular group. To establish indirect discrimination it must be shown that the requirement or condition was applied equally to persons of any group but a considerably smaller proportion of a particular group can comply with it. Third, Section 71 of the Race Relations Act 1976, is another area, which uniquely places a duty on local authorities to make appropriate arrangements with a view to ensuring that their various functions are carried out with due regard to the need to eliminate unlawful racial discrimination, and to promote equality of opportunities and good 'race' relations between people of different racial groups. The effect of this part of the Act has diminished with the reduction in influence and power of local authorities in service delivery, such as education and the provision of council housing. Finally, the positive action aspects of the legislation in advertising and training can be seen as based on 'group justice' by giving employers scope to help members of under-represented groups to compete for jobs on an equal footing with the rest of the workforce (see Chapter 3 for a fuller discussion of these aspects of the legislation).

In this way, the British legislation is more limited than that in the USA which allows for 'class action' cases to be taken against employers on behalf of groups of workers. In the USA, if an employer has to pay compensation for discriminating against a particular employee, they have to pay compensation to all employees in that class. This can be a severe financial penalty. In Britain, the employer only has to pay an individual and compensation levels were low so that 'by making discrimination cheap [the law] virtually ensures the ineffectiveness of the rights approach' (Lustgarten and Edwards, 1992, p. 274). Also, the British system does not allow quotas like the USA based on labour market percentages. As Lustgarten (1989, p. 18) pointed out in the area of 'race' the effects on employers were very limited: only the individual who brings a successful case of racial discrimination is compensated and not similar employees. This is also true for cases of sex and disability discrimination.

Another label for the 'equal opportunities' legislation is 'protective'. It involves the creation of rights, which the weaker party can assert by means of litigation, in the traditional mode of private law. It is not a proactive or preventative law. It tells people what they must not do and punishes them for wrong doing, rather than setting up environments that would be conducive to 'equal opportunities'. For the law to work, the protected person must invoke the legal process or the penalties must be so credible that the very existence of the law is a goad or deterrent in itself: the *'in terrorem'* effect. However, this has not been the case for 'equal opportunities' legislation. The success rate of cases has been very low, and the penalties for defaulters in the past has been very low, although this may change with the lifting of the upper limit for compensation by the ECJ.

What happens when people take cases? The Sex Discrimination Act, Equal Pay Act, Race Relations Act, and Disability Discrimination Act all give individuals direct access to industrial tribunals. This can be a problem because anti-discrimination laws are specifically designed to challenge many commonly held assumptions, therefore calling for a sensitive and enlightened approach from members of industrial tribunal panels, a good grasp of complex legal principles and a readiness to criticize established employment practices. This means that the success rate of cases has been low, even when successful compensation has been low in the past. Many complainants have experienced difficulty in getting the employer to pay, some never receiving the money they had been awarded. Victimization of the applicant and deterioration of relationships in the workplace also often occurred. Two reports have been published by the EOC which studied the victories and defeats of applicants in sex discrimination and equal pay cases at industrial tribunals. The titles of the reports were illustrative of the problems incurred. The report on successful cases was called *Pyrrhic Victories* (Leonard, 1987). Pyrrhus was a leader of an army who won a battle in Greek mythology, but only at the cost of the death of most of his troops. The report on unsuccessful cases was called *Trial by Ordeal* (Gregory, 1989). Interestingly, in 1996, the EOC reported that for the first time more men than women had made formal complaints against sex discrimination. These were often through men's failed attempts to get low-paid jobs, which employers considered to be 'women's jobs'. In the past men would not have considered these posts but with the reduction in traditional male occupations they were trying to compete with women for 'women's work' (EOC Annual Report, 1996a).

Where there is more than one piece of legislation to deal with one sort of discrimination, as in the case of sex discrimination, this also causes difficulties and cases can fall between two stools and through the legislative net. An example of this was the case of Meeks v. National Union of Agricultural and Allied Workers. A part-time secretary took a case under the Sex Discrimination Act, because she was paid less per hour than full-timers. Unfortunately, the Equal Pay Act, which was intended to cover such circumstances, was of no use because all the secretaries were women and no male comparator was available. The industrial tribunal considered that a requirement making it necessary for an employee to work for 35 hours per week in order to qualify for the higher hourly rate was indirectly discriminatory. It constituted a condition with which proportionately fewer women than men could comply and which the employer could not justify. However, the industrial tribunal went on to say that the discrimination in question was not unlawful since it concerned the payment of money which is excluded from the scope of the Act.

The underlying assumption behind both the 'individualistic' and 'protective' approach to 'equal opportunities' legislation is that the prevailing system is essentially a fair one, although there may be isolated cases where a particular individual is treated unfairly. This, it is implied, can simply be put right by a policy of treating individual women, ethnic minorities or disabled people as though they were men or White people or non-disabled, an approach which in the area of 'race' was dubbed 'colour-blind'. Lustgarten and Edwards (1992) argued that the law is weakened because of this adherence to individualism. The effect of this approach is to leave existing structures substantially intact. While it is agreed that women, ethnic minorities and disabled people may be unfairly distributed within the labour market, it is suggested that this can be redressed by redistributing them a bit: that is, appointing a few ethnic minorities to senior posts or women into 'male' jobs. What is not questioned is the nature of the structures themselves. There is never a hint that the division of labour which they embody or the values, which are used to decide the rewards assigned to the various groups within them, might in any way be inherently sexist, racist or disablist.

Gregory (1987) presented a penetrating analysis of such legislation. She suggested that although 'anti-discrimination legislation can be seen as a response to the demands of oppressed groups for the removal of historical barriers to the achievement of full equality . . . The state . . . assumes a conformative role, using the legislation to control those employers whose practices fall short of acceptable notions of equal opportunity, and to evolve institutional structures for channelling the conflicts'. She argued that 'it is important to disperse the cloud of mystification surrounding the legislation, so that it is clearly recognised as part of the processes of containment. It is on the statute book in order to protect, not threaten, the fundamental structures of capitalist society, and therefore cannot by itself constitute the vehicle for achieving a non-racist, non-sexist society.' Blakemore and Drake (1996) agreed that in the area of racial inequality, 'in the future, whatever legislative framework exists for equal opportunities policies, a much tougher approach will be called for if the creation of a permanent rift or gulf between these minority communities and the majority is to be avoided' (p. 136).

Equal treatment, which is clearly the guiding principle of the 'equal opportunities' legislation, merely ensures that all may, theoretically, enter the competition. But it does nothing to recognize the handicaps carried by some entrants, some of which may be so severe as to prevent them from even reaching the starting line. In contrast, special treatment for women, ethnic minorities and disabled people, in the form of additional rights, positive action or even positive discrimination, might be said to advance the cause of 'equal opportunities', but this is at the cost of equal treatment. In such circumstances, the argument that according special treatment to women, ethnic minorities and disabled people implies discrimination against men, White people and non-disabled people, has to be faced. At the moment, women only have special additional rights which relate to biology: pregnancy and childbirth. These measures are designed to recognize and compensate for disadvantage. In the present climate, any additional positive discrimination which sets out to treat women, ethnic minorities and disabled people more favourably is inconceivable and faces difficulty on both the theoretical and practical levels.

Possible changes to the law

The fundamental question remains: can the law be changed to be a successful instrument of social change? Smart (1989) said no. She argued that, 'It is important to think of non-legal strategies and to discourage a resort to law as if it holds the key to unlock oppression'. This was because it has been consistently shown that the law works better for White middle-class men than for anyone else. However, Morris and Nott (1991) counter-argued that, while 'equal opportunities' was not achievable solely through the law, there was still an essential function for it in the pursuit of that goal, mainly because the law purported to represent the values and mores of society at a given time. Therefore, it was an important part of the armoury in fighting for 'equal opportunities'. But Morris and Nott (1991) argued that to continue as such, important changes needed to be made. The legislation needed to be less complicated and more user-friendly, the separation of the Equal Pay and Sex Discrimination Acts was untenable and they needed to be combined, the burden of proof should be shifted from at present on the employee to prove discrimination on to the employer to prove non-discrimination; legal aid should be available for complainants and levels of compensation need to be raised.

It is helpful to look at the changes in the legislation that the Commissions (CRE and EOC) responsible for its review and monitoring on behalf of the government have advocated. In the area of 'race', the CRE has called for tougher legislation to combat racial discrimination in companies and institutions that still persists despite many years of the Race Relations Act. Despite the introduction of a voluntary code of practice by the CRE (1984a), Home Office funded research on the legal enforcement of the Race Relations Act (McCrudden *et al.*, 1991) concluded that the Act had largely failed to achieve its aims of reducing discrimination and promoting 'equal opportunities' in employment. Therefore, the CRE using as models both the American legislation and 'Fair Employment Law' in Northern Ireland has called for several changes:

• Compulsory ethnic monitoring. (At present, only about one-third of major employers, and a higher proportion of public sector employers, follow some form of ethnic monitoring).
• More public money in terms of legal aid to be extended to individual 'race' complaints before industrial tribunals.
• Provision in the Act for class actions for affected groups and the possibility of establishing precedents.
• Tougher penalties for offenders. Companies and individuals often ignore 'race' relations legislation because the penalties are not severe enough.
• Racial harassment and attacks to be made a specific crime. (There are arguments for and against this. The CRE argued that this change would give it due importance and significance. However, counter-arguments included the fact that if a racial motive could not be proved the assailant would get off as they can only be charged with one offence. At the moment judges have the discretion to give tougher sentences for attacks that have a racial motive).

There has also been criticism of the CRE itself and calls for its radical overhaul (McCrudden, 1991). It has been argued that the CRE has concentrated too much on advisory and promotional work and not enough on legal enforcement: 'too much carrot and not enough stick'. Where investigations took place in the form of formal investigations into employment practices within organizations these were poorly handled and there was no system for carrying out 'post-mortems' to learn for the future, nor any significant follow-up with employers.

In the area of gender, we can see that the EOC has been more conservative in its demands than the CRE. It has not called for legal aid in discrimination cases, nor for employers to keep records relating to the sexual composition of the workforce. However, it has called on the government to update the legislation. It wants to see a sweeping reform of the Equal Pay Act, described as a 'paradise for lawyers, but hell for women'.

In 1991, the EOC launched its 'Equality Agenda':

• New legislation to combat discrimination against women at work. The Equal Pay Act and the Sex Discrimination Act to be abolished and replaced with an Equal Treatment Act, which would prompt speedier tribunals and protect women from being sacked for becoming pregnant. The Act would give tribunals the power to recommend reinstatements and higher compensation awards

- A national strategy for childcare to overcome one of the main barriers to sex equality. Employers have been looking at ways of financing childcare for their employees. But feasibility study after feasibility study has shown that they cannot do it by themselves. The EOC wants a high-level inquiry into setting up a national strategy and says childcare should be a partnership between government, employers and parents
- Family policy which looks at flexible working for women and men with young children

Possible weaknesses of the Disability Discrimination Act 1995 have also been identified by the disabled people's movement as areas that they would like to see changed:

- Unlike the Commissions in the areas of 'race' and gender the National Disability Council was only given the role of advising the government. This means it has even less power than the CRE and EOC for influencing change
- The Act advocates greater opportunities for disabled people 'without imposing undue burdens on business or employers'. The meaning of this clause is very vague and contestable
- The definition of impairment in the Act is very tight. For a disabled person to be covered by the legislation, their impairment has to have 'a substantial and long-term effect on his [sic] ability to carry out normal day-to-day activities'
- Employment clauses of the Act do not apply to employers with fewer than 20 employees
- An employer must make 'reasonable' adjustments to job and premises. The definition of 'reasonable' is again unclear and contestable
- The Disability Discrimination Act amends and repeals provisions of the Disabled Persons (Employment) Act 1944, the most important being the quota system. This is seen by many commentators as being a retrograde step and in fact many other European countries use systematically and strongly enforced quota systems to promote disabled people's opportunities

Ultimately, it can be argued that the most essential requirement for the pursuit of 'equal opportunities' is a genuine political will by governments to achieve that goal as a matter of basic civil liberties. 'The whole concept of equality of opportunity depends on a recognition that, left to its own devices, society does not organise itself in a truly egalitarian, non-discriminatory fashion' (Morris and Nott, 1991). Successive British governments have failed to demonstrate this will, and have given clear messages that equality of opportunity or even equal treatment is not a social priority. Evidence to support this argument comes from both the underfunding and ignoring of the EOC and the CRE, which are charged with keeping gender and 'race' legislation under review and suggesting changes to make it more effective.

The repeated and most prominent call from the EOC for the provision of childcare by the government has been largely ignored. The CRE's second review of the Race Relations Act (1991) demonstrated not only their criticism of law but also their own limited powers to act. They argued that:

While there is no evidence that the racial discrimination covered by the Race Relations Act 1976, which the Commission tackles through its law enforcement powers is increasing, it is not decreasing at all fast enough ... In the case of racial discrimination, those in positions of power and authority ... are in a position to adopt, implement and monitor the kind of comprehensive equal opportunities policies that would put an end to discrimination and enable all our citizens to realise their full potential and make their full contribution to society regardless of their ethnic origins. That racial discrimination still exists at substantial levels indicates that far too few have done so (CRE, 1991, pp. 16–17).

The arguments put forward by the EOC and CRE to change and strengthen the legislation have fallen on closed minds. It is unlikely that the government will agree either to compulsory ethnic monitoring or enlarging their role in childcare.

Cameron (1993) found that 'equal opportunities' policies fail to deal with the underlying causes of discrimination, and have often been 'quickfix' attempts unrelated to the needs of either people or business. The CRE has found that despite the vast majority of the largest UK companies having made a paper commitment to racial equality policies, only half of these had begun to translate these into action plans (Ollerearnshaw and Waldreck, 1995). Both the CRE and the EOC are beginning to speculate as to whether a better response from employers would be forthcoming if the emphasis was placed on how 'equal opportunities' policies can improve employee initiative, effectiveness and productivity. This would be done in an attempt to persuade them to take action because 'equal opportunities' policies were 'of direct benefit to themselves' (Ollerearnshaw and Waldreck, 1995, p. 24). However, Blakemore and Drake (1996) posed the sceptical question as to whether this approach was a genuine step forward in the field or whether it is a cynical exercise in rhetoric which was attempting to sell the policies, but would only succeed in watering them down to ineffectiveness. Instead it may be a more fruitful argument to maintain that the law has played and can play an important part in the improvement of opportunities for women, ethnic minorities, and disabled people. The fact that it currently appears to do so little is due not simply to the inherent limitations of the law, for which there are proposed changes, but also to the indifference of those who formulate the laws and those who interpret them.

Summary

This chapter forms the concluding chapter to Part One of this book. First, it has widened the consideration of the influences on 'equal opportunities' in this country by examining the past, present and possible future impact of the legislation emanating from the European Union (EU) in the areas of gender, 'race' and disability. It analyses the different types of EU legislation categorized by 'regulatory policy' and 'soft law'. What we see from this analysis is that despite resistance from the UK government, the EU has been both active and effective in making changes in the area of gender. The legal framework of Community law regarding equal treatment of the sexes consists of several directives, treaty terms, decisions of the European Court of Justice and the general principle of the removal of sex discrimination as a fundamental right. However, in the areas of both 'race' and disability the EU has been much less proactive. In fact, the lack of or even negative activity in the area of 'race' is revealed in stark contrast to the area of gender. Not only has the EU failed to develop legislation against racial discrimination, it has also created a 'Fortress Europe' immigration policy, which has created a dominant image of the EU as White European and created a detrimental effect even on ethnic minorities who are EU nationals. In the area of disability, the EU has used 'soft law' in the form of action programmes, recommendations and resolutions developed to promote the social and economic integration of disabled people. Therefore, we see variations in action taken on disability across the Member States.

The final section of the chapter examines current national legislation and its potential impact on 'equal opportunities'. It considers the arguments that the legislation has limited thinking about the subject in several ways. First, the legislation is criticized for its 'individualistic' approach with very little recall to 'group justice'. Second, the fact that it is 'protective' rather than proactive, and it is legally complex, leading to many unsuccessful cases in industrial tribunals, is examined. This leads to a discussion of the effectiveness of legislation in playing a part in providing 'equal opportunities'. The recommendations for strengthening the law put forward by both the EOC and CRE and the criticisms of the Disability Discrimination Act by the disabled people's movement are considered. The final conclusion is that once strengthened, the law does have an important part to play providing it is supported by the will of legislators and the judiciary.

Equal opportunities and the key areas in social policy

INTRODUCTION

Part Two of the book will examine the key areas of social policy for 'equal opportunities' issues and developments in the fields of gender, 'race' and disability. The social policy areas covered in Chapters 5, 6 and 7 are generally accepted as the core of social policy's concerns with welfare provision: education, employment, income maintenance, social services, health and housing. As Hallett (1996) points out: 'These services are at the core of the welfare state' (p. 2).

Chapter 5 considers the areas of education and employment, Chapter 6 looks at income maintenance and social services, and Chapter 7 examines health provision and housing. The chapters contain literature and research evidence from examples of 'equal opportunities' developments in these areas. They will examine policies, procedures and the implementation of 'equal opportunities' practice in service delivery and welfare provision, looking at the effectiveness and appropriateness of these policies and service outcome for women, ethnic minorities and disabled people. The major developments in each of the key areas will be examined separately for gender, 'race' and disability implications. This is not because I wish to argue that these fields should be separated from each other, but rather that it reflects the way policies have been traditionally divided with their differential impact on different groups and therefore how accompanying research has developed. Where there is variety in the length of sections on different policy areas and in the fields of gender, 'race' and disability this reflects the amount of work that has been undertaken in the appropriate area.

The separation of the sources of disadvantage for study in these chapters does not aim to deny that there are considerable overlaps between the disadvantages in social policies for all three groups: women, ethnic minorities and disabled people. They are often the most vulnerable to changes, especially withdrawal and retraction of public resources in the field of welfare. We cannot build equality for one group on the basis of inequality for others: all equalities need to be considered and it is essential to have policies that are comprehensive and coherent. Therefore, while this book will retain the categories of gender, 'race' and disability when examining 'equal opportunities' in welfare provision, it will at the same time attempt to acknowledge diverse experiences and access within these groups.

CHAPTER 5

Social policy areas: education and employment

This chapter will examine the social policy areas of education and employment.

Education

Gender

Girls' and women's disadvantage at all levels of education was well documented in the 1970s and 1980s. Research investigating gender and schooling examined girls' unequal access to educational opportunities, and identified problems in classroom interaction and practices. It encouraged the development of anti-sexist policies in schools, which looked at curriculum access, language, textbook biases, and the gender values and bias of teachers. The idea of core subjects was seen as a way to combat girls' underrepresentation in science and maths (Byrne, 1978; Deem, 1980). By the mid-1980s, 'equal opportunities' policies in the area of gender were well established in many local education authorities and then into schools and colleges under their control (Arnot, 1985; Arnot and Weiner, 1987).

We now appear to be experiencing a reversal in the differential educational success of girls and boys, which is beginning in the school system. A report from the Equal Opportunities Commission, looking back over ten years from 1984 to 1994, confirmed that girls have overtaken boys in all subjects at GCSE level and were catching up rapidly at A level. Tests on seven-year olds showed a gap emerging from an early age. However, this phenomenon must be treated with some caution. If it is a reversal of fortunes, which continues, it will take many years to work through the higher levels of the educational system and into the labour market where it will face different obstacles and challenges. To date, women's education has left them with lower earning power and more limited job opportunities than men (EOC, 1991). Boys continued to do better in vocational qualifications and maintained their lead in the top grades of most A level subjects, as well as obtaining a higher percentage of first class degrees at university (Central Statistical Office, 1995). Women continued to be underrepresented and underachieving in certain subjects, which contributed to a gender-divided labour market. Some areas of the curriculum, both formal and informal, were male-gendered and there was a tendency on the part of teachers and lecturers to pay more attention to male pupils and students (Acker, 1992; Bagilhole, 1993b).

This has led some analysts in the 1990s to claim that 'equal opportunities' policies in education have not been that successful and they have called for more systematic and far-reaching polices (Arnot and Weiler, 1993; Weiner, 1994). Also, it was argued that educational reforms aimed at restructuring the education system (greater parental choice, more involvement of lay people in governing bodies, the introduction of market principles, the devolution of financial control to schools and colleges, the emphasis on centrally controlled National Curriculum and centrally monitored educational standards) had not taken gender issues on board (Middleton, 1993). As to whether the National Curriculum, although not established to increase the representation of girls in certain subjects, will have this effect is too early and difficult to evaluate fully (Deem, 1996).

The reduction in the power and influence of local education authorities through the local management of schools and some opting for grant-maintained status has meant that 'equal opportunities' policies and practices which were initiated by the local authorities may have been watered down or given less emphasis. The reforms also had an effect on female educational staff. David (1993) pointed out that the demand for more flexibility in hours taught, the extension of the working day and week, and a reduction in holiday entitlements had disproportionately affected women lecturers in further education. Deem (1996) also showed that women teachers who make up the vast majority of those in primary education were affected by schools' greater financial instability through the increase in short-term and temporary contracts.

Deem *et al.* (1995) highlighted the gendered effect of the introduction of more lay people on to governing bodies of schools and these bodies' increased influence and power. More men were in positions of power on influential resource subcommittees than women, and women's voices were heard less. A heading in the *Guardian* (1996b) summed up the situation: 'Girls are doing better than ever in the classroom and the majority of teachers are women, but schools are still run by men.' The article reported a study by East London University, which showed that women applicants for head teachers' posts suffered discrimination from governors.

Gender and Higher education

Research has identified discrimination against both female students and staff in universities, which was perpetuated through structural and cultural ways (Bagilhole, 1993b, 1993c, 1995a, 1996c; Bagilhole and Woodward, 1995). Women graduating from British universities outnumbered men for the first time in 1994, making up 51 per cent of students getting first degrees. But women made up less than a quarter of lecturers in 'old' universities, and barely more than 5 per cent of professors (Goode and Bagilhole, 1996a, 1996b, 1997 forthcoming). In its first report, the

Hansard Commission (1990) saw universities as 'bastions of male power . . . it is likely that the persistence of outdated attitudes about women's career aspirations constitutes the main barrier stopping women from reaching the top in academic life. It might be thought somewhat ironical that institutions dedicated to the unravelling of truths are themselves still wrapped in the myths of the past.' Since then the changes that have taken place in higher education with the dramatic increase in student numbers, external research and teaching inspection, an increase in temporary and short-term contracts, and the extension of hours of work have all disproportionately affected women academics, already in a small minority (Bagilhole, 1995b).

In its second report the Hansard Society (McRae, 1996) recommended that all universities needed to take action to improve the representation of women at all levels, but particularly Oxford and Cambridge, which were seen as places to influence and guide future generations of leaders, industrialists, policy-makers and opinion-formers. By 1995, 32 universities in Britain had joined Opportunity 2000. Oxford and Cambridge jointly joined in autumn 1993. Each has established clear achievable objectives, an 'equal opportunities' committee, and monitors recruitment and promotions. These initiatives have produced improvements. At Oxford University, in 1985, 14 per cent of lecturers and 5 per cent of professors were women; by 1995 this had increased to 18 per cent and 7 per cent respectively. At Cambridge, in 1986 women made up 8 per cent of lecturers and 3 per cent of professors; by 1995 this had increased to 14 per cent and 6 per cent respectively.

Opportunity 2000 (1996) has also launched a new initiative focusing specifically on increasing the number of women in science, engineering and technology (SET), where they are seriously underrepresented. This was an attempt to tap the growing and increasingly high achieving source of new talent that girls represent. In the past, it was argued that women's underrepresentation in SET disciplines reflected their underachievement in science and maths subjects at the ages of 16 and 18. The traditional view was that women do not have the same aptitude for science and engineering subjects as men. But in 1988 science became a compulsory subject for all school children aged between 5 and 16, and evidence from national testing at 7, 11 and 14 years of age and GCSE examinations at 16 showed that girls and young women performed equally as well as boys and young men. Physics was the only subject in which boys outperformed girls. But comparatively few young women go on to study SET at A level, and even fewer at university.

Why do women turn their backs on SET education as soon as they can? Opportunity 2000 (1996) argued that when young women studied SET subjects at university, 'the male-dominated culture of science and engineering departments is at least partly responsible for their subsequent exit from SET careers . . . women pay both personal and social costs when they cross the threshold into a "male domain" because they find themselves working with values, systems and performance criteria which have been set up for men not women' (p. 7). It was argued that 'women are more likely to be interested in scientific problems if they have a social relevance and could produce social benefit' (p. 7). Girls' alienation from SET included inappropriate teaching methods and course design and a shortage of female role models (Grundy, 1992).

'Race'

There was a growth in research into 'race' and schooling during the 1970s and 1980s. The Swann Report revealed discriminatory patterns of behaviour in the classroom, and pointed to discrimination in the allocation of pupils to lower sets and streams (Parekh, 1992b). An investigation in Birmingham showed different levels of suspensions that could not be explained by factors other than 'race', and several studies showed Black Caribbean pupils were much more likely to be suspended and excluded from school than White children, and were over-represented in special needs schools and units for children with behavioural problems (CRE, 1984b; Bourne *et al.*, 1994). Ethnic minorities in general were also underrepresented among those with power in the education system, such as governors, administrators, inspectors, teachers and lecturers. As a result of concern over the effect of mainstream education on ethnic minority children and perceptions of its lack of cultural understanding, some communities set up complementary and compensatory schooling in the form of supplementary schools outside of normal school hours (Chevannes and Reeves, 1987).

When looking at Asian girls' educational experience, Brah (1992a) argued very strongly that racism compounded by sexism was present. This was seen to be either 'direct or indirect' and 'conscious or subconscious'. Therefore, it manifested itself either through 'implicit stereotyped assumptions made by teachers or other educationists about Asian girls and boys', or it was 'institutionalized in the routine structures and practices of the school, as, for example, when the school curriculum neglects, negates or misrepresents the history and cultures of Asian and other black groups' (p. 74). Brah argued that explanations for underachievement that were sought in the culture of ethnic minority groups, not only unjustifiably blamed the victim but were also overly simple because there was a wide variation among Asian parents' attitudes to their children's education, as there are in any community. Ethnic minority children felt devalued if there were very few or no ethnic minority teachers in schools or in other areas of education. The stereotype of 'passive' Asian girls led them to receive even less attention than White girls, who in turn received less than boys. Assumptions were made that they would not be allowed to go on into further and higher education by their families, and there was little support or information provided for those that wished to do so (Brah and Minhas, 1983; Mirza, 1992).

In the past, claims of general under-achievement of ethnic minority communities in Britain in terms of educational qualifications and levels of attainment were clearly justified (see Chapter 1 for statistics on educational underachievement). However, the situation today is far more complex. Recently, we have seen a narrowing of the gap in levels of educational attainment between Whites and ethnic minorities and a gap opening up between ethnic minority communities (Jones, 1993). Despite this, we must be cautious of going too far down the diversity road, because the idea of ethnic minority cultural pathologies have in the past served to reduce the emphasis on the problem of racism in the education system (Brah, 1992a; Rattansi, 1992). This approach can be fuelled when one ethnic group suffers a particular type of discrimination and another does not. For example, children of Black Caribbean origin were said to have little motivation at school, exhibit more disruptive behaviour and to be less academically able. In contrast, Asian children were seen as highly motivated, hard-working and deferential. Thus it was claimed that the problem was not racism, but the fault must lie in the Black Caribbean family and culture. This assumption has been challenged by research that highlighted teachers' general lower expectations of achievement of Black Caribbean children and the differential treatment these children received in schools (CRE, 1984b; Bourne *et al.*, 1994).

Schools have for a long time been aware of issues of 'race' in education. Initially, they introduced 'multicultural', and latterly anti-racist policies. Evidence showed that these policies within schools produced real benefits in classrooms, and had a positive impact on the achievements of ethnic minority children (Richardson, 1992). However, the 1988 Education Reform Act with its tightening of the National Curriculum and introduction of local management of schools has had an effect on this progress (Ball *et al.*, 1990; Gill *et al.*, 1992). We have seen to some extent the marginalization and undermining of the multicultural and anti-racist initiatives by local authorities through 'financial and political expedience' (Law, 1996, p. 191). It was argued that policies and legislation, which attempted to introduce a market-led education system encouraged the likelihood of increased 'racial' segregation between schools and were 'likely to impede . . . the educational outcomes and aspirations of black minorities' (Law, 1996, p. 192). The following example demonstrated the likelihood of this. Using the argument of parental choice, parents of a five year old White girl won the right for her to be transferred to another primary school because her present school was 90 per cent Asian. This was fought by the Commission for Racial Equality because it was based on racial factors, but they lost (Runnymede Trust, 1992).

Race and higher education

The higher education sector has been much slower in coming forward with policies and initiatives to deal with the underrepresentation of ethnic minorities (CUCO, 1994; Bagilhole and Robinson, 1997; Westcott, 1996), despite evidence being found of discrimination (Banton, 1994). For example, a CRE investigation (1988) into St George's Hospital Medical school admissions revealed a sophisticated process of computerized racism and sexism. An attempt to computerize initial selection decisions led to academics' previous decisions being reproduced in a computer program. However, to duplicate the academics' previous pattern of decisions a score bias against 'non-Caucasians' and women had to be written into the program. Computerized racism was probably a rarity. But if these academics' decision making was typical, it showed a society where ethnic minorities and women may succeed despite their 'race' and gender, but where these created a significant handicap. Studies have continued to identify discrimination. Ethnic minority applicants to medical schools were shown to be less likely to be successful than White applicants with the same qualifications at all levels of A level scores (Esmail *et al.*, 1995; McManus *et al.*, 1995).

Taylor (1993) showed two clear differences between the 'old' universities and the former polytechnics. The latter both received a larger proportion of applicants from ethnic minorities and accepted a higher proportion. The highest acceptance rates for 'old' universities were for Whites (54 per cent), the rate for ethnic minority applicants was much lower (27 per cent) and those for Asian groups somewhere between the two (34–47 per cent). There was a reverse picture in the former polytechnics. Whites had the lowest acceptance rates (37 per cent) and there was less variation between the ethnic minority groups, all being between 42 and 46 per cent. For this reason, Taylor (1993) argued that 'old' universities needed to look at their admissions policies and criteria, train admissions tutors and have a code of practice on the admissions of students. Other factors which disproportionately affected ethnic minority applicants was that they were likely to have obtained A levels through resits. Also, Asians were almost twice as likely as Whites to apply to university with other qualifications than A levels, and Black Caribbeans were nearly five times as likely. Tanna (1990) found three reasons for a higher incidence of resits among South Asians: many were taking other qualifications at the same time, they were more likely to have already taken an unconventional route in education, and finally 'poor teaching' and 'bad schooling'.

Disability

The policy dilemma of 'integration versus segregation' that has been identified by many writers as the most important issue in the area of education and disability has not been resolved (Ford *et al.*, 1982; Tomlinson, 1982). This is despite the creation of special separate schools and schooling for disabled children being outrightly condemned by many analysts. Oliver (1996) argued that segregated schooling actively invalidated the fundamental function of education, which was 'to ensure the integration of individuals into society' (p. 78). The persistence of segregated education was seen to fail disabled children in terms of personal and social development by not preparing them for an independent life; instead it socialized them into accepting a reduced role, excluded from mainstream social and economic life (Gilroy, 1993, p. 29; Oliver, 1996). Blakemore and Drake (1996) showed that another consequence was the fact that the 'lack of mainstream education has prevented a high proportion of disabled people from gaining academic and professional qualifications' (pp. 144–5).'For too long education in all sectors has colluded with the demands of the labour market to keep disabled people out of the workforce' through 'socialising disabled people into accepting a life without work and by failing to give disabled people the necessary skills to enter the labour market in the first place' (Oliver, 1996, pp. 90–1).

The development of state education in Britain shows a long history of excluding disabled children. Although the 1944 Education Act appeared to be committed to the education of disabled children in mainstream schools, it led to the establishment of a system of segregated education (Tomlinson, 1982). The questioning of this system in the 1960s and 1970s led to the setting up of the Warnock Committee, which reported in 1978 and supported the principle of integration. The Committee identified the issue of integration as complex, distinguishing between functional, locational and social integration. From this came the 1981 Education Act, but this legislation held two important and debilitating factors for the policy of integration. First, it made clear there would be no extra money available and, second, it contained a 'disablist' statement that integration should not adversely affect the education of other children (Oliver, 1996). Since then, despite the fact that the number of special schools has declined, it is still the case that most disabled children are educated separately. This is despite reports from Her Majesty's Inspectors of Schools that have condemned the accommodation, facilities and curriculum in large numbers of special schools (Barnes, 1991). Oliver (1996) blamed this on several factors: 'A government that is not really committed to it and has not resourced it properly, it has been deliberately sabotaged by recalcitrant local authorities, professionals have used their power to prevent it, and educational administrators are too incompetent to ensure its implementation' (p. 86).

Whereas educational literature appeared to view the issue of integration as relatively simple and a technical problem of the provision of support services and organizational changes within schools (Moore and Morrison, 1988), it was perceived as more complex by sociologists. Hegarty and Pocklington (1982) argued that integration should be seen not just as physically bringing disabled children into mainstream schools, but as part of an acceptance that the purpose of schools was to educate all children, 'a process geared to meeting a wider range of pupil needs'. Oliver (1988, 1991b) condemned the debate around the integration or segregation of disabled children as being narrowly technical and lacking in the required political consciousness and passion that segregation on the grounds of 'race' provoked. Although it had been acknowledged that the curriculum and resources used to deliver it, such as books and assessment procedures and practices, needed examination and change because of their potential sexist and racist content (Mason and Reiser, 1990), in the area of disability this has been largely ignored (Oliver, 1996).

Underpinning the concept of the integration of disabled children into mainstream schooling was also the idea of having to 'tolerate' disability and to persuade teachers, parents and other children to accept it, given the dominant idea of 'normality' to which children with special needs may not conform. This has been challenged and an alternative perspective put forward that the ideal of 'normal' children with identical needs did not exist: instead, we had to accept difference and diversity as not necessarily inferior (Abberley, 1987; Oliver, 1989). Oliver (1996) argued that the very term 'integration' should be renamed 'inclusion' to acknowledge this approach.

Finally, the Education Reform Act 1988 made a significant change in the debate about the education of disabled children with the introduction of the National Curriculum shifting 'the focus of the debate . . . from issues of where it should take place to what it should be about' (Oliver, 1996, p. 81). However, the Act continued the segregation of disabled children through the curriculum. It did not give disabled children the right to the same curriculum as other children. Instead it allowed the modification of the National Curriculum for disabled children at the discretion of the head teacher.

Disability and higher education

There is very little literature or research in the area of disability and higher education. What there is shows that the majority of universities have ignored this issue. The first comprehensive investigation of British universities' 'equal opportunities' policies and practices (CUCO, 1994) revealed that disability was the area that had been tackled least compared with gender and 'race'. Only 36 per cent of the universities had a code of practice on the employment of disabled people, and even fewer (33 per cent) had introduced any flexible working arrangements and schemes to accommodate the needs of disabled employees. The follow-up study (Bagilhole and Robinson, 1997), while showing an increase in the number of universities that had taken action in this area, highlighted that very few were aware of the implications of the Disability Discrimination Act 1995 or had considered what changes they needed to make to fulfil their obligations under it.

Employment

Gender

Women are continuing to enter the labour market in ever increasing numbers. An Equal Opportunities Review survey (EOR, 1994b) forecast an increase of 600 000 in the number of women employed in the 1990s alongside a decrease in the number of men. The Hansard Society (McRae, 1996) acknowledged that 'women are continuing to enter the labour market in increasing numbers, and in some parts of the country they outnumber men at work. Mothers with young children are now a permanent feature of the workplace and employers are increasingly taking steps to accommodate a diverse and changing workforce' (p. 5).

On an individual level they recorded some very public improvements: a woman speaker in the House of Commons, the appointment of the first woman Chief Constable and the fact that women can now be ordained as priests in the Church of England. However, despite these achievements, looking at the progress of women in decision making, influential and powerful positions in the public and private domain, their general conclusion was that: 'There is as yet, however, no room for relaxation' (p. 19). Despite numerous attempts to eliminate discrimination in employment by legislation, both national and European (see Chapters 3 and 4), women remain disadvantaged. For example, in the private sector services of retailing, banking and finance, where women are concentrated, Britain had the largest wage gap between women and men in Europe, and in all non-manual work Britain again emerged the lowest with women earning less than 60 per cent of men's earnings (Commission of the EC, 1992, p. 151).

A major reason for women's disadvantage in the labour market and the lack of effect of 'equal opportunities' legislation in the area of gender has been identified as persisting occupational segregation (Bagilhole, 1994a). This segregation was evident both horizontally, where women and men worked in different occupations, and vertically where women worked in the same occupations as men but were concentrated at the bottom levels of the organizations. Women have been particularly drawn to the public sector. In fact, the growth of the service sector meant that women entered the labour market without displacing men (Commission of the EC, 1992). The lack of adequate, affordable child care also forced many women to participate in lower paid part-time work or home working, which is particularly prone to exploitation (Bagilhole, 1986).

Looking at the private sector, Gregg and Machin (1993), in their study of top executives and managers, argued that the 'glass ceiling' was still intact. They found evidence of men overtaking women in lower and middle management to the higher levels. Only 8 per cent of senior executives were women and they were paid 6 to 8 per cent less than male counterparts. This illustrated in one sector how women were excluded from the positions of power where resources are controlled and key decisions made. The concept of the 'glass ceiling' or perhaps more appropriately the 'sticky floor' depicted the barriers women face in reaching the higher levels of management or even leaving the low-paid sector. These two different but related problems can cause dilemmas for 'equal opportunities' policies as Coyle (1989) illustrated in her study of local government: 'The concerns of manual women workers are the exploitation of low pay and part-time working, and they cannot always share the concerns of women in higher grades, who are seemingly better off' (p. 47).

However, one area where women do share a common cause is in the problem of sexual harassment. As a form of discrimination, it has been shown to be widespread, prevalent across all types of work, and predominantly used by men to maintain their power and control in the workplace (Bagilhole and Woodward, 1995). Collier (1995) reported that according to an Industrial Society review more than 93 per cent of those harassed were women. Coussey and Jackson (1991) reported that more than half of all women in paid employment experienced at least one incident of sexual harassment, though many chose not to report it for fear of victimization. This problem has been recognized by the European Union (EU) with the publication of their code of practice and an expression of desire by the Commission to produce a binding directive on it for all Member States (European Commission, 1994).

Little has been introduced in Britain in terms of 'family friendly' policies. There have only been limited plans for developments in the area of childcare. The highly publicized introduction of nursery vouchers in 1995 was criticized for going nowhere near answering the problem of the lack of adequate and appropriate child care. The Statutory Maternity Allowance compared unfavourably with other European Union countries. For example, in Britain it only covered a period of 10 months with 90 per cent of earnings for only six weeks, 12 weeks at a low flat rate, and then nothing, whereas in Germany, maternity benefit was paid at 100 per cent of earnings for six weeks before and eight weeks after birth and 18 months parental leave allowance was available at a low fixed rate for six months and means-tested for the remainder (Rapoport and Moss, 1990). Shared parental leave in Britain has been completely absent from the agenda. In 1994, the European Union attempted to phase in paternity policy, but as Britain has opted out of the post-Maastricht social legislation there was no legal right to this in Britain (EOR, 1994c, p. 14). It is interesting that the limited advances and moves to increase women's equality with men in the labour market have all been 'role-related policies; that is, measures or provisions which were designed to ease women's entry to the workforce but not to undermine or challenge traditional assumptions about their family roles' (Blakemore and Drake, 1996). These types of measures can be seen as a dual-edged sword: while giving women rights in the area of childbirth and child rearing, they reinforce women's traditional roles.

It is important to note that the situation for ethnic minority women in the labour market is even worse than for White women. A large body of research has demonstrated that ethnic minority women suffer from discrimination at work (Brown, 1984; Jones, 1993; Bagilhole and Stephens, 1997a). They are to be found in the lowest status, lowest paid grades where they work longer and more anti-social hours. Also, because ethnic minority women are more likely to work full time compared with White women, their child-care needs are even less addressed than women in general. Beechey and Whitelegg (1986) showed that in contrast to women's general concentration in the service sectors, Asian women are more commonly found in low-paid, semi-skilled and unskilled manufacturing jobs, particularly in the clothing and textile industries. Asian women also have an unemployment rate twice as high as White women (Owen, 1994). One of the reasons is that they are concentrated in industries that have been particularly hit by the recession and are vulnerable to technological change and relocation out of the country (Mitter, 1986).

Bruegel's analysis (1989) of data from London showed that 'black women are not only at the bottom of the pile, but their position has got worse relative both to black men and white women over the last few years' (p. 49). She showed that White women earned 23 per cent more per hour than ethnic minority women. In turn, ethnic minority women earned only 63 per cent of ethnic minority men's weekly wages compared with an equivalent figure for White women compared with White men of 72 per cent. Mama (1992) argued that: 'The sexist and racist devaluation of black female labour in Britain is not only historical but also a contemporary fact, and the situation, far from improving, appears to be deteriorating' (p. 85). It has been well chronicled that ethnic minority women in the labour market were affected by complex divisions that can be described as vertical and horizontal segregation affected by gender, 'race' and class (Mama, 1984; Bruegel, 1989; Hallett, 1989; Cook and Watt, 1992; Phizacklea, 1994).

Mama (1992) argued that: 'The positions of black and white women and men are inextricably related and often resonate against each other' (p. 82). The low wages of ethnic minority men has drawn ethnic minority women into the labour market. For example, initial migration from Asia was almost entirely male and Asian women immigrated as dependants, but because Asian men on average earned substantially less than White men, this has drawn more Asian women into full-time work out of economic necessity (Brah, 1992a). Brown (1984) found differences between the economic activity patterns for different Asian groups. The rate for Sikh and Hindu women, in the age group 16–24, was higher than for White women, whereas for Muslim women, fewer than one-fifth were in employment. Brah (1992a) argued this cannot be accounted for by using only 'culturalist explanations', such as that Muslim families do not allow women to work outside the home. She suggested that later migration, the difference between the rates of economic activity between groups of Muslim women from different countries, regional variations in the proportion of Muslim women working, and their previous socioeconomic status before migration, needed to be considered. Age was also a factor, with Muslim women showing similar patterns of labour market participation to non-Muslims among young Asian women (Brah, 1986).

'Race'

In general terms, ethnic minorities experience significant inequalities in the employment field in the types of jobs they obtain, their earnings levels and their vulnerability to unemployment. One important, determining factor in this is the practice of racial discrimination. The extent of job opportunities limited by discrimination was demonstrated by a series of tests in the 1960s and 1970s. Trial applications for advertised vacant posts showed a substantial proportion of employers rejected those with obvious ethnic minority names (Daniel, 1968; McIntosh and Smith, 1974). A Policy Studies Institute repeat of the survey undertaken in the 1970s (Brown and Gay, 1985), revealed that more than one-third of employers in London, Birmingham and Manchester who advertised vacancies in the press, discriminated against ethnic minority job applicants, a similar figure to the previous survey. A formal investigation by the CRE of the Beaumont Leys Shopping Centre, Leicester, found that although Asians were adequately represented as applicants for jobs compared with their proportion in the local job market, they were underrepresented among those selected; they were four times less successful than Whites. The employers could not explain the disparity on non-racial grounds. Research into accountancy and graduate employment in the late 1980s showed ethnic minorities suffering both direct and indirect discrimination (CRE, 1987a, b). Ethnic minority young people have also been shown to be excluded from the parts of government training schemes most likely to lead to permanent employment (Cross and Smith, 1987) and diverted by careers advisers away from employers that choose to exclude ethnic minorities (Wrench, 1990).

Brown (1984) showed clear evidence of racial discrimination with ethnic minority men earning less than White men in equivalent job levels and occupations. However, patterns of employment have shifted and greater diversity has appeared between ethnic minority groups. An academic study of the 1991 census figures (Peach, 1996) predicted that Britain's Black Caribbeans face an 'Irish future' while Asians face a 'Jewish future'. This was explained by the fact that predominantly the Black Caribbean population was working class, in manual work, state-educated and council-housed, while the Asian population will become self-employed, owner-occupiers and white-collar workers with professional qualifications.

Despite this divergence, Jones (1993) pointed out that unemployment and employment in the lowest paid service and manufacturing industries remained high in the Pakistani and Bangladeshi communities and some sections of the Black Caribbean community. Also, the proportion of ethnic minority men in all age groups participating in the labour force was lower than for Whites. In the young age group this was largely because more are staying on in education, but in older age groups this probably reflected hidden unemployment and greater difficulty in getting a job. As already observed, when looking at women's labour market participation rates we saw different patterns. They were extremely low for Pakistani and Bangladeshi women, but higher than Whites for Black Caribbean women, even when they have children, and about the same among African Asians, Africans and Indians.

Brown (1984) reminded us that 'the original migration to Britain was the consequence of a labour shortage, and that process did not put the minorities on an equal footing with whites – rather . . . it established the inequalities that have persisted since' (p. 63). He argued that major underlying processes which contributed to the persistence of racial disadvantage in the British employment market were 'racial exploitation and exclusion' (p. 46). Immigrant workers were given jobs vacated by Whites who had progressed to better employment. These were in the lower paid public sector and were industrial jobs with long hours, shift-work and unpleasant conditions. Until the second Race Relations Act in 1968, racial discrimination in employment was legal. Openly discriminatory job advertisements were seen as natural and legitimate. Overall job patterns reflected this with a concentration of ethnic minorities in semi-skilled and unskilled manual work. There were far fewer managers and supervisors than among the White population, and a notable proportion of Indian and Pakistani workers were self-employed. A general pattern for immigrants was a downgrading of their previous jobs in other countries and concentration into distinctive sectors of the economy: manufacturing, transport and communications industries. A similar pattern occurred with later immigrants, for example the East African Asians who were expelled from Uganda in the late 1960s and early 1970s. A substantial proportion had worked in professional and business occupations in Africa, but were absorbed into manual work in Britain.

Brown (1992) showed that by the beginning of the 1970s immigration legislation had effectively halted ethnic minority immigration for work. However, there was a persistence of a high degree of racial segregation in the labour market with about 80 per cent of ethnic minorities still doing manual work despite their qualifications. By the 1980s, we can see that: 'The impact of the Race Relations Acts on discrimination in the job market was at first encouraging but in the long term disappointing' (Brown, 1992, p. 56). The distinctive pattern of ethnic minority employment was still firmly set, and the gap in unemployment levels between ethnic minorities and Whites was becoming wider as unemployment rose generally. By 1982, the ethnic minority unemployment rate approached 20 per cent, nearly double the White rate, not falling below this until 1987. This was caused by the concentration of ethnic minority manual workers in industries that have been most badly hit by recessions, the marginal nature of jobs held by ethnic minorities and racial discrimination (Brown, 1984).

More recently, there have been changes in the employment patterns of ethnic minorities, but they have still not converged with Whites. Brown (1992) showed that this phenomenon cannot be explained by educational differences because the gap was greater among those with higher qualifications. Important differences have opened up between ethnic groups and age groups; unemployment was much higher among Black Caribbeans, Pakistanis and Bangladeshis than among Indians, and the rate is much higher among young people than old. For Black Caribbeans aged 16–24 unemployment exceeded 30 per cent for a time, and exceeded 40 per cent among Pakistanis and Bangladeshis of the same age group (Brown, 1992).

There has been a significant increase in self-employment among Asians since the mid-1970s. About one-quarter of Indian men were self-employed, almost double the proportion for White men. For Pakistanis and Bangladeshis the figure was 17 per cent, again higher than average. For Black Caribbeans the figure was lower than average. There has been a gradual drift upwards in the average job levels of ethnic minorities in the 1980s. This improvement was largely because of changes in the job patterns of young people. Overall the gap between Whites and ethnic minorities remained high with a disproportionate number of ethnic minorities in semi-skilled and unskilled jobs.

As identified in Chapter 3 of this book, it would appear that a business case for 'equal opportunities' has been accepted by the public and private sector, and the government. This approach has been strongly advocated by the Commission for Racial Equality. An example of this was their publication *Racial Equality Means Business* (CRE, 1995d) where they argued that 'equal opportunities' policies 'contribute to an organisation's competitive edge' by allowing them to 'draw on the skills and talents of a diverse workforce, value and nurture diversity, reach out to all sectors of the community, as employers, customers, clients and suppliers, and respect the interests of those communities in which it is involved, and respond to their needs' (p. 5).

How have employers responded to this approach? Two CRE surveys of large employers in the private and public sectors have looked at this question and found the answer to be favourable (Coussey, 1995, pp. 21–2). First, when employers in the private sector were asked for reasons for introducing 'equal opportunities' policies for ethnic minorities they all cited business reasons: 48 per cent mentioned the recruitment of higher calibre staff, 44 per cent goodwill, 41 per cent obtaining a broader skills and experience base, 26 per cent improved morale, and 18 per cent the encouragement of ethnic minority customers. Action taken included race-equality training (49 per cent), regular monitoring (51 per cent), encouragement of applications from underrepresented groups (29 per cent), pre-employment access training (24 per cent), targets (10 per cent) and including 'equal opportunities' in performance objectives (8 per cent). In the public sector, information was sought from 41 local government authorities in areas with high ethnic minority concentrations. The vast majority (36) monitored their workforce for 'race', 35 collected data on applicants, 21 analysed some recruitment data, and half monitored progress within the organization. In terms of positive action, 20 authorities had introduced training for special needs, 19 applicant training for access to senior levels, and 23 training for their own ethnic minority staff, for example in management development.

It would appear that 'equal opportunities' in the area of 'race' had been accepted and adopted by many employers especially the large ones. We might presume that this will reduce racial disadvantage within the labour market. However, 'equal opportunities' policies have been shown to have been limited in the area of reducing racial inequality in employment because they impact particularly on people already in work or those with a chance of recruitment. They cannot touch the unemployed. Blakemore and Drake (1996) argued that in fact the consequence of this is that part of their effect may be to increase inequalities between different minority communities.

Disability

A comprehensive survey showed that fewer than one-third of the two million disabled people of working age in Britain were in employment (Martin *et al.*, 1989). Even those in employment are disproportionately represented in lower status and lower paid jobs (Barnes, 1991). Berthoud *et al.* (1993) demonstrated a direct correlation between the severity of a person's disability and their employment status. Before the Disability Discrimination Act 1995 disabled people could legally be refused employment simply because they were disabled, even though their disability was irrelevant to the job for which they applied (Barnes, 1991). Disabled people are disproportionately affected by unemployment both in the size of the problem and the duration (Lonsdale, 1986; Glendinning, 1991). Therefore, it is not surprising that 'for many people the demand for access to work is seen as a crucial component of the struggle for equality' (Abberley, 1996, p. 70).

Honey *et al.* (1993) found that larger organizations were more likely to employ disabled people than small ones, but most employers had stereotypical views, such as reservations about disabled people's ability to do certain jobs and their level of productivity. Nearly one-half saw no benefits in employing disabled people, and only one-quarter had a clear written policy on disability. Before the Disability Discrimination Act, the main way that the government sought to increase disabled people's employment by the quota scheme (as discussed in Chapter 3) had little effect. A study (Morrell, 1990) undertaken to investigate the role of the Employment Department's Disablement Advisory Service, which sought to encourage companies to employ disabled people and provided advice, revealed that there was some willingness by employers to employ disabled people tempered by the fear that this could create problems. However, small employers had very little awareness or understanding of their obligations under the quota system: fewer than three-quarters had heard of the scheme and half of these were unaware of their legal obligations under it. Even three-quarters of the large employers who were aware reported that it did not influence their recruitment and employment policies because of lack of enforcement.

Finkelstein (1993a) argued that 'the predominant factor contributing to the disablement of different groups is the way in which people can participate in the creation of social wealth' (p. 12). He argued strongly for solidarity in the disability movement around the social model of disability and against acceptance of the medical model. Taking this approach, it was argued that the fact that many disabled people are not in paid work did not mean that they cannot work: rather, that the segregated, special education system to which they were consigned failed to equip them with the necessary skills and socialized them into accepting a life without paid work. The way in which the labour market operated also mitigated against their inclusion (Oliver, 1991a; Berthoud *et al.*, 1993; Lunt and Thornton, 1994). The Code of Good Practice on the

Employment of Disabled People (Department of Employment, 1984), endorsed by the CBI and the TUC, recognized that 'most disabled people have the same skills and abilities to offer as able-bodied people and are effective as employees without the need for any special help; many other disabled people have as much to offer as able-bodied people given the use of appropriate help which is readily available; when the abilities of disabled workers are overlooked, companies are missing out on the contribution of potentially valuable employees'.

Oliver (1991a) has argued that attempts to reduce inequality for disabled people in the labour market have failed because they concentrate on the labour-supply side of the equation. In other words, how can disabled people be adapted to make them suitable for employment? There have been no attempts to provide incentives to change the work environment, which contains so many barriers to disabled people. In the past, government attempts to tackle the issue of disabled people and unemployment have centred around welfare-based initiatives, such as Employment Rehabilitation centres, Adult Training centres, Institutionally Secured employment, Sheltered workshops and Sheltered placements. These have been criticized as offering low-paid or unpaid work in segregated sectors with little or no opportunity to join the mainstream workforce (Barnes, 1991). Lunt and Thornton (1994) argued that the individual disabled person was viewed as 'in some way less than whole and as deficient, and thus the employer requires compensation in order to employ him/ her'. Therefore this concentration on individuality not only ignored the working environment and its institutional discrimination but also 'precludes recognition and discussion of a number of other positions including structural disadvantage' (p. 225).

Although still based on the labour-supply approach, in the mid-1980s, a more innovative and less traditional method developed through social service and health authority funding, to attempt to increase employment for people with learning difficulties: supported employment initiatives. These have been defined as 'real work in an integrated work setting' (Lister and Ellis, 1992). They were seen as challenging the conventional 'work-readiness' approach, which it was argued was ineffective for people with learning difficulties because of their difficulty in learning and transferring generalized work skills and the normal lack of support once in employment. The new approach used a 'place and then train model' as opposed to 'train and then place' (Pozner and Hammond, 1993). Pozner and Hammond's (1993) research indicated that these initiatives were effective in that 'clients are finding real jobs with real wages in regular settings' and retaining their jobs. However, the provision was found to be 'sporadic, fragile and a long way from meeting the extent of need' (p. 1).

Abberley (1996), while understanding the political attraction and short-term tactical reasons for adopting the social model approach to disability, argued that this stance has led to an over-reliance on the idea of equality for disabled people by their total inclusion into the world of productive labour and a refusal to place impairment under the social and political gaze. He viewed this as a too simplistic version of the social model stemming from the fight for the removal of social barriers and access restrictions. Some academics have called for a more complex approach, which continues to recognize the importance of the impact of an individual's impairment while still acknowledging the potential dangers of this approach to political contingency (Morris, 1992a; Shakespeare, 1994). Abberley (1996) argued that total adherence to the social model 'seems to . . . pass over an essential issue for disabled people, obscured by the romanticism of productivity – that even in a society which *did* make profound and genuine attempts to integrate impaired people into the world of work, some would still be excluded by their impairment' (p. 71).

Abberley (1996) was not advocating the view that impairment was an individual's natural problem unaffected by social, cultural, economic and political factors, but rather the contrary. He argued that it was important 'to work out a way of incorporating the material reality of impairment into social theories of disablement' (p. 63). He cited examples of such impairments as cataracts and erosion of the hip joint as proving that it was not only disability that was socially constructed and part of an historical context. He argued that the differential availability and accessibility of desired treatment to different groups in different societies was one way that 'what was once the substratum of impairment also slid into the superstructure of disablement, and thus of oppression' (p. 64). Another way that this happened was the way in which 'the technical possibility of "cure" comes to be experienced as a moral imperative by the impaired person and her family, because a social system organised around the taken-for-granted desirability of independence, work and physical normality cannot admit exceptions to this worldview' (p. 64).

Gooding (1994) tempered this view slightly by pointing out some very small chinks of a rights-based approach to social policy for disabled people. The passing of the Disability Discrimination Act 1995 was a major development in this approach. Gooding (1994) gave other examples, which included the 1991 and 1993 Education Acts, which held up desegregation of education as a goal, and the Chronically Sick and Disabled Persons Act (CSDPA) 1970, amended in 1976 to include places of employment. However, Topliss and Gould (1981) have shown that decisions on cases have favoured employers and discouraged local authorities from taking action under the CSDPA.

Some employers and organizations have attempted to take practical steps to enhance the employment of disabled people. One important example of an initiative demonstrating what can be done, even without anti-discrimination legislation, was that undertaken by Lambeth Borough Council. They took dramatic action by deciding that from the end of May 1986 onwards they would not apply for exemption and no non-disabled people would be recruited until the Council had reached its 3 per cent quota of employees registered as disabled. Although this was perfectly legal, it did provoke a great deal of debate. They used targeted advertising, open days for disabled people and the guarantee of an interview for disabled people with the appropriate paper qualifications. The council was able to increase their proportion of disabled workers. The scheme was only in existence for three months, but in that time the Council had almost achieved its 3 per cent target from its original position of 0.9 per cent. In the end the scheme had to be abandoned, because not enough suitably qualified and skilled disabled candidates could be found (Leach, 1989).

During the 1980s, we saw the growth of optimistic views on the potential of new technology, in terms of technological aids, computerization, and the possibility of home-based employment, for enabling disabled people to participate more fully in the labour market, based on the prominence of the rehabilitation approach which 'emphasised the way in which technology corrects or normalises the impaired person' (Roulstone, 1993, p. 241). However, Roulstone (1993) argued that, while there was some evidence of more and wider employment opportunities for disabled people, there was 'little evidence to show that new technology is redefining the notion of disability' (p. 242). This was even though it had the potential to challenge the view that physical ability was any longer such a useful skill in modern society and to back the social model of disability by showing environmental and attitudinal barriers to be the true source of disability. 'The ... fundamental point is that technology has generally been seen to "correct" the deficits of the impaired individual, rather than the prime focus being on the impact of technology on employment barriers (physical and attitudinal)' (Roulstone, 1993, p. 247).

As Roulstone (1993) pointed out, 'there is nothing inherently egalitarian about technology' and 'no guarantee that [it] will be used in an enabling way' (p. 244). The problem of disabled people's access to new technology and their ability to shift into technology-based jobs was, therefore, obscured by the emphasis on technical help. Most disabled people have been educated in segregated schemes with the concomitant lack of qualifications and confidence to be independent (as discussed above in the section on education and disability), and were reliant on welfare benefits or employed in low-skilled manual work. As part of the post-Second World War welfare-based initiatives to increase disabled people's employment, there was the Special Aids to Employment Scheme which functioned as 'the main gatekeeper of technological resources' for disabled people (Roulstone, 1993, p. 245). Roulstone (1993) saw many limitations to this scheme. The main one is its corrective, individual approach led by a traditional view and financial restrictions as opposed to a social model of disability with its accompanying rights-based approach. Applicants were only eligible for help if they had or were about to obtain work. Even more detrimental to disabled people was the requirement that the technology requested must have 'unique' benefits for the disabled worker over and above what they would provide for a non-disabled person.

Summary

This chapter has examined employment and education, two of the key social policy areas, for implications and issues in the fields of gender, 'race' and disability. In the area of education, the issues shared by women, ethnic minorities and disabled people are underachievement, differential access and discrimination. However, for women and ethnic minorities the previous patterns of underachievement are altering substantially. In the field of gender, we are seeing evidence of a reversal in the differential educational success of girls and boys, which is beginning in the school system. Nevertheless, it is predicted that this will take many years to work through the higher levels of the educational system and into the labour market. Higher education remains an area where women experience discrimination and lack of support, particularly in disciplines where they remain underrepresented, such as science, engineering and technology. To date, women's education still leaves them with lower earning power and more limited job opportunities than men. For ethnic minorities, claims of general underachievement in terms of educational qualifications and levels of attainment were clearly justified in the past. However, recently there has been a narrowing of the gap in the levels of educational attainment between Whites and ethnic minorities generally, and differential achievement occurring between ethnic minority groups. Even so, notes of caution are being sounded so that we do not ignore the issue of racism in the education system by taking a too simplistic explanation for this diversity based on cultural approaches. Certainly, in higher education there has been very little action to attempt to deal with the underrepresentation of ethnic minorities. A policy area of particular significance for disabled people is the issue of 'segregated' education, and the detrimental and excluding effect this has for them. Although this problem has diminished in terms of bringing more disabled children into mainstream schools, it still persists, and appears to be reproduced in the right to exclude disabled children from the National Curriculum at the discretion of educational professionals. The majority of higher education institutions have taken very little action on and continue to ignore the issue of disability.

Employment is not distributed equally in Britain. Those in higher paid, higher status and higher powered jobs are more than likely to be White, non-disabled and male. Despite women entering the labour market in ever-increasing numbers, they remain disadvantaged largely because of persistent occupational segregation. They are often segregated into women's jobs, but when they do compete with men the 'glass ceiling' remains a barrier to them. Sexual harassment has been shown to be widespread and prevalent across all types of work. Little has been introduced in terms of 'family friendly' policies, such as child-care provision, adequate maternity benefits and parental leave. Finally, ethnic minority women are shown to be in an even worse position than White women in the labour market, suffering racial discrimination and being in the lowest status, lowest paid grades, where they work longer and more anti-social hours.

In general terms, ethnic minorities experience significant inequalities in the employment field in the types of jobs they obtain, earnings' levels and vulnerability to unemployment. One important, determining factor in this is the practice of racial discrimination. Despite this, patterns of employment have shifted and greater diversity has appeared between ethnic minority groups. However, unemployment and employment in the lowest paid jobs remain high in certain ethnic minority groups, and the employment patterns of ethnic minorities have still not converged with Whites. The original migration to Britain of ethnic minorities as a consequence of a labour shortage established the inequalities that have persisted.

More recently, the Commission for Racial Equality has advocated the business benefits of 'equal opportunities' in the area of 'race'. This appears to have been successful, particularly among large employers where we see an increase in the introduction and implementation of policies. However, it is important to note that these can only impact on ethnic minorities already in work or those with a chance of recruitment. This may have the unintended consequence of increasing inequalities between different ethnic minority communities.

Disabled people are far less likely to be in paid employment than non-disabled people. Before the Disability Discrimination Act 1995 they could be legally refused employment simply because they were disabled, even though their disability was irrelevant to the job for which they applied. If in employment, they are disproportionately represented in lower status and lower paid jobs. Most employers have stereotypical views, such as reservations about disabled people's ability to do certain jobs and their level of productivity. To combat this, many analysts have argued for solidarity in the disability movement around the social model of disability and against acceptance of the medical model. This is an attempt to move away from the concentration on the labour-supply side of the equation, which tries to make disabled people suitable for employment rather than looking at barriers to their involvement. However, caution has been sounded that, because of certain individual impairments, there cannot be total inclusion of all disabled people into the world of productive labour. Optimistic views emerged on the potential of new technology to challenge the view that physical ability was still a useful skill in modern society and to back the social model of disability by showing environmental and attitudinal barriers to be the true sources of disability. However, to date technology has generally been used to 'correct' the deficits of the impaired individual, rather than impacting on employment barriers. On the positive side some innovative and less traditional attempts to increase the employment of disabled people have been made, and there have been some examples of a rights-based approach to social policy for disabled people.

CHAPTER 6

Social policy areas: income maintenance and social services

This chapter follows on from Chapter 5 by examining two more key social policy areas: income maintenance and social services. As in Chapter 5 these areas will be investigated by gender, 'race' and disability.

Income maintenance

Gender

Women are over-represented among the poor in contemporary Britain. Poverty for women is associated with motherhood, lone parenthood, the unequal distribution of income in families, low pay, part-time work, old age, reliance on benefits and responsibility for unpaid household duties and caring work (Pahl, 1980; Land 1983; Glendinning and Millar, 1992; Groves, 1992; Vogler and Pahl, 1993; Callender, 1996; Millar, 1996a). The social security system has been shown to have done little to alleviate this problem, despite women being the main recipients of benefits (Lister, 1992). On the contrary, prior to enforced changes by the European Commission and the European Court of Justice, the rules and regulations of welfare benefits in Britain directly discriminated against women, particularly married women (Millar, 1989; Whitting, 1992), and have continued to discriminate indirectly in practice (Lister, 1992). The division of labour between men and women, with women taking the main responsibility for the private sphere of domestic and caring work meant that, where they were employed, they were more likely to be in the sort of jobs which did not provide access to benefits: low-paid, part-time, casual work (McLaughlin, 1991; Lonsdale, 1992; Bagilhole, 1994a). Therefore, because women were often not the breadwinners in their family, there was the assessment that 'there is no need for the state to pay them benefits if they lose their jobs' and 'the assumption of the financial dependency of women on men continues to structure women's access to resources in . . . the social security system' (Millar, 1996a, p. 59).

The social security system in Britain has been structured from the start with traditional assumptions about the differing roles of men and women in society. Beveridge (1942), who laid the foundations, held the view that married women would be housewives and supported either through their husbands' paid work or entitlement to benefits from their husbands' National Insurance contributions. The only benefits considered suitable for married women were those that reinforced their marital and parental role, such as maternity benefits and children's allowances. If married women were in paid employment, they were offered the 'married women's option' to pay a lower contribution to National Insurance with the ensuing lack of entitlement to benefits (Lister, 1992). This option was not removed until 1977.

Only during the 1980s were further changes made to the openly differential treatment of women and men. Mostly because of pressure from the European Commission, through the 1979 Directive on Equal Treatment in Social Security, women could be the named claimant of income support for a couple, claim invalid care allowance and for their husbands as dependants, and disabled women no longer had to undergo the 'household duties test' (Millar, 1996a). However, in practice: 'The current social security system provides the main source of income for many women but it fails to provide adequacy and security' (Millar, 1996a, p. 62). It continued to treat women and men differently.

If we look at the contributory system of benefits first, one of the main reasons for this differential treatment is that it was based on a traditional male model of employment. It therefore does not provide for those in part-time, low-paid, casual, non-permanent jobs: that is, most women. Lister (1992) pointed out that about 2.25 million women were not entitled to benefits, such as unemployment and/or maternity pay, because they earned below the minimum level for contributions to the National Insurance system. Women's common interrupted pattern of employment made them more vulnerable to inadequate contributions for a full pension in their own right (Walker, 1992), which was particularly significant if they divorced (Joshi and Davies, 1991). Even if we look at benefits specifically for women, such as statutory maternity pay, we see restrictive regulations (much more so than other European Union countries) that many women cannot fulfil, again because of the type of work they find themselves in and their employment patterns. Maternity-pay entitlement is restricted to those who earn over the National Insurance threshold and then paid at a higher or lower rate depending on the length of the women's employment history with her current employer. To claim the higher rate of benefit women have to have worked for their present employer for either at least 16 hours per week for two years or eight hours per week for five years (EOC, 1996b). McRae (1991) found that only 69 per cent of employed pregnant women were entitled to maternity pay and less than half (42 per cent) at the higher level. Child benefit, paid specifically to women for their children and highly valued by women, particularly those who are not in paid employment, as 'money of their own' (Walker *et al.*, 1994) was frozen throughout much of the 1980s.

There has been a move by the government to restrict reliance on contributory benefits and to place more emphasis on means-tested benefits, family responsibility and private provision in the names of 'targeting' of benefits, and a desired reduction in 'dependency culture' and public expenditure. In the case of means-tested benefits, this had major implications for women because, as Millar (1996a) pointed out, 'The concepts of breadwinner men and financially dependent women remain strong in the rules surrounding means-tested benefits' (p. 61). Income support, which was the main benefit paid to those out of work, was paid to a family based on their total income assuming the erroneous idea of equitable distribution of income within families (Vogler and Pahl, 1993). The reliance on total family income meant that female partners of employed men who themselves became unemployed were not likely to be eligible for this benefit. There was also a financial disincentive of loss of benefit if a woman remained in employment if her male partner became unemployed (Millar, 1989).

In terms of the encouragement of family responsibility, the Child Support Act 1991 aimed to get absentee fathers to pay money for child support and, where they were already paying, to increase the amount. Where this was achieved, it did not benefit many lone mothers and their children because if they were dependent on benefits the child support they received was deducted pound for pound from income support. Also, in cases where child support was set at the same level as their benefit and wiped it out entirely, this resulted in a worse financial position for them. This was because previous passport entitlement to other benefits, such as housing benefit, was removed (Millar, 1996b).

Two ways of changing the social security system to make it non-discriminatory have been suggested, but both have their critics and limitations. First, there was the issue of providing benefits on an 'individualized' basis with all adults and children having an entitlement to benefits in their own right and no assumptions about women's financial dependency on men. Criticisms of this approach argued that 'individualized' benefits were likely to involve even more means-testing and would be more costly (Duncan *et al.*, 1994). Second, it has been suggested that there should be a return to more reliance on contributory benefits, but also that they must importantly be based on a gender-aware employment pattern. In other words, they should take into account women's position and pattern of employment in the labour market. However, a warning was sounded about benefits paid to those who stay at home to care, that may act to 'lock women further into their caring role in the "private" sphere of the family and out of the labour market and the "public" sphere more generally' (Lister, 1992, p. 68). This would therefore be another example of social security benefits supporting and facilitating a traditional family structure and gender roles.

'Race'

Racial discrimination and inequality are crucial factors that determine the 'ethnic divide' in British society (Amin, 1992). There are plenty of statistical data to demonstrate the general inequalities in income between ethnic minorities and White people in Britain. Using the 1990

General Household survey, Hills (1995) showed that over one-third of ethnic minority households' gross incomes were in the poorest fifth category compared with 18 per cent of White households. The 1991 Census data showed that Bangladeshi households were the most likely to be on low incomes followed by Pakistani and Black Caribbean households. Over half of Bangladeshi households were in wards classified as the most disadvantaged nationally by unemployment, economic activity or lack of car ownership (Green, 1994).

This position of ethnic minorities in Britain had an effect on their experience of poverty and their entitlement to benefits (Cook and Watt, 1992). This is particularly evident if we look at contributory benefits determined by National Insurance. Being linked to earnings, they necessarily excluded those in the lowest paid and most insecure jobs who were most vulnerable to unemployment. As shown above, feminist analysis showed us that women were disadvantaged in the benefits system because it was founded on a male model. Amin (1992) extended this idea to show that entitlements were based on a White male norm of continuous full-time employment, which formally excluded many ethnic minorities from the right to claim. Bhavani (1994) highlighted this as being of particular and increasing importance for Black women: because of their present and predicted disadvantaged position in the labour market, 'Black women may increase their employment levels but in a deteriorating situation' (p. 12). Ironically, though, as Black women were more likely to work full-time than their White counterparts, they were more likely to be covered by National Insurance even though they were low paid.

An area that is specifically detrimental to Black people's rights under the benefit system is the link between immigration controls and claiming social security benefits, which has resulted in racial discrimination. Immigration and social security legislation included regulations to limit certain groups access to welfare benefits through such rules as residence tests and the preclusion of a 'recourse to public funds' (Gordon, 1986; Williams, 1989; Cook and Watt, 1992; Law, 1996). The issue of asylum-seekers' rights to claim benefits has been a prominent issue since the mid-1990s. Their right to claim benefit was withdrawn in February 1996. However, this was reversed by an Appeal Court judgement later in the year which ruled it illegal. The government proposed new legislation to reverse this judgement.

Despite statistical evidence that showed greater poverty among ethnic minority communities and their lower take-up of social security benefits (Brown, 1984; Gordon, 1986), relatively little research has included the issue of 'race' and its effects on the experience of claiming and the take-up of social security benefits (Craig, 1991; Sadiq-Sangster, 1991; Cook and Watt, 1992; Ginsburg, 1992; Marsh and McKay, 1993). Also, there was no ethnic monitoring of benefits services, which could give a more systematic and informed view of the issue.

A notable exception to this has been a small-scale qualitative research study undertaken by Law *et al.* (1994) in Leeds. They found a complex picture with significant differences between ethnic minority and White claimants, but also between different ethnic minority communities in terms of their perceptions of the system and experiences of claiming. Contrary to the common view that ethnic minority communities were 'spongers' and a burden on the state, they found evidence of large amounts of non-claiming, underclaiming and a delay in claiming among ethnic minority communities, particularly among the Bangladeshis and Chinese who had a strong idea that claiming carried shame and stigma with it. They attributed this idea to cultural and religious factors, which led to negative views about using the benefits system, and feelings of insecurity among communities with a constant play on the issues of immigration control by the government. This had created 'a climate of secondary citizenship [which] has cast doubt for many black minority households on their entitlement to benefits' (Law, 1996, p. 64). This insecurity has been created and maintained by ethnic minority claimants being subjected to 'racially discriminatory scrutiny and suspicion'. Their passports were checked and they were asked for proof of birth, age, marriage or immigration status. They therefore became 'second-class claimants' (Gordon, 1991). Gohil's (1987) study of Asian claimants in Leicester showed that many of their concerns centre on the fear of unnecessary questioning about their immigration status, rather than language difficulties or lack of knowledge. The CRE (1985a) found evidence of stereotyping, confusion and the incorrect use of ethnic minority claimants' names, misinterpretation of such areas as capital and property held overseas, the sharing of household incomes, and family separation and divorce, which had led in some cases to denial of benefits. Ethnic minority claimants made a much greater use of community welfare advice agencies, family and friends than White claimants. Law's (1994) study cast doubt on the idea of 'dependency creation' by the benefits system. He found that claiming benefits created a sense of independence for some ethnic minorities who did not see this as a barrier to obtaining work. There was a 'dynamic shift' into and out of claiming and little evidence of dependency being passed down from one generation to another.

Bloch (1993) undertook research for the DSS on the take-up of benefits by ethnic minorities. However, in many respects it predetermined its recommendations of the need for interpreters and translated information by focusing from the beginning on ethnic minority claimants' information needs. While this was acknowledged as important, Law's (1994) study showed that more than this was needed to ensure the take-up of benefits entitlement by ethnic minority communities. There was a need for welfare rights advocacy work to overcome dominant perceptions of shame and stigma, which were attached to the idea of claiming, and the need for more information to be disseminated about the system through the informal networks within the communities (Law et al., 1994). There was also the need to counter any racist attitudes and stereotyping by benefits agency staff through training, guidelines and employment and the promotion of ethnic minority staff (NACAB, 1991; CRE/BA, 1995).

Disability

Beveridge (1942), the father of the British welfare state, argued that a system of social security should meet the needs of disabled people: i.e. 'The inability of a person of working age, through illness or accident, to pursue a gainful occupation' (p. 124). In other words, disabled people were to be supported by non-disabled people working and contributing to National Insurance and social assistance schemes for their benefit. There was no indication that disabled people might be aided in the pursuit of their own working lives. Instead there was a call for the provision of disability benefits and industrial pensions, medical services within a National Health Service and rehabilitation.

Taking the social model of disability discussed in Chapter 2, it has been shown that impairment led to the handicap of poverty (Lonsdale, 1990; Barnes, 1991). As for women and ethnic minorities, as demonstrated above, the fact that benefits were linked to earnings necessarily excluded those in the lowest paid, most insecure jobs who were most vulnerable to unemployment. This analysis is particularly important for disabled people because of their singularly worst disadvantage in the labour market as shown in Chapter 5 in the section on employment. The norm of the non-disabled claimant works to exclude disabled people from their rights to claim.

The dominance of the medical model of disability has translated into social security policies and rules whereby disabled people's access to income maintenance was constructed not only by means-testing but also by medical criteria (Barton, 1989). The prevalence of the medical model of disability interpreted into the social security system was demonstrated by the way that particular categories of disability are used as criteria for qualification for different types of benefit and variable amounts of money (Department of Social Security, 1994, p. 163). Despite the fact that access to benefits for disabled people has widened, they were always and continue to be controlled by judgements made by medical personnel about the capacities of individual disabled claimants. Some social security benefits for disabled people were means-tested, such as Income Support and the Disability Working Allowance (DWA). Non-means tested benefits included the Severe Disablement Allowance, the Attendance Allowance and the Disability Living Allowance which included a mobility component (Blakemore and Drake, 1996, p. 144).

The restrictive rules and regulations surrounding the benefits system available to disabled people, particularly invalidity benefit, Severe Disablement Allowance and the therapeutic earnings rule limited the scope for their part-time work. Roulstone (1993) pointed out that this was particularly true where the disabled person needed a gradual move or re-entry into the labour market. Blakemore and Drake (1996) argued that viewed through the more recent social model of disability, 'The benefits system takes on a very different cast, social security becomes a compensatory device intended to mitigate the exclusion of disabled people from the community in general and from paid work in particular' (p. 145).

The system can be shown to be even more proactive than this in maintaining disabled people's dependence even through a benefit, which was introduced with the pronounced aim of assisting disabled people in work. Pozner and Hammond's (1993) study of supported employment initiatives for disabled people discussed in Chapter 5 in the section on disability and employment revealed that a 'benefits trap' had a major detrimental impact on their outcomes and advantages for disabled people. Many disabled clients were restricted to part-time posts below their full potential, otherwise they would have been financially worse off and prejudiced their housing situations if they worked longer hours. All the agencies involved in supported employment initiatives emphasized the 'constraining role' of the benefits system. Only a small minority had been able to utilize the Disability Working Allowance for clients, and the vast majority, who had not, gave the following reasons: 'clients will end up worse off, client's housing benefits may be affected, the complexity of the benefits system, and the perception of risk of losing other benefits essential to clients' (p. 21).

Obviously some form of income maintenance will always be required by disabled people whose disability prevents them from working despite a barrier-free environment, but the Disabled People's Movement have argued for these to be based on the rights of citizens rather than a charitable approach. Until then the disability benefit system has been shown to inadequately cover the costs of impairment and to discourage independence (Oliver, 1996).

Social services

Gender

Women predominate 'on both sides of the front line of the personal social services' (Davis, 1996) as the users and providers of personal social services, both professionally and through informal, voluntary and community care. As Pascall (1986) summed it up for women: 'Looking after people is either done for no pay, within the family, or for low pay in the public sector' (p. 29). Looking first at the large presence of women as clients of social services we see that there have been two main reasons for this. First, women outnumbered men very significantly as care providers for those in society whose care was the primary concern of the legislative base of social work and social services departments. Most women cared for a young child at some stage of their lives. The task of community care for the elderly, sick and the mentally ill fell on women either as family members, neighbours or volunteers (Bagilhole, 1996a, 1996b). It appeared that care for the elderly, disabled people or the sick only fell to men if there were no women available (Hallett, 1989). Second, women outnumbered men in two sections of the community where social services were concentrated: among the increasing numbers of poor (Glendinning and Millar, 1992) and the elderly (Tinker, 1981).

Community care in effect meant care by the family which has worked to the disadvantage of women (Bayley, 1982; Finch and Groves, 1983; Finch, 1984, 1986, 1989; Ungerson, 1990), despite the fact that 'there is no suggestion in the phrase that women are implicated more than men' (Finch, 1986, p. 15). It was argued that: 'By defining this in rosy terms as informal, intimate, flexible, and by portraying it as both the service of choice for the consumer and the relationship of choice for the carer, the uncomfortable exploitation of carers can be glossed over' (Brown and Smith, 1993, p. 188). 'The community was thus perceived as an inexpensive and humanitarian source of care for dependent adults . . . however, the reality of the community as a source of care means that the majority of care is provided by women' (Tester, 1996, p. 134). Research which has looked at the care of the elderly suggested an order of preference for care givers: first a spouse, then a daughter, a daughter-in-law, a son, then another relative or non-relative (Qureshi and Walker, 1989).

However, many studies have shown that the service provision offered to women carers was often insensitive to their needs. It could lead to a deep mistrust and lack of confidence in social workers themselves and a preference for dealing with voluntary workers whom carers felt were less judgemental, less threatening, more supportive and thereby provided a more appropriate service (Bagilhole, 1996a). Women seemed to be expected to carry a heavier burden of care than men. Several small studies indicated that the provision of services, such as home helps, were more related to the sex of the carer than the needs of the client. It appeared that male carers of disabled people were more likely to get meals-on-wheels, rehabilitation and assessment services and long-stay care for their dependants, while female carers got day care or short-stay care for more disabled dependants (Fawcett, 1988). It has also been shown that disabled women were less likely than disabled men to be given help with household tasks because of assumptions about the division of labour in the home (Arber and Ginn, 1991). Ungerson (1985) neatly summed this up by identifying 'two cross currents, namely the identification of women as the pivotal characters in family life and the preferential allocation of certain social services to men where a woman is in some sense "absent"' (p. 187). She argued that these features worked at an ideological level to socially control women and limit their access to this service resource.

Social services have failed to address ethnic minority women's needs in similar, but also particular, ways. Bryan *et al.* (1985) argued that ethnic minority women's experiences and relationship with welfare state services demonstrated more clearly than any other area the effect of institutionalized racism. This failure by social services has led to a response whereby ethnic minority women have organized, mostly through voluntary and informal organizations, to provide appropriate services to the ethnic minority community (Mama, 1993) and in some areas this has received backing from the social services departments. However, it can be argued that this let social services off the hook in providing adequate and appropriate services for all (Bagilhole, 1992).

The rhetoric of community care in Britain took women's natural caring role for granted. As traditional state-provided welfare was removed and the material conditions of those needing care deteriorated, we saw the increasing use of the labour of women relatives and volunteers to offer sophisticated and sometimes intensive care within the community. Feminist analysis exposed this increase in women's caring burden. This ideology of women as social carers was incorporated in the British welfare state from the start, and was seen by many feminists as the core of women's oppression (Wilson, 1977; Barrett, 1980; McIntosh, 1981; Stacey, 1981; Land, 1982; Dale and Foster, 1986). A woman's life cycle consisted of periods of caring for children, caring for husbands, caring for parents or in-laws in mid-life, and continually caring for neighbours and friends. Aronson (1990) described how the 'cultural assumptions and realties' of women's lives worked to sustain the existing pattern of care, but she argued that 'it comes at a high cost to women'.

If there was no support from the state, the policy increased the care asked from women within kinship relations and as voluntary work. While women were exploited in providing unpaid work in the community, this was both undervalued and not given due recognition by social services who did not provide adequate assistance or support for these women (Langan, 1992a; Walker, 1992). Little account was taken of these women's needs, still less their wishes. Caring for a dependent relative was undoubtedly emotionally as well as physically exhausting. Yet the daughters, daughters-in-law and other women relatives and neighbours who were urged to take on these responsible tasks were usually in late middle age, at a stage when having to retire from paid employment led to severe financial hardship. The proportion of women who gave up jobs to care should not lead us to forget that most women worked *and* cared; women were not absolved from domestic responsibilities just because they were in the labour market (Beechey and Whitelegg, 1986). Graham (1993) argued that because most women could not afford to pay for care for their relatives they had to provide it themselves and thus became financially dependent. There is great value in allowing disabled people and the elderly to make genuine choices about remaining in their own home, or about residential care, but social workers should be equally sensitive to the impossible stress on women.

Waerness (1984) saw 'care' as a 'compassion trap' for women similar to Land and Rose's (1985) 'compulsory altruism', where women lacked the choice of whether to perform caring tasks, in the absence of viable alternatives. However, it was important at the same time to recognize that women were not solely the victims of policy changes. It may be that, at the grass-roots level of the welfare state, care-giving and care-receiving was as Brown and Smith (1993) cited 'the service of choice for the consumer' and 'the relationship of choice for the carer'. What was needed was financial resources and professional support for this form of care. This can be demonstrated if we consider the area of volunteering. Here women's altruism could be seen as ambiguous. In some ways it perpetuated the structures which exploited and oppressed women, but it could also provide empowering opportunities. The everyday world for women of providing and receiving care through volunteering was complex and can be emancipating for both groups. There were shown to be advantages for women from volunteering and receiving the help of a woman volunteer (Bagilhole, 1996a).

The vast majority of those employed by social services departments are women. They form the largest proportion of women working in any part of the welfare state. Most of these women work part-time, and their predominance at the lower levels and scarcity in management positions remains constant. Nottage (1991) showed that even though 86 per cent of workers in social services were women, 89 per cent of directors of social services were men (90 per cent in 1971). Ethnic minority women were even more scarce in senior levels than White women (Davis, 1996). The reorganization of personal social services into generic departments in 1971 and the subsequent reorganization in 1974 decimated the numbers of women in senior positions who had previously been in control of the old children's departments. 'The world of the local authority personal social services is one in which mainly White, often part-time women workers serve the front line of the service negotiating the distribution of scarce resources (including their own time and skills) in the face of the needs of (predominantly women) service users, while the majority of the full-time White men are employed to supervise and manage resources' (Davis, 1996). In other words, as Grimwood and Popplestone (1993) argued, 'Women's talents are being wasted, women are suffering discrimination, important decisions are being taken by men, [and] organisations are being run to suit men' (p. 3).

Periodically the absence of women from social work management received passing attention in the professional journals. But the very marked discrepancy between the proportion of women and men entering the occupation and reaching the top was never accorded the sort of attention it deserved. While it has begun to be recognized that to provide an appropriate service for all the community, ethnic minority workers should be employed at all levels, this has not generally been accepted for women (Ahmad, 1990; Grimwood and Popplestone, 1993). Research showed that women's careers in social services were hampered by several factors, but the major barrier to their career development was seen as the culture of the organization dominated by a male style of management and the lack of support mechanisms to empower women to challenge this (Eley, 1989; Lancelot, 1990; Allan *et al.*, 1992). In the organizational structure of personal social services, caring roles and management roles have become distinct and separate with women in the former and men in the latter. It has been argued that 'the development of a macho management style has contributed to the repression of social work values and passion about social issues' (Pryde, 1991) and that, accompanying this management style, new managerialism led the service to be more market and externally performance-orientated (Langan, 1992b).

Grimwood and Popplestone (1993) showed that not only did personal social services underpin the role of women as carers among clients but also the gendered way that work was distributed within the structure of the organization 'confined' women to low-status care and support jobs.

A stark example of this was in the home-care and home-help organizations, because of the nature of the role and tasks home helps are expected to carry out. These tasks could include intimate and personal care such as bathing and attending to incontinence. Despite a recent rise, home carers were still paid a very low wage. Very few men were employed in this poorly paid work. This phenomenon was even more starkly demonstrated by ethnic minority women's position in personal social services where 'they find themselves in the majority as care assistants in residential establishments in cities, in the lowest-status, worst-paid jobs, involving the most intimate caring tasks and with the least prospects of promotion' (Grimwood and Popplestone, 1993). The introduction of compulsory competitive tendering in local authorities meant that the areas where women's work is concentrated, particularly ethnic minority women in cleaning, catering and laundry services, were disproportionately marginalized and affected with subsequent lowering of working conditions, pay and loss of security and related benefits (Newman, 1994).

This segregation of jobs where women in personal social services found themselves concentrated in particular jobs can be described as horizontal segregation. Howe (1986) had also drawn attention to vertical segregation occurring where women and men shared the same positions, with women being predominant in dealing with client groups that were of lower status. Women social workers were more likely to work with elderly, disabled and mentally ill people, and women predominated in residential work, particularly with the elderly. This pattern was even more stark for ethnic minority women (Watt and Cook, 1989).

Several recommendations have been offered to attempt to remedy the gendered nature of both personal social services employment opportunities and its concomitant service. In the area of employment, these included anti-sexist training courses for all workers, and 'equal opportunities' for women workers to go on training courses, which were run at appropriate times alongside career counselling. In terms of service delivery it has been proposed that consideration of women's issues should be included along with other aspects of assessment, in particular the service to carers which needed vast improvement. Facilities for children at social services reception needed attention with staff being available to care for children. While participation of women clients and staff in reviews and case conferences must be enabled and valued in a way which research indicated it was not, in family cases it should not be acceptable for workers to deal only with the mother. Finally, it has been suggested that research was needed to find out the number of women clients being dealt with and to identify how resources should be more appropriately allocated.

'Race'

Generally, there has been shown to be a low take-up of social service provision by ethnic minority communities, despite evidence of their need.

Explanations for this phenomenon concentrated either on the lack of knowledge and information about the services on offer, which led to calls for translated leaflets and provision of interpreters, or misplaced assumptions by professionals of extended family support among these communities. Atkin and Rollings (1993) highlighted ignorance of or lack of understanding of the needs of ethnic minority communities based on myths, stereotypes and generalizations. Law (1996) highlighted the need for a more dynamic conception of the culture and ethnicity of communities. This was because there have been changes in family and household structure, and geographical mobility; and immigration legislation has played its part in dividing families.

Relatively less attention has been focused on the appropriateness of service provision itself. As Gilroy (1993) pointed out, although language issues were important for the take-up of services, 'Issues of race cannot be reduced to matters of language . . . making a change from an anglocentric service provision is more important than translating leaflets for minority groups for whom little provision is made' (p. 36). We need to ask various questions of the service itself. Examples include: Does it monitor its clients by 'race'? Does it consult with the local communities and make use of community centres and voluntary organizations to enhance take-up? How many local social services authorities have meals on wheels which cater for vegetarians, Black Caribbeans or those who eat halal food? How many elderly people find themselves excluded from a service because it does not take account of their needs?

Dominelli (1986), in her critique of social services, argued that norms related to the White middle-class family were the standard by which others were judged. Since then there has been a definite if reluctant move from this previous 'colour-blind' approach to provision of services (Bagilhole, 1993a). Anti-racism has at least been established in the professional training of social workers (Dominelli, 1986), but this has led to government criticism of an over-concentration on 'race' and accusations of 'political correctness'. Also, Law (1996) questioned the efficacy of this approach. He argued that: 'The documentation of racist ideologies in social work has directly informed the developments of anti-racist approaches, but the failure to adequately document their connection with discriminatory practice . . . has led to the confinement of anti-racism to either simplistic rhetoric or ineffective policy and practice guidance' (p. 146). Watt and Cook (1989) argued that although there have been discussions and debates on the issues of the 'needs of ethnic minorities' and 'service delivery to ethnic minorities' for about 25 years, this had only confirmed 'the resistance to change from most of the social services departments which have paid lip service to challenging racism and working towards anti-racist strategies' (p. 73). Blakemore and Boneham (1994) argued that, in this respect, the presence of Asian practitioners and welfare workers could be extremely beneficial to service users, especially older Asian women.

It has been argued that further research was needed into the perception of the services among the ethnic minority communities (Law, 1996).

Do certain ethnic groups associate feelings of shame and stigma with their use? Is the demand or take-up of services concomitant with a reaction of service providers which involves perusal of individual's immigration status and rights linked to citizenship? Law (1996) put forward three interconnecting factors to explain the non-take-up of social services by ethnic minority communities. These were negative perceptions of social service departments, uncertainty about their eligibility and lack of perceived need. Atkin and Rollings (1993) showed that departments are perceived as unwilling to understand ethnic minority communities' needs, difficult to communicate with and slow to respond or change.

Law (1996) argued that: 'Local authority social services has long been a battleground in the local politics of race' (p. 113). This had centred around controversial issues and struggles, such as the admission and treatment of ethnic minority children in residential care, and the rights and wrongs of same 'race' fostering and adoption. Barn's (1990) study of ethnic minority children in local authority care showed this to be a complex issue in practice. Although there was no dispute about the high incidence of ethnic minority children in care, there was diversity among the communities with very few Asian children being present – and even Black Caribbean and mixed origin children were more likely to enter care on a voluntary basis than White children. If we look at the trans-racial versus same 'race' debate around fostering and adoption, we find that this is also complex. Initially, what had been categorized as a White liberal perspective viewed trans-racial placements as not only acceptable and preferred to long-term institutional care, but also as making a contribution to promoting 'race' relations (Tizard, 1977). Then came a radical perspective which was opposed to trans-racial placements and argued that the apparent measured success of previous placements was only achieved by researchers failing to include the issue of 'ethnic identification' in their research (Gill and Jackson, 1983; Rhodes, 1992). By the mid-1980s, several local authorities had adopted the policy of same 'race' placements and set about recruiting ethnic minority foster parents. This created a backlash and accusations of 'political correctness' from the government, who called for the downplaying of 'race' issues. The Children Act 1989, in the area of child-care decisions, called for the recognition of 'religious persuasion, racial origin and cultural and linguistic background' not to be given preference, but to be placed alongside other considerations like the detrimental effect on children of delaying placements if same 'race' families were not available.

So what we found was evidence of contradictions in the provision of social services to ethnic minority communities (Skellington and Morris, 1992). While there was a failure to provide accessible and supportive elements of the service, at the same time there was an over-provision of the social control side, for example, the over-representation of Black Caribbeans in compulsory detention for mental health problems. This allowed contradictory evidence to be cited as evidence for institutionalized racism, either the low or high take-up of different services.

Another contradictory area was the perception by service providers of the notion of the pathology of ethnic minority families. This led to both the perceived need for social work intervention or, on the other hand, the idea that these families have less need of social workers because of a higher level of family and community support than White families. Dominelli (1989) argued that this left us with racially discriminatory forms of provision and practice. What we then saw was the lack of an overall strategy on the part of social services and, instead, a pattern that was variable and uneven within and between different local authorities (CRE, 1989b).

As one response to the recognized inadequacy and ineffectiveness of service provision to ethnic minority communities, we have seen the emergence and development of a reliance on ethnic minority voluntary agencies to fill the gap. Patel (1990) demonstrated the primacy of these agencies in providing culturally sensitive and appropriate services, particularly to the elderly. However, these developments have to be treated with caution, even though they may be the clients' preferred form of service, because they can be used as an excuse for lack of change and proper resource allocation by social services departments. By relying too heavily on culturally appropriate service provision through separate services, they have acted as a suppressor of political action to ensure fair mainstream services (Patel, 1990; Bagilhole, 1993a).

The NHS and Community Care Act 1990 introduced an initiative, which could be seen as praiseworthy: the involvement of all interested groups in care decisions – the users, carers, voluntary groups and the local community. Ethnic minority communities were specifically mentioned in this light (Department of Health, 1989). Despite this there has been no evidence to support the view that there was an improvement in the effective assessment of ethnic minorities' needs by social service departments. Watt and Cook, 1989; Sumpton, 1993; Butt, 1994; Butt *et al.*, 1994; Baylies *et al.*, 1993, found a general deficiency in service provision for ethnic minority patients discharged from psychiatric hospitals. There was a lack of preparation for return to the community, and problems of poverty, unemployment, homelessness and racial harassment. Reasons cited for the persistent problems in constructing 'care packages' for ethnic minorities have been various: the assumption that they could adequately express their demand for culturally appropriate services, the inadequate provision of such services in some areas, especially outside inner cities, the over-reliance on referring potential clients to community groups, tokenistic consultation with ethnic minority groups and, finally, cash-limited budgets (Walker and Ahmad, 1994; Begum, 1995).

Cameron *et al.* (1989) demonstrated that community care services were inappropriate for the needs of the ethnic minority elderly 'in the provision of unacceptable aids, adaptations, often costly, that were not used because they did not meet cultural requirements, and bath nurses turned away because their help with washing was interpreted as unhygienic (rinsing not being done in the customary way) or as an invasion of privacy' (p. 245). Patel (1993) argued that authorities and professionals have legitimated their continued neglect of ethnic minority elders by using traditional stereotypes of extended caring families or the notion that the elderly will retire to their countries of origin, and arguments about their relatively small numbers. In considering the NHS and Community Care Act 1990 for ethnic minority elders, Patel identified direct and indirect racism in service delivery, operating at different levels and in different guises.

It is likely in the future that unless changes are made there will be increasing gaps between the needs of the ethnic minority communities and the resources available. Cash-limited budgets do not favour the seeking out of unfulfilled need and new areas of service provision. Law (1994) found that even the ethnic minority community with the highest socioeconomic position – people of Indian origin – found it difficult to access suitable social services. In his study of Sikh elders Law found a great lack of professional support despite an urgent need for personal and domestic help, and advice on benefits among this group. Importantly, Law (1996) pointed out that even in the process of restructuring care provision into the community nothing would change unless the issues already identified in inadequate social service provision to ethnic minority communities were dealt with. 'Each new edict from central government indicates that service providers must listen more carefully to the "Voice" of black ethnic minority groups. The gulf between official claims and actual practice "on the ground" remains disturbingly wide' (p. 145).

Disability

Oliver (1996) argued that: 'At present it remains true that welfare services are failing, and are likely to continue to fail to accord disabled people the entitlements of citizenship' (p. 58). Sainsbury (1995) identified three broad periods in the post-war development of personal social services for disabled people, which she gave the following labels: 'promotional welfare', 'rights, choice and control', and 'the burden of care'. The first period, 1948 to 1963, was characterized by an open-ended commitment to service provision. The type of services provided and the attitude to disabled people's rights were underpinned by the National Assistance Act 1948, which gave local authorities the 'power to make arrangements for promoting the welfare' of disabled people. Given the post-war shortage of labour, a commitment to the underpinning of the welfare state by full employment, and the Disabled Persons (Employment) Act 1944, which supported the important right of disabled people to work, local authorities established sheltered workshops, hostel accommodation for disabled workers and home-working schemes. However, as Sainsbury (1995) pointed out, 'From the outset, there had been a clear bifurcation on gender lines between local authority services: those associated with employment and disability were allocated overwhelmingly to men, while those associated with "the handicapped" aided disabled women in the home' (p. 188).

Sainsbury's (1995) second period of 'rights, choice and control' was when the government supported public spending and encouraged local authorities 'to increase their expenditure on all personal social services, including those for disabled people' (p. 190). There was also a shift in policy from an emphasis on residential care to a commitment to community care, despite the fact that in practice expenditure on residential care still dominated (Davies, 1968). The emergence of the disability lobby, influenced by the civil rights movement in the USA, pressed for financial help for individual disabled people, and participation in the management of residential homes. This led to the development of some half-way houses where provision was provided to prepare disabled people to live independently although aided by volunteer carers (Dartington *et al.*, 1981). Therefore, service provision moved away from an emphasis on employment to care and the replacement of domestic labour, such as home helps, meals on wheels, and aids and adaptations to houses. However, underpinning these developments was legislation which appeared contradictory. In 1970 the Chronically Sick and Disabled Act, and the Local Authority and Social Services Act were passed. The former emphasized community care by strengthening the duties of local authorities to adapt homes, provide home helps and ensure access to public buildings. Whereas the latter Act, by bringing together all the different specialisms in social services and creating a generic social worker, effectively restricted the development of specialist services for disabled people (Sainsbury, 1986), and limited the attention and resources that could be given to the Chronically Sick and Disabled Act (Topliss and Gould, 1981).

Sainsbury's (1995) final period of concerns over 'the burden of care' from 1976 led to criticisms of the previous period as economically irresponsible. Successive Conservative governments, since their election in 1979, accelerated cuts in public expenditure. This led to the NHS and Community Care Act 1990, which Oliver (1996) pointed out is central to the strategy aimed at 'stimulating the private and voluntary sectors to act as providers of services and for the statutory authorities to act as enablers and purchasers of services rather than sole providers' and, importantly, 'at the cheapest cost' (p. 55).

There has been a questioning of the quality of community care in private households, particularly by informal carers, as being more acceptable than residential care and professional carers (Owens, 1987; Morris, 1993a). Community care was criticized by feminists for two reasons. First, it was seen as against the interests of carers, predominantly women who lacked support from the state (Finch and Groves, 1980); second, it accepted the male model of disability, which ignored disabled women's service needs (Lonsdale, 1990; Morris, 1993b). Sainsbury (1995) raised several other possible disadvantages for all disabled people in the provision of community care. A central problem to the reforms was an inherited one from the past: the problem of achieving a needs-led assessment within a limited and restricted budget. Because the main thrust of the provision was to keep people out of expensive residential care, service was only provided for those who, without it, were on the edge of entering residential care. Disabled people's voluntary organizations also lost their campaigning and advocacy role by having to separate it from their service provision to be eligible to be providers of service under contract to local authorities. Finally, the reduction in the power and resources that local authorities held increased the role of the NHS in the control of services, with the danger of the reassertion of the dominance of the individualistic 'medical model' of disability. However, Oliver (1996) did indicate some areas for limited optimism. He identified a growing demand from service users to have a voice in the services provided as statutory authorities become purchasers rather than providers of services, and that the legislation provided, at least in theory, greater opportunities for user involvement.

The problem was how effectively this was translated into practice. Despite the stated aim of reducing professional dominance and the 'dependency culture' through community care, this did not happen for disabled people. Davis (1993) pointed out that 'our lives are substantially still in their hands. They still determine most decisions and their practical outcomes' (p. 199). Morris (1993b) did not place much faith in the provision of appropriate service for disabled people at all; instead, she argued very strongly for the replacement of service provision by money so that disabled people could be in control and purchase from the market what they needed and wanted. Otherwise, she argued that 'their opportunities to be independent citizens will disappear'. Disabled people had rights to see and contribute to their care plans, but they were allocated a care manager who was a professional responsible for decisions on purchasing their care and they had no access to legally enforceable grievance procedures. Assessment of needs was an exercise in power (Hugman, 1991) and despite some improvements, fundamentally the 'power and control of those services' remained in professional hands (Oliver, 1996, p. 56). Oliver (1996) argued that 'there is no direct relationship between the needs of disabled people and the services they receive. Rather, disabled people have their needs defined and interpreted by others' (p. 124) and in the context of the allocation of scarce resources. Evidence showed that disabled people were not being involved in the planning and delivery of services as the legislation required (Bewley and Glendinning, 1992; Ellis, 1993; Hoyes *et al.*, 1993). This was particularly so when professional decisions on the provision of care were also influenced by stereotyped views on ethnic minorities' needs and racism (Begum, 1994).

Like services for physically disabled people, services for people with a learning difficulty have grown in number and developed over the twentieth century, and similar criticisms of them can be made. Questions about who the services were provided for were particularly pertinent for this group of clients. Were they designed to meet the needs of people with learning difficulties, their carers, society or the professionals involved? The complexity of this question was highlighted with a discussion of the issues involved for this client group around the area of human rights and empowerment. As Todd (1995) pointed out, Britain signed the United Nations Declaration of Human Rights in 1948. Rooted in this was an important issue that individual freedom was constrained by accompanying responsibilities not to impede the freedom of others. In the light of this, Todd reported that disputes and difficulties have arisen when people with learning difficulties have attempted to assert their human rights, often because many were reliant on relatives, carers or professionals as advocates. This led to two problems. First, 'decisions over rights . . . can be perceived as paternalistic and promoting dependence' and second, 'the effect of applying a right may not have equal consequences for all those concerned' (p. 63).

The concept of empowerment has been articulated by disabled people as part of their demands for control over their own lives and as a counter to their experience of powerlessness, but it was a radical political phenomenon which has been described as containing 'inherent tensions' (Gilbert, 1995). The concept of empowerment created similar dilemmas to the articulation of human rights for people with learning difficulties. It 'inevitably raises questions about the power relationship between disabled people and their immediate carers, but it also raises questions between disabled people, professionals, managers and politicians' (Gilbert, 1995, p. 114).

What we saw in reality was that, combined with this growth in services, professionals consolidated their control by developing more sophisticated methods of assessment for determining needs and producing solutions to them. In fact, 'It is professional staff who play the key role in identifying and subsequently meeting needs they themselves have defined' (Todd and Gilbert, 1995, p. 3). However, this meant they were faced with ever-increasing demands for a limited budget with 'continuing reluctance on the part of society to support the cost of providing such services' (Earwaker and Todd, 1995, p. 5). Therefore, Earwaker and Todd (1995) made the important point that 'the nature of service provision is determined by both professional and political considerations' (p. 6).

The main services provided for people with a learning difficulty were day services and short-term care. Day services took the form of community adult-training centres about which Earwaker and Todd (1995) were quite scathing: 'Little can be established abut the purpose of these centres, although it is assumed that they are intended solely to provide a supervised form of occupation, which was in some way productive' (p. 8). The productive side may be challenged, as a survey of one local authority's day centres revealed that the majority of centres took in menial work from factories in the form of 'outworking', such as packing razor blades or sweets, which occupied the attenders at the day centre and often staff for quite long periods of the day and for which the centres received a pittance (Bagilhole, 1989). The provision of short-term care was usually provided within institutions such as hospitals or residential homes. It was frequently called 'respite care' and Earwaker and Todd (1995) argued that this term demonstrated that the service was seen as being provided more for the carer than the person with learning difficulties, and could often lead to distress or feelings of rejection on their part. Some innovative schemes provided short-term care in the person's home, but these were few and far between. Residential care was often the only option for people with severe or multiple disabilities (Hubert, 1991) and was more likely to be used for ethnic minorities with learning difficulties (Stalker, 1991). Earwaker and Todd (1995) ended their assessment of services provided for people with learning difficulties on a rather pessimistic but challenging note. They argued that we could not rely on those in control of the services, professionals and politicians, to administer the necessary changes to make them more appropriate for their clients. 'People with learning difficulties and their advocates must look elsewhere if they are hoping for any real change. If they wait for the services to undergo a metamorphosis, then it will be too late' (p. 31).

The definition of disability, as either an individual attribute or con-structed by the structure of society, remained a disputed area, which demanded different policies and services. Oliver (1983, 1990) argued very strongly that an adequate practice for social work and effective policies for disabled people could only be built on the basis of a model that recognized that disability was a social phenomenon and not an individual problem: 'It is a social problem concerned with the effects of hostile physical and social environments upon impaired individuals, or even a societal one concerned with the way society treats this par-ticular minority group' (p. 2). The acceptance of this analysis therefore demanded that social work practice with disabled people should be broadened. Oliver (1996) criticized professional social work for inter-vening on an individual level only with disabled people, which in fact further disabled them particularly in the environment of residential care.

As we have seen there were still many areas of concern around the provision of social services for disabled people. Finkelstein (1993b) argued that: 'The modern challenge is to provide alternatives to current practice so that workers and disabled people can share expertise in barrier identification and removal, both at the personal level ... and the social level, where public facilities need to be made truly public' (p. 41). Leach (1989) highlighted how social services departments did not employ disabled people in sufficient numbers. Anti-discrimination policy needs to ensure both that provision is made for the special needs of disabled people and that they have equal access to general services. Equal access may be denied for several reasons: disabled people may not know about the services, physical inaccessibility (for example, no transport to day centres or lunch clubs), inadequate provision for special needs, and direct and indirect discrimination, including institutionalized racism and sexism. To combat this measures to ensure equal access include information and publicity materials that portray positive images of disabled people, and the translation of information into Braille and on to tape. There also needs to be appropriate consultation with disabled people on their services, for example, a thorough review of criteria for assessing need and charges with disabled people, and the appointment of disabled people to consultative bodies. Disabled people need access to ordinary lunch and social clubs, not just day centres or meals-on-wheels, and there needs to be integration of disabled children and adults in day nurseries, residential homes and adult training centres. Finally, there should be a complaints procedure for disabled people who need to contest the withdrawal or limitation of particular social services.

Summary

This chapter has examined the social policy areas of income maintenance and social services. First, looking at income maintenance, we have seen a growth in poverty and unemployment, and therefore a reliance on social security benefits. There has also been an emphasis on private caring and means-tested benefits in Britain, which has disproportionately hit women, ethnic minorities and disabled people. Walker (1996) argued that social security 'is not just about preventing poverty. It is one of the principal ways in which the State . . . acts to reduce inappropriate inequality' (p. 15). However, the first section of this chapter shows that, certainly in the areas of gender, 'race' and disability, it is not achieving this aim. Women's entitlement and access to benefit is severely limited because of policies being based on assumptions about women's traditional role. The crux of the matter is the linking of benefit entitlement to paid work. This also impacts on ethnic minorities and particularly disabled people who find themselves in the lowest paid most insecure jobs – if in paid work at all. The added dimension of disadvantage for ethnic minorities is the actual and feared use of immigration rules, which limit their right to draw on public funds. For disabled people the system of income maintenance has been mainly based on the 'medical model' of disability, not on supporting their access to the labour market, which has discriminatory implications.

The second section has considered the area of social service provision. Social services have been described in terms of meeting the needs of dependent individuals such as children, the elderly and disabled people and their families to assist their social functioning. However, the idea of need as the determining force in the provision of services has been challenged and the second section of this chapter identifies many other factors, which impact on the provision of social services for women, ethnic minorities and disabled people. Despite the fact that women predominate as the users of social services, their needs are not being appropriately met. The development and emphasis on community care has disproportionately and detrimentally affected women. Their caring role has been taken for granted and the service provision offered to women carers has been insensitive to their needs. Although women also predominate as service providers in this area, they are to be found concentrated in lower level jobs with least decision-making power. We see both the horizontal segregation of women into different jobs than men and their scarcity in management positions. Therefore, women have less influence on the way services are provided.

Despite evidence of their need, there has been shown to be a low take-up of social service provision by ethnic minority communities generally. Explanations for this phenomenon have concentrated either on their lack of knowledge and information about the services on offer or misplaced assumptions about the culture of ethnic minority communities. This has led to the inadequate investigation of the appropriateness of service provision. Although anti-racism has been established in the professional training of social workers, it has not been translated into practice. So what we see is the lack of an overall strategy on the part of social services and, instead, a pattern that is variable and uneven within and between different local authorities. This means that community care services have been inappropriate for the needs of the ethnic minority community and there has remained a gap between official claims for service provision and actual practice.

Despite the move through different identified phases in the provision of social services to disabled people, they have continued to be criticized. Community care is a crucial area of policy, which has been questioned from the position of disabled people and their carers. The main problem for disabled people is that, despite the stated aim of reducing professional dominance, this has not happened in any meaningful way. In fact, it is argued, professionals have consolidated their control. Fundamentally, the definition of disability from either an individualistic or social perspective is viewed as important for social work practice. It has been argued that adequate and effective policies for disabled people could only be built on the basis of a model that recognized that disability was a social phenomenon and, because this has not happened, social work with disabled people is founded on too narrow a base.

CHAPTER 7

Social policy areas: health services and housing

This chapter follows on from Chapters 5 and 6 by examining the final two key social policy areas identified by Hallett (1996): health services and housing. As in the previous chapters these policy areas will be investigated by gender, 'race' and disability.

Health services

Gender

As Foster (1996) pointed out: 'Health care is predominantly a woman's world' (p. 101). However, this statement needs to be qualified by adding that this is only true at a simple numerical level. Women form the largest group of consumers and providers of health care in Britain. This can be seen across many areas. Women have been shown to have used the GP service, occupied hospital beds, been admitted to psychiatric units and consumed more drugs and medicines than men (Kane, 1991). They also comprise nearly 80 per cent of the labour force of the NHS and provide most of the unpaid health care within the family and community. However, health care is not a 'woman's world' in terms of the control of health services or the provision of adequate or appropriate health care for women.

Although women are such a large majority in the NHS labour force, they are mainly in the lower levels of the hierarchy: nurses, cleaners, caterers, home helps and carers. The general underrepresentation of women at senior levels was highlighted by Goss and Brown (1991), whose study detailed the small proportion of women at senior levels in clinical professions, in senior administrative and clinical grades, and at all levels of management. Women only occupied 15 per cent of all consultant posts, 3 per cent of surgical consultant posts and 18 per cent of all general managers' posts. The various barriers to women's progression were identified as including: lack of flexible working arrangements, undervaluation of part-time work and the widespread use of patronage and 'head-hunting' for senior posts, which favoured male employees. Harding (1989) argued it was predominantly sex discrimination that excluded women from supervisory and management positions in the NHS, rather than any lack of skills or qualification. This discrimination maintained an ideal of a male career structure where full-time working was valued above part-time. Maddock and Parkin (1994) argued that NHS hospitals were still dominated by a male medical tradition which did not welcome or even accept women doctors as equal colleagues. They identified a 'discouragement culture', which discriminated against both women and ethnic minorities, resisted change and maintained inflexible working arrangements, which made it difficult for women to combine a career and a family, and thus worked to protect men's careers. Even where there were women doctors (most of whom are White), they were employed in the lower status and prestige areas of medicine such as geriatrics (Allen, 1988). Also, Hayden (1991) found that women still felt discriminated against when applying for posts outside of hospitals in general practice, which was often considered to be a softer career option.

An Equal Opportunities Commission (EOC, 1991) survey of all regional and district health authorities in England and Wales and health boards in Scotland found that 'equal opportunities' management practices were not being effectively implemented in the NHS. Parkin and Maddock (1995) argued that the commercial climate in the NHS 'is a breeding ground for smart macho managers' who were 'driven by extreme competitivity' (p. 76) and expected all staff to conform to working extremely long hours as they did themselves, thus excluding or at least discouraging women.

Nursing has always been seen as women's work. However, even in this area women took longer to gain promotion than the few men working within this area. Davies and Rosser (1986) found a disproportionate number of men in manager grades. While men took on average 8.4 years to progress from their initial qualification to a nursing officer grade, women with the same qualifications took more than twice as long, on average 17.9 years. Despite the majority position of women in the NHS, Davies and Rosser (1986) identified its climate as 'hostile to women'. While men were confident of putting themselves forward for promotion and sometimes 'informally encouraged to do so', managers viewed women's family responsibilities as a problem for their promotion.

Ethnic minority women tend to be employed in certain sectors of the NHS. In Doyal *et al.*'s study (1981), they found 81 per cent of qualified nursing staff, 78 per cent of ancillary workers (half of whom were women), 84 per cent of domestic and catering workers (among whom 78 per cent and 55 per cent respectively were women) were from overseas. This demonstrated that in the past, ethnic minority immigration provided a cheap source of labour for the NHS. Where ethnic minority women were employed as nurses, this was usually as lower status State Enrolled Nurses (SEN) and nursing auxiliaries rather than as State Registered Nurses (SRN) (CRE, 1995c). A study by the King's Fund Equal Opportunities Task Force (1990) showed that racial inequality was widespread and deep-rooted in nursing. It confirmed that ethnic minority nurses were concentrated in enrolled nurse grades and also on night shifts without equal access to training and career development opportunities. Ethnic minority nurses and, in fact, ethnic minority doctors who were predominantly male were also disproportionately represented in the lower status and more unpopular areas of medicine, such as geriatrics and mental health (Radical Statistics Health Group, 1987).

Since 1983, government policy on compulsory competitive tendering has disproportionately affected the areas where ethnic minority women work, often being the first areas to be contracted out, such as catering, cleaning, laundry and hospital ancillary work. Although these areas have always been low paid, compulsory competitive tendering has led to intensified exploitation through longer hours, lower wages, less bargaining power and fewer people employed even where contracts have been won by 'in-house bidders': that is, their previous public service employers (Milne, 1989).

The health service could be criticized for having done little to acknowledge and meet health needs as expressed by women themselves, including the different requirements of ethnic minority and disabled women. One of the reasons for this was that the low pay and the low status of women's work in the service was matched by few women at decision-making levels in the service. Some of the few sensitive and special services for women have been threatened, undermined or lost in recent years, such as the South London Hospital for Women, which was closed in 1984. This hospital was the last in the country to guarantee that patients would be treated and nursed by women and was the only one that enabled doctors to train as consultants and surgeons exclusively with other women.

Male doctors have been criticized for being patronizing and holding stereotypical views of women. Ussher (1989) highlighted the long and continuing tradition of the medical profession's view of women as genetically mentally unstable. In the nineteenth century, women were considered to be governed by their wombs which caused unique women's conditions, such as hysteria. Ussher (1989) argued that the modern versions of this were premenstrual syndrome and post-natal depression. As Miles (1988) showed, women consulting their GPs about problems of depression or anxiety were often told it was caused by hormonal imbalance or, in other words, 'It's just your age' (p. 120). In her study of women's experiences of ante-natal care and childbirth, Oakley (1980) showed that doctors frequently ignored and dismissed women's knowledge about their own bodies, their lives and their health-care needs. Pollock (1984) found that doctors often ignored women's reporting of side-effects from taking the contraceptive pill.

Women experience a lifetime of interventionist medicine often revolving around their fertility. This was described by Foster (1996) as 'the increasing medicalisation of women's lives' (p. 104), which failed to address the underlying social and economic factors in women's health problems (Burns and Phillipson, 1986; Ussher, 1989). Young women were given the contraceptive pill; during pregnancy there was close medical control; and middle-aged and older women were given drugs for depression and anxiety and Hormone Replacement Therapy (HRT) during the menopause. As an example, Foster (1996) offered the argument that the promotion of HRT 'encourages older women to seek a medical elixir of youth rather than to challenge the sexist and ageist attitudes which lead our society to devalue and discount middle-aged women whilst admiring more powerful middle-aged men' (p. 106).

Another new area of treatment for women which Foster (1996) saw as a dramatic example of the 'medicalisation of women's lives', which had received much attention, was high technology infertility treatment, such as *in vitro* fertilization (IVF). Foster argued that this had been at the expense of the under-researching of the primary causes of infertility, despite the treatment remaining relatively unsuccessful and expensive. It had also been shown that doctors were highly selective about the type of woman they treated and made decisions based on social and economic factors over and above clinical factors. Douglas *et al.* (1992) showed that to get on the NHS waiting list for fertility treatment, women in Manchester had to have lived with a male partner for at least three years and the couple had to fulfil the criteria laid down for adoptive parents.

In the areas of fertility and contraception, ethnic minority women also experienced health care in a qualitatively different way to White women because of stereotypical views and prejudices. They were more likely to be given long-term contraception with increased risk to their health, abortions and sterilizations (Bryan *et al.*, 1985; Williams, 1989). Asian women had campaigned to place the issue of women's differential reproductive rights on the agenda. They had exposed the use of the contraceptive drug Depo-Provera on ethnic minority and working-class women, and thereby challenged the primacy of the feminist abortion rights issue with some reported cases of the involuntary sterilization of some women because of the stereotyped assumption about the reproductive capacities of Asian women (Brah, 1992a). There was evidence to show that ethnic minority women had to face services that were inappropriate to their particular need, for example, communication in an appropriate language, and examples of overt racism, such as being told that they should not have any more children (Larbie, 1985; Randhawa, 1986; Hennings, 1993).

Despite these examples of the 'medicalization of women's lives' the health services have not met the requirements of women in many ways. Two examples of specific programmes for women – cervical and breast-cancer screening – demonstrate this. First, screening for cervical cancer grew and developed in an unplanned way. Despite GPs actively encouraging women patients to receive regular smear tests (Ross, 1989), it had disappointing results (McPherson and Savage, 1987). One reason was that younger middle-class women were more likely to have regular smear tests than more vulnerable older working-class women (Townsend and Davidson, 1992). The possible underlying causes of cervical cancer were also under-researched, despite evidence of the strong possibility of its link with industrial pollutants (Robinson, 1981).

The second example showed that, despite an efficiently planned and administered national breast-cancer screening programme, Britain had the highest mortality rate in the world: 52 deaths per 100 000 women (Faulder, 1993). The government's White Paper *The Health of the Nation* (Secretary of State for Health, 1991) detailed the aim 'to reduce breast cancer in the population invited for screening by 25 per cent by 2000 compared to 1990'. However, for several reasons, scepticism existed about the effectiveness of this screening programme and its ability to achieve this aim. Some medical experts had taken to condemning women for putting the whole programme at risk by failing to attend for screening in sufficient numbers (Roberts *et al.*, 1990). However, breast screening by mammography had inherent weaknesses. It produced a relatively high level of false positive test results creating a great deal of stress for women who were called back for unnecessary further tests (Skrabanek, 1988). Also, some of the tumours found by mammography were latent or so slow growing as to pose no threat (Klemi *et al.*, 1992).

Until recently the standard treatment for breast cancer was the removal of the breast, which was both disabling and disfiguring. Despite proof that mastectomy was no more effective in prolonging women's lives than lumpectomy, which conserved the breast, it was still offered as the safest form of treatment by some surgeons. A disturbing development in this area was a very controversial and radical new form of medical intervention emerging for healthy women. In the USA, women who came from families with a high incidence of breast cancer were being offered preventative 'prophylactic surgery': the removal of both breasts (Brown, 1992). Also, in Britain, Evans *et al.* (1994) stated in euphemistic terms that: 'An energetic attempt to reduce the risk of breast cancer would include the option of prophylactic bilateral mastectomy' (p. 186).

'Race'

There is a growing body of evidence that ethnic minorities receive a qualitatively and quantitatively worse service from the NHS. So far, health services have failed to address satisfactorily the concerns of ethnic minority health workers and consumers. There was a pattern of lack of knowledge and treatment in the NHS of conditions more commonly suffered by ethnic minority people (Torkington, 1991). For example, work on sickle-cell anaemia in those of African descent had concentrated on family planning rather than prevention and treatment (Grimsley and Bhat, 1988). There was a need for the screening of all babies at risk, planned, organized and coordinated treatment of known cases, counselling services and specialist clinics. Smaje (1995a) estimated that there would be 6000 cases of sickle-cell anaemia per year by the year 2000. However, there was some room for optimism with evidence of positive developments and good practice in some local health-care developments based on community-based groups. One example was Liverpool's developments which included a 'race' and health patient's charter, and specialist posts including link workers (Share, 1994).

Despite an increase in research, this has had minimal benefits in improving health care for ethnic minority communities (King's Fund,

1991; Bhopal and White, 1993; Sheldon and Parker, 1993; Stubbs, 1993). 'Race' and health was discussed at length in the Chief Medical Officer's Report *On the State of the Public Health*, which pointed out that 'the NHS must address the particular needs of the black and ethnic minorities living in this country and take positive steps to eliminate discrimination' (Calman, 1992). Balarajan and Raleigh (1993) analysed this White Paper in terms of 'race'. The paper identified five key areas in which substantial improvements in health could be achieved: coronary heart disease and stroke, cancers, mental illness, AIDS and sexual health, and accidents. The epidemiological evidence to date suggested that for most of the key areas ethnic minority communities were at greater risk. There was a much greater risk of coronary heart disease among Asians in England and Wales compared with the national average. Mortality from this cause in 1979–83 was 36 per cent higher in Asian men and 46 per cent higher in Asian women with a rising trend. Black Caribbeans were at much greater risk of stroke than the population nationally. Mortality from this cause during 1979–83 was 76 per cent higher in Black Caribbean men and 110 per cent higher in Black Caribbean women. Although Asians and Black Caribbeans had lower mortality rates for cancers overall, they had higher rates for some. The rate of diagnosis of schizophrenia was reported to be several times higher in Black Caribbeans, and young Asian women had suicide rates well in excess of the national average. There was a low take-up of family-planning clinics, especially among Asian women. Accidents were linked to social and economic disadvantage and therefore predominant among ethnic minority communities.

Law (1996) argued that for the NHS 'challenging racism and racial inequality have yet to arrive on the national policy agenda' (p. 150). Research in the area of 'race' and health has been criticized on several counts. First, an over-emphasis on a cultural approach had resulted in a failure to examine structures both outside and inside the NHS, which determined the health of ethnic minority communities. The outcomes of this type of approach were the call for cultural awareness training, and the location of the problem of 'race' and health back in the ethnic minority communities and their supposedly deviant or deficient cultural practices and inadequate language abilities. An example of this was the assumed causes for particularly high infant mortality, which was found among Pakistani-born mothers, attributed to the cultural practice of marriage between relatives, which led to a higher prevalence of genetic abnormalities. Ahmad (1994) criticized this explanation and categorized it as an example of the 'demonology' of ethnic minority cultures. He showed that there was evidence of high levels of genetic abnormalities among communities with a low incidence of relatives marrying. There has also been a failure to seek other causal effects, such as the poorer quality antenatal care for ethnic minority mothers which had been identified (Bowler, 1993).

Second, research was seen as lacking clarity over basic essential concepts such as the classification of different ethnic groups and over-emphasizing their homogeneity with little attention to the differentiation within and between them producing a 'naïve empiricism and cultural reductionism' (Ahmad, 1993). Law (1996) demonstrated the dangers of accepting data on 'race' and health without careful analysis. He looked at the 1991 Census data on ethnic origin of those reporting a long-term illness and found many problems with their interpretation. There was a problem with the too high aggregation of the classification of ethnic groups, for example: Indian Sikhs, Muslims and Hindus were undifferentiated even though different practices among these groups may play a significant part. There was no accounting for the effects of age, gender or socioeconomic conditions of the different groups, and there was evidence of the under-reporting of chronic illness among ethnic minority communities. Therefore, he argued that although 'the gradual introduction of ethnicity into health information systems throughout the 1990s will lead to increased opportunities for improvements in health planning . . . this will crucially depend on the quality of the data analysis' (p. 161). The over-reliance on mortality rates in much of the research was also seen as inappropriate given the younger age profile of ethnic minority communities; and gender differences and the incidence of disability had been largely ignored (Smaje, 1995a). Finally, and most importantly, Ahmad (1993) pointed out that very few benefits in terms of the improved health of ethnic minority communities had resulted from the research undertaken.

An example of this has been the research undertaken over the last three decades around the very high levels of diagnosis of schizophrenia and the over-representation of Black Caribbeans among those compulsorily detained in psychiatric hospitals and units (Dunn and Fahy, 1990; Sashidaran, 1994). Studies had shown anything between a three to six times higher chance of such a diagnosis than in the White population (Balarajan and Raleigh, 1993). However, two different and opposing explanations and concomitant policy proposals have been mooted. Law (1996) labelled these as the 'anti-racist perspective' and 'ethnic vulnerability perspective'. The first perspective criticized the role of racism, both within the mental health-care service leading to stereotypical misdiagnosis, and in the wider community, leading to low material conditions, such as high unemployment, poor housing and racial harassment. The second perspective assumed that the high incidence of diagnosis and the admission to hospital of Black Caribbeans for schizophrenia and their compulsory detention was proof of a higher prevalence of the disorder among that community, indicating an ethnic or genetic propensity to mental ill health, violence and dangerous behaviour.

The first perspective based on racism has been questioned. Smaje (1995a) pointed out that if racism in the mental health-care service was the primary cause of the over-diagnosis of Black Caribbeans as schizophrenic, then it would have had to be on a massive scale, which was highly unlikely. However, Smaje (1995a) did not want to deny the existence of racism altogether. He suggested that various factors came into play to explain the over-diagnosis, including differential levels of racial discrimination between different hospitals and consultants, and higher levels of racial discrimination against 'non-compliant' Black Caribbean men. In terms of the second perspective, higher ethnic or genetic vulnerability to mental ill health, Balarajan and Raleigh (1993) had shown this was difficult to argue with lower suicide and attempted suicide rates among Black Caribbean communities generally, although Raleigh (1996) identified a more recent raised suicide rate among young Black Caribbeans. The rates of admissions to hospital for schizophrenia were higher among Black Caribbeans in Britain than that reported in Jamaica (Hickling, 1991), and higher among second-generation British-born Black Caribbeans than first generation Black Caribbeans (McGovern and Cope, 1987) making the link between genetics very unlikely. Also, Law (1996) showed that the gender differences between admission rates for schizophrenia were very significant. Women's rates of admission were lower than men's and, although rates for Black Caribbean women were generally higher than for other women (181 per 100 000), they were substantially lower than Black Caribbean men's (272 per 100 000) and Irish men's (191 per 100 000). Law argued that this gender difference was likely to indicate an explanation based in the different patterns of interaction between the health service by men and women.

The NHS underwent major reforms in terms of the removal of the influence and power of district health authorities who in the past held the responsibility for 'equal opportunities' policies and their implementation within the NHS. Many individual units gained independent trust status and there was the change to the all-pervading ethos of contracting as suppliers and receivers of services. Ahmad (1993) argued that any advantage of the introduction of market forces to patient care depended to a large extent on the idea of an 'active well-informed consumer' able to make rational choices, but this was unlikely to be the case for disadvantaged and discriminated against groups, such as women, ethnic minorities and disabled people. While these reforms in the control of the NHS presented the opportunity for greater flexibility in addressing equal opportunity issues by individual trusts, they also carried the risk that the pressures from other issues at the local level, such as balancing budgets, business planning and contracting, might push 'equal opportunities' into the background. The devolution of decision making to managers meant that implementation was likely to be fragmentary and piecemeal, and depended heavily upon the particular managerial culture prevailing within individual trusts (Bagilhole and Stephens, 1997b). The issue of who was in control was also important. The continued lack of representation of ethnic minority communities in nonexecutive positions in the NHS caused concern. The King's Fund (1989) demonstrated the underrepresentation of ethnic minority communities among the membership of the old health authorities. A study by Jewson *et al.* (1993) showed that after the NHS reforms, the representation of ethnic minority communities and women fell even further.

A survey carried out by the Equal Opportunities Review (EOR, 1994d) of individual trusts' main 'equal opportunities' policies and initiatives undertaken or planned achieved only a 32 per cent response rate, perhaps suggesting the low level of importance attached to this area. Although all but one of the respondents had a written 'equal opportunities' policy, despite the EOC (1991) recommendation that trusts should appoint an 'equal opportunities' officer, few have done so, and only two-thirds had drawn up wider 'equal opportunities' action plans, which varied in scope and detail. The picture that emerged was one of wide variation in action being undertaken by individual trusts. Some negotiated a wide range of 'equal opportunities' agreements, while others achieved relatively little. As the King's Fund Final Report (1990) said, 'real and consistent progress throughout the service will only be achieved when action to ensure "equal opportunities" becomes a formal and routine part of the duties and responsibilities of all health service managers'. Even though the CRE (1992) launched their code of practice in primary health care to encourage sensitivity to the needs of ethnic minority communities and equality in access and provision, it only made recommendations and was not enforced by law. Ward (1993) criticized this approach which consisted of organizational and staff development, and ethnic monitoring as inadequate.

Despite being the largest employer of ethnic minorities, the NHS had been exposed as promulgating discrimination and unequal opportunities in the area of 'race' across the many and varied types of jobs within it. Studies carried out between 1986 and 1990 by the King's Fund Equal Opportunities Task Force (1990) revealed a number of barriers that ethnic minority workers faced in the NHS. The Final Report by the Task Force found that health authorities had made only limited progress in tackling racial inequalities. Most authorities had adopted an 'equal opportunities' policy, but few had translated that policy into a timetabled programme of action, and most had failed to produce data on the ethnic composition of their workforce, or to monitor recruitment. The Report also highlighted the lack of promotion prospects for ethnic minority staff and their underrepresentation in management.

In response to this state of affairs, a working group, chaired by Virginia Bottomley, the then Secretary of State for Health, was set up in September 1992, to advise on ways of promoting 'equal opportunities' for ethnic minority employees (EOR, 1994d). A programme of action to address the barriers facing ethnic minority staff was launched in December 1993. Its overall aim was to achieve 'the equitable representation of minority ethnic groups at all levels in the NHS (including professional staff groups), reflecting the ethnic composition of the local population'. The programme recommended that all NHS employers took the following first steps: adopt a written 'equal opportunities' policy and action plan; collect and analyse ethnic-monitoring data and use the information to draw up plans for remedial action; carry out a detailed monitoring of personnel procedures; and provide training in selection procedures for staff.

Although there was also a concern with 'equal opportunities' employment issues for women within the health service, much of it failed to address the issues of ethnic minority women. This was because it focused on the need to allow more women to enter into the higher levels of management and clinical practice, which were mostly beyond the immediate horizons of many ethnic minority women. According to EOC research (Bhavani, 1994; Owen, 1994) they were more likely to work longer hours, to be lower paid, to enjoy lower occupational status, and to be employed predominantly in manual and ancillary jobs, despite being as well qualified as White women. The King's Fund (1991) argued that the service of ethnic minority nurses in the NHS had been undervalued and talent had been squandered. This had been reflected in the quality of care, which ethnic minority citizens received through less accessible services. Ward (1993) pointed out the process of channelling ethnic minority nurses into low-status sectors such as geriatrics, psychiatry and services for people with learning difficulties, and away from further training. Bhavani's (1994) review of existing research confirmed that ethnic minority women were much more likely than their White counterparts to be employed within the NHS as ancillaries, and as nurses were more likely to be found in low-status specialisms, such as community and mental-health nursing. Bagilhole and Stephens (1997a) highlighted the relatively high levels of racial and sexual discrimination and harassment experienced by ethnic minority women health workers at all levels in the NHS.

The lack of ethnic minority staff in decision making and powerful positions in the NHS has important consequences for the type of service provided. There was evidence of the persistence of stereotyping and negative attitudes towards ethnic minority patients by White staff among GPs (Ahmad *et al.*, 1989) and midwives (Bowler, 1993). Bhopal and White (1993) also demonstrated a problem of poor knowledge and misrecognition of priorities in health care for Asian communities by health professionals. They identified communication and language problems as priorities, as opposed to the high incidence of certain diseases such as coronary heart disease. Smaje (1995b) argued that a more sophisticated approach to identifying the health needs of ethnic minority populations must be impressed on senior managers. Confusion existed, with little information available on the efficacy of policy interventions in this area. The King's Fund's recent report (Smaje, 1995a) showed that ethnic minorities generally had poorer quality contact with health services, widely interpreted as evidence of racism in service provision, often of an indirect nature and based on stereotypes of particular ethnic cultures. Despite an increasing awareness of ethnic minority health issues among managers, it remained fragmentary. 'Few would deny the need to enhance communication between ethnic minority patients and health professionals' (p. 28).

A Health Education Authority (1994) survey demonstrated the need for health services supported by trained interpreters and translators. While the majority of young people preferred advice in English, middle-aged and older sections of the ethnic minority population generally preferred mother-tongue materials. Interpreting needs increased across age bands and were significantly higher among women. Bagilhole and Stephens (1997a) showed a high reporting from the ethnic minority women health workers, at all levels, in their study, of the informal and unrewarded use of their translation and interpretation skills, approachability, and their knowledge of cultural and religious requirements. They argued that it was important that greater imaginative use of ethnic minority language ability was made as one of the criteria in the selection process. It was essential to recognize and reward the variety of languages spoken by staff and their knowledge of their communities as valuable assets.

Finally, there was evidence of racial discrimination in access to medical training (CRE, 1988; McManus *et al.*, 1995). The CRE's (1996) formal investigation on the appointments of consultants and senior registrars in the NHS showed that ethnic minority doctors, even if they did manage to receive training, were less likely to be given senior positions than Whites. The report stated that there was 'great cause for concern' in the way appointments were made. 'The disparities in success rates for different ethnic groups were so marked and consistent and the omission of procedural safeguards so routine, that the possibility of discrimination cannot be ignored'. A wide gap was identified between 'equal opportunities' policy and practice that 'can only be attributed to lack of will, because there is no shortage of detailed guidance on the subject'. The CRE (1996) argued that it was possible that NHS changes have exacerbated the problems as independent trusts made their own appointments and 'equal opportunities' programmes were likely to be less developed than when consultants were appointed by regional health authorities. The report included the recommendations of training selectors and the ethnic monitoring of applicants and appointees.

Disability

Rather than being criticized for the underdevelopment and lack of services, as in the area of 'race', the health service has been accused of over-intervention in the area of disability, and taking over the control of decisions from disabled people by dictating the form of intervention in purely medical terms, which are allowed to define disabled people's needs. Medical practitioners were seen to be the controllers and gatekeepers for disabled people's access not only to health services but also to other services and benefits by the over-concentration on medical interpretations of eligibility. The medical model of disability still dominated legislation and provided the categories for access to services and benefits, despite being heavily criticized (Oliver, 1981). Manning and Oliver (1985) preferred to use the term 'the medicalisation of disability' to show recognition of its all-encompassing influence in all areas of welfare. What the health service did not seem to provide was an equal and accessible service for disabled people but, instead, one that was still heavily skewed towards the desire to cure and normalize their behaviour and appearance.

Finkelstein (1993a) argued that the dominant role given to medical practitioners as gatekeepers to disabled people's access to all welfare services, not just medical, had led to their image of dependency and the view that disability was a medical problem only. 'The concept of the disabling society is not one which is seriously considered when delivering health services to disabled people' (Silburn, 1993, p. 224). Baird (1992b) argued that: 'Doctors and paramedics colonised disability, and turned disabled people into material for research and experimentation' (p. 5). This medical and therapeutic intervention in disabled people's lives began even before birth. Oliver (1996) described this intervention as 'genetic engineering' with screening for certain disabilities putting pressure on some couples not to reproduce and providing criteria for abortions. Morris (1992b) identified the problem as the fact that disabled people were excluded from the analysis of what makes a healthy society.

Oliver (1996) saw it as a stark choice between 'one which seeks to eradicate disease, illness and pathology or one which seeks to welcome and celebrate difference' (p. 121). Medical intervention and dominance in disability issues took the form of striving for 'normality' in behaviour and appearance, to cure and rehabilitate. This meant the medical interpretation of disabled people's needs, such as the promotion of painful and sometimes unsuccessful surgery to enable people to walk as opposed to recognizing the validity of using wheelchairs and providing an accessible environment. Silburn (1993) argued that the medical model 'is the rehabilitation service, which still dominates the health service's view of what disabled people need from it. It still strives to produce normally functioning individuals, with the definition of "normal" being "as they were before they were disabled"' (p. 224). 'Yet it is questionable to what extent disabled people would want to be rehabilitated if they lived in a world where the struggle to learn to walk a few yards on crutches was made pointless by decent wheelchairs and a barrier-free environment' (Silburn, 1993, p. 224).

Finkelstein (1993a) demonstrated that the beginnings of classifying and interpreting disability in medical terms came about originally because there was a desire to divide the poor into deserving and undeserving: that is, those who could not support themselves because of infirmity from those who were non-disabled but lazy and indolent. The former, identified and classified by doctors, were to be given food and shelter, but also importantly from this perspective, to be made as 'normal' as possible through rehabilitation and special aids to make them employable. This dominance of the medical profession has meant that disabled people did not play a part or have a say in their own classification. 'By the middle of the twentieth century all disabled people were being routinely classified and registered by many different agencies according to medically defined categories' (p. 13). These professional medical classifications increased in sophistication and complexity in the 1970s and 1980s to accommodate the need to qualify for different health treatments, aids, welfare services and special social security benefits. This role of 'gatekeeper' and controller of access to resources for doctors was becoming more controversial and being challenged. However:

Hospital doctors . . . are still expected to have the last word about their patient's discharge dates, or about their transfer to other institutions, or to decide whether they should be offered facilities such as regular readmission to relieve carers. These are not necessarily medical decisions, but the constant demands of the hospital service require someone to take responsibility . . . The real problems are the need for assessment at all, and that doctors who undertake the responsibility may not be adequately trained (or experienced) for the task (Harrison, 1993, p. 213).

Harrison (1993), a medical practitioner, argued that disability and medicine were 'inextricably linked' because 'anyone with an illness or injury of any severity is disabled for as long as the condition lasts' (p. 211). However, he recognized that medical training and practice was also intrinsically inadequate as a service for disabled people because it differentiated and favoured 'acute' conditions (something of recent onset and short duration) over 'chronic' conditions (that which had lasted and would last for a long time). As he argued: 'Doctors are essentially interventionists, trained to diagnose, treat and either cure or admit defeat. This ethos fitted the "acute" model far better than the "chronic" one' (p. 211). Medical education was rooted in the natural sciences, largely ignoring social science, and students 'rarely see patients outside hospital buildings'. Doctors were trained to take responsibility and expected control of decisions unchallenged by patients, 'a poor environment for learning correct approaches to disability' (p. 212). There were some signs of optimism that criticism of the medical model meant that professionals were beginning to move away from medical control by the health service to social and welfare interventions in the community. Harrison (1993) argued that some areas of medicine were better than others, such as outpatient clinics and general practice, where there was inevitable involvement with patients and their families over longer periods, although he acknowledged that, even in these areas, specific education about disability remained uncommon.

Oliver (1993) offered an example of what he described as the 'medical hegemony' in special education: 'medical need still predominates over educational need' (p. 55). Children were withdrawn from classes for physiotherapy. He argued that: 'If children are brought up to believe, through experiencing a range of medical and paramedical interventions, that they are ill, we cannot be surprised if they passively accept the sick role' (p. 55). Silburn (1993) gave an indication of the changes that professional workers needed to make to enable disabled people to not only take part in, but to control decisions made about themselves. She described the process whereby health professionals' decision that money should be used to build a young disabled unit in a local authority was overturned by a survey, which found disabled people's own priorities to be community services (Silburn, 1988). These services have been founded within the 'philosophy and practices . . . firmly rooted in the social model of disability' (Silburn, 1993, p. 220), 'empowering, offering choices and focusing on society as the problem, rather than the individual' (pp. 224–5). An example of the success of this team was their work with disabled people who had been inappropriately admitted to hospital when their real needs had proved to be 'a lack of accessible housing, poor technical aids and not enough support for either the disabled person or the family carer in the form of practical help or emotional/social release' (p. 222).

However, the need to acknowledge and take account of the views of disabled people seemed to be very slow in materializing and there was a danger that control would pass from one set of professionals to another. Finkelstein (1993a) called this the 'administrative model of service intervention' with a different set of 'experts' still seeing 'the lives of disabled people as in terms of problems to be solved and their role as providing solutions' (p. 15). Finkelstein argued (1993b) that the medical model and the rehabilitation service needed to be remoulded into the social model of disability (see discussion of this model in Chapter 2 of this book) and services for disabled people should be located in the Department of Environment rather than Departments of Health and Social Security to allow the expertise of engineers and architects to be enhanced in the provision of services to disabled people. 'In effect this means that the goals, extent, duration and nature of medical interventions should be guided by an analysis of the social and personal barriers to be overcome rather than by any functional limitations of the individual' (p. 41).

When seeking health and medical care, disabled people should be able to use the same general services as the non-disabled and have specialist services provided for their particular needs. This principle of integrated accessible services applied equally to disabled people in the community and those coming out of long-stay hospitals. This policy required coordinated planning and service provision at every level of the NHS and with other statutory services and user representatives with direct experience of disability. Interdisciplinary teamwork was advocated 'so that the medical approach to disability becomes just one part of a response involving a whole range of agencies, professions and interests. And the team must always include the disabled person in question, besides key members of the family and friends' (Harrison, 1993, p. 215).

Many changes were needed to ensure an equal service to disabled people. Some examples included the development of regional strategies to ensure that all services were fully accessible and included plans for specific provision for the differing needs of groups of disabled people, in particular for the growing number of elderly disabled people, ethnic minority disabled people, people coming out of long-stay hospitals and those at risk of coming into institutional care, including young physically disabled people leaving special schools. Programmes of staff training also needed to be introduced in various areas, for example, in making information accessible to people with sensory disabilities or learning difficulties; obligatory basic and in-service training for doctors and other health professionals in the management of disability, including the effects of physical and social access barriers and non-medical factors; and training of family-planning advisers and all staff in maternity services to ensure the non-discriminatory treatment of disabled people and provision of specialist counselling, treatment and support if required.

Disabled people are under-represented as workers in the health service. Chinnery (1991) showed that the caring professions in general have never come near meeting the 3 per cent quota established by the Disabled Persons Employment Act. French's (1986) study showed that despite positions in the NHS that required empathy and the understanding of disability, disabled people were never specifically invited to apply in the advertisements. Most arguments put forward against appointing disabled people in the health service hinged on their assumed inability to cope and the likelihood of having accidents (Chikadonz, 1983; French, 1986). This was the case even though it was acknowledged that disabled people could provide a better service by having a unique asset and greater rapport with similarly impaired people than non-disabled professionals (Shearer, 1981; O'Hare and Thomson, 1991). French (1986) found that all the disabled professionals she interviewed could see major advantages to patient service in their being disabled, having carefully chosen their specialisms and places of work, including greater empathy, patience, understanding, instilling confidence, communication, breaking down professional barriers, acting as role models and changing the attitudes and understanding of professional colleagues. This suggested that 'disabled professionals are no less capable than their able-bodied colleagues and may have unique assets to bring to these professions' (French, 1993, p. 209). Despite this, they experienced a need to work harder and be more determined to prove themselves.

Housing

Gender

When looking at the issues of women and housing, Dutta and Taylor (1989) argued that: 'Sexism affects all women in all aspects of their lives because it prescribes the roles and behaviour that are deemed to be acceptable'. In other words, for access to good-quality affordable housing, women needed to have a male partner (Morris and Winn, 1990). As Gilroy (1994) somewhat cynically expressed this, 'The woman has to find her prince before she gets her palace' (p. 54). Apart from this, there were only three other 'socially acceptable models for home ownership by women: separated and divorced women usually retain the family home and stay there to raise the children; widows live their lives out in their married locations; and single "spinsters" might inherit a home from their parents' (Card, 1980, p. 216).

Woods (1996) pointed out that the 'direction of national housing policy since 1980 has created difficulties for female-headed households with regard to accessing good-quality affordable housing' (p. 65). 'Women find it much harder to gain access to housing which is allocated by ability to pay rather than by housing need' (Muir and Ross, 1993, p. 1). Therefore, the continuous trend in government policy to increase home ownership to the detriment of provision of public sector housing 'produces increasing disadvantage for women' (Muir and Ross, 1993, p. 1). Women were less likely to be owner-occupiers because of low earnings and their greater reliance on means-tested benefits, and were therefore more dependent on the rented sector which did not fulfil their needs (Watson, 1986; Brion, 1987; Munroe and Smith, 1989; Morris and Winn, 1990; Sexty, 1990; Muir and Ross, 1993).

This phenomenon was starkly shown when looking at men and women without a partner. In 1991, 39 per cent of single men and 44 per cent of divorced and separated men were buying a property with a mortgage, compared with only 25 per cent of single women and 33 per cent of divorced and separated women (Department of Environment, 1993). Also, even where women did get into owner occupation, it was often at the poorer end with a lower standard of amenities. Women mostly could not afford to take on a mortgage and those who did so had to commit more of their earnings than men (Nationwide Anglia Building Society, 1989). Both direct and indirect discrimination by building societies in providing mortgages to women was identified (Glithero, 1986; Watson, 1988). Muir and Ross (1993) calculated that, using women's average earnings and looking only at the lowest tenth of flat prices in London, only 15 per cent of women could afford to buy a flat and only 19 per cent a bedsit. These issues provoked a debate as to whether, in the interests of women, owner occupation should be made easier or if rented accommodation should be invested in and raised from its second-rate position.

The consideration of women's housing needs was becoming increasingly more important. First, women were outliving men into old age. Woods (1996), using the General Household Survey, calculated that 62 per cent of the population aged over 75 were women, and 59 per cent of these were living alone compared with 30 per cent of men in this age group. Despite 46 per cent of women aged over 65 owning their own home outright, Sykes (1994) showed that they were in a vulnerable position, often with low incomes perpetuated from their earlier labour market position, and being concentrated in the older, less well-repaired housing. Brotchie and Hills (1991) showed that it was difficult for them to get aids and adaptations to cope with their growing disabilities. Under these circumstances, older women in both the rented sector and private owners had a limited choice of suitable housing (Sykes, 1994). From the rented sector, they might be able to move to sheltered housing, if there was an adequate supply in their area. For owner–occupiers their option of 'trading down' into cheaper property depended on the value of their home and had been made less viable with the housing slump. Sheltered housing was also becoming less affordable with the rising costs of service charges.

Second, there was a higher incidence in the breakdown of relationships. This was one of the main reasons women gave for applying as homeless to local authorities (Woods, 1996). There were also many female lone parents without a permanent home who stayed with family and friends (Bull, 1993). In the owner–occupier sector, McCarthy and Simpson (1991) showed lone fathers were more likely to remain in their home than lone mothers. Women, on the other hand, were in a particularly difficult position if their relationship had broken down within ten years. They were likely to have young children, be unwaged, and live in cheaper property. Gilroy (1994) highlighted the fact that the Child Support Act presented a new problem for divorcing mothers. There would be less likelihood of an exchange of the marital home instead of maintenance. Roberts (1991) argued that in housing design, affordability needed to be calculated on the basis of women's earnings, not the now, often out-moded, idea of a male wage-earner being present in a household.

Gilroy (1993) showed that the government policy of the 'right to buy' council property, most purchases of which had been of the better housing stock, had worked to the detriment of women 'by decreasing the quantity and quality of stock at a time of increasing female reliance on the rented sector' (p. 116). In short, women had less good-quality accommodation available to them in a market-dominated housing sector (Brion, 1987; Morris and Winn, 1990; Sexty, 1990; Woods, 1996). Drake (1989) argued that women needed public housing by showing that women's housing needs differed from men's in two ways. First, they were more likely to need their housing to accommodate their respons-ibility for children, and care of disabled, sick or elderly people. Second, their housing needs often arose out of an unexpected or sudden life event, pregnancy, relationship breakdown and physical violence.

Despite the reduction in council housing, it still remained an import-ant sector for women, with female-headed households and women under 30 more likely to be found in this form of tenure than their male counterparts. In 1991, 39 per cent of divorced or separated women were in rented council housing compared with 25 per cent of men, and 41 per cent of women under 30 compared with only 14 per cent of men (Department of the Environment, 1993). Prescott-Clarke *et al.* (1994) showed that affordability was the most important reason for applicants being on council waiting lists and lone parents (the vast majority of whom are women) had the lowest incomes. However, female-headed households also received poorer quality housing in this sector. They were more likely to be housed in maisonettes or flats, clustered in the more run-down estates and allocated to areas with high scores on a deprivation index (Woods, 1996). Private renting also created problems for women, some of which they shared with men, such as insecurity of lettings, availability and cost. However, they also encountered the additional risk of sexual harassment from their landlords (Watson and Austerberry, 1986; Miller, 1990). A Greater London Council study found that 12 per cent of women living alone in privately rented accommoda-tion had experienced 'serious molestation' (Thornton, 1990).

Ethnic minority women had particular problems in the housing sector across all housing tenures. Their particularly low pay made it harder for them to be owner–occupiers (Oppenheim, 1993) and they had to wait longer for council accommodation and were offered poorer quality property (Rao, 1990). An added problem for access to local authority accommodation for some ethnic minority women was their vulnerability under immigration legislation if their relationship broke down. Dhillon-Kashyap (1994) highlighted the fact that under immigration regulations, newly married couples had to live together for 12 months ('the 12-month rule'), and if a woman had been sponsored by her husband to join him (the case for 99 per cent of ethnic minority women), it was on the commitment that he could provide for her financially 'without recourse to public funds'. This meant that not only could local authorities refuse these women accommodation but they were also obliged to report them to the immigration authorities. Even for women who were not contravening immigration regulations there were difficulties in accessing local authority accommodation. Mama (1989) found that ethnic minority women who approached councils because of relationship breakdown and domestic violence encountered insensitivity and hostility from housing officers.

Domestic violence was a major cause of women's homelessness. 'Having somewhere to go is probably the single most important thing in enabling a woman to leave her husband and in this sense housing policy and practice can make it either possible or impossible for women to leave their husbands' (Morris and Winn, 1990, p. 126). Yet the provision of refuges (about 200 across Britain with about ten for ethnic minority women and few providing access for disabled women) remained inadequate and their funding under threat. Niner (1989) demonstrated that only women with children who were escaping from a violent partner, not women on their own, were seen as priority for rehousing.

Dibblin (1991) found that only 17 per cent of local authorities usually accepted young people as homeless, and Cheeseman (1992) found that more men than women were helped. This was probably because of the nature of the preference given to those sleeping rough, who were more likely to be men. Douglas and Gilroy (1994) highlighted both under-counting and a 'great gender divide' when looking at the 1991 census count of rough sleepers: 2397 men and 430 women. This gender gap might be explained by the hidden nature of women's homelessness. Daly (1993) established this when looking at European homelessness. She reported that men's homelessness was 'precipitated by material changes and is more public in its manifestation. Women's homelessness typically arises from relationship problems and is "solved" through private channels'. Dealing with those who slept rough was the main aim of government-funded programmes, hence the fact that 74 per cent of those helped by one specific scheme, the Housing Corporation's Roofless Package, were men (Cheeseman, 1992). It is interesting to note that 51 per cent of the women helped were from ethnic minorities compared with only 17 per cent of the men, and 78 per cent of the women were under 25 years compared with 43 per cent of the men (Cheeseman, 1992).

Women were at a disadvantage in housing employment. The National Federation of Housing Associations (NFHA) (1985) found that despite making up only 38 per cent of workers, men were three times as likely to be managers and twice as likely to be professional staff. In contrast, at the lowest end of the wage scale there were almost five times as many women. Brion (1994) showed that there were some grounds to be optimistic in terms of the increasing numbers of women who were becoming fellows of the professional organization the Chartered Institute of Housing, although they only made up 19 per cent. However, she also argued that women were experiencing considerable discrimination when being considered for higher grade posts and in the technical functioning of housing.

ROOF (1990) found that the number of women in chief officers posts in housing had actually fallen from the very low 5 per cent in 1986. Despite the fact that women dominated as housing managers when the profession evolved in the 1920s, Coatham and Hale (1994) could identify only ten for their research, just 3 per cent of all chief housing officers in the latter half of 1989. They reinforced Brion's (1994) description of discrimination against women by showing that the majority of the women chief housing officers had to make the choice between their career and having children. The majority had no children. Coatham and Hale (1994) argued that housing management attracted a different type of person during the 1990s with local government's generally more 'business-like' and 'market-orientated' approach. Also, women were found to be under-represented in unpaid but decision-making positions in housing. They only represented 30 per cent of those on housing association committees of management (Kearns, 1991).

'Race'

'The character and extent of racial discrimination in the various sectors of the housing market constitute one of the most well-established aspects of racial inequality in modern Britain' (Law, 1996, p. 81). Using 1991 census data, Owen (1993b) showed that ethnic minority households were in poorer quality housing and had a greater housing need than the White population generally. This was because ethnic minorities' choices in housing were more limited than the White population. One reason was that, being disadvantaged by the employment market, they were more likely to be found in low-waged work. Another factor was racism and discrimination in the housing sector.

It had been shown that discrimination existed across all forms of tenure in the housing sector, ranging from blatant exclusion and refusal of mortgagees to regulation of access to council housing (CRE, 1989c, 1989e, 1989f, 1990a, 1990b, 1992, 1993; Skellington and Morris, 1992). An investigation of Liverpool City Council in 1986 found that ethnic minority families had to wait longer for a council house than White people and had less of a chance of getting the better quality housing with central heating and a garden. The CRE (1989d) found that 20 per cent of accommodation agencies discriminated against ethnic minorities.

In the same year they found that an Oldham estate agent had discriminated against Asian clients by controlling information about properties in order to segregate people by 'race'. The agency also unlawfully accepted discriminatory instructions from sellers (CRE, 1989f).

Even the predominance of owner occupation among Asian families was an indication of their lack of choice in the housing sector leading to the purchase of low-cost, low-quality properties in run-down areas (Rex and Moore, 1967; CRE, 1985b; Karn et al., 1985). 'Asian households have been caught in a "catch 22" situation' (Amin, 1992, p. 22). Also, the General Improvement Area programmes and Housing Action Areas aimed at this sort of property did little to benefit this group in spite of their eligibility for grants (Rex and Tomlinson, 1979; Brown, 1984). Ethnic minorities were also found in poor-quality rented accommodation (CRE, 1984c; 1989c). Ratcliffe (1992) argued that ethnic minorities' housing needs were missed because there was no policy for dealing with the worst housing first.

Housing tenure varied widely between different ethnic minority groups. About 80 per cent of Indians and Pakistanis owned their homes compared with 45 per cent of Bangladeshis, and just over 40 per cent of Black Caribbeans. Only one in ten South Asians was in local authority rented accommodation compared with over one-third of Black Caribbeans who were also four times more likely to rent from a housing association than South Asians (CRE, 1995a). Also, ethnic minorities were more likely to live in flats (35 per cent) rather than houses compared with the White population (20 per cent) (CRE, 1995b).

There was a different pattern of housing tenure among Black Caribbeans and South Asians to the White population. Jones (1993) demonstrated that in the early days of immigration very few ethnic minority families managed to obtain council housing. However, by 1991, although the proportion of South Asians (11.1 per cent) remained much lower than Whites in council housing, the proportion of Black Caribbeans (35.7 per cent) grew higher than Whites (21.4 per cent) (Owen, 1993b, p. 8). Peach and Bryon (1993) argued that this was at least partly explained by the high proportion of lone mothers among this community who enhanced access to local authority housing. From 1982, because of government policies and financial incentives, owner–occupation grew among the general population and spread to lower socioeconomic levels. There was a high level of owner–occupation among South Asians (77.1 per cent), and there had been a growth in owner–occupation in the Black Caribbean population (48.1 per cent) but it was still below White households (66.6 per cent) (Owen, 1993b, p. 8).

Jones (1993) showed that the type of property owned by the different communities remained consistently differentiated. In 1982, while 54 per cent of White households lived in a semi-detached or detached house, only 23 per cent of Black Caribbeans and 26 per cent of South Asians did so. This did not change greatly in the 1980s. In 1982, the majority (59 per cent) of South Asians lived in terraced housing, and half at the end of the 1980s. In 1982, while only 3 per cent of White households had more than one person per room, 16 per cent of Black Caribbeans, 26 per cent of Indian, 47 per cent of Pakistani, and 60 per cent of Bangladeshi households did so. These figures had only narrowed slightly over the last decade with the general pattern remaining.

Overall, ethnic minorities lived in poorer and more overcrowded accommodation than Whites. Whereas the vast majority of White households (98 per cent) had at least one room per person, this was true for only 53 per cent of Bangladeshi and 70 per cent of Pakistani households. Also, while information on homelessness broken down by ethnic group was not published at a national level, several studies showed that ethnic minorities are more likely to be homeless than Whites. A study in 1991 of single homeless people in England found that ethnic minorities are over-represented among the residents of hostels and bed and breakfast accommodation among young people and women. They made up one-third of those under 25 and half of all the women. In London, ethnic minority households formed 53 per cent of those registered homeless in 1992–93 even though they made up only 15 per cent of all households in this area. In Tower Hamlets, Bangladeshi families made up 59 per cent of all the homeless families, while they only represented 10 per cent of all families in the borough (CRE, 1995b).

In all the forms of housing tenure there were geographically racially concentrated areas, ranging from certain council house estates and whole areas of cities to particular streets. Virdee (1995) argued that one aspect of this phenomenon was explained by the choices ethnic minority households made in response to fear of racial violence. Dhillon-Kashyap (1994) showed that this was even more pertinent for ethnic minority women living alone or with children, even if they lived with a male partner, as they were more likely to be alone at home when taking children to school and shopping. Mama (1989) found that ethnic minority women were extremely concerned about their personal safety on the streets and in their homes. Harrison (1995) also argued that in practice 'geographical concentration actually can be advantageous for minority ethnic residents in some respects; in terms of security for households against racist attack, for political organisation, for religious, educational or voluntary activity, to maintain family networks, to benefit from the presence of one's own linguistic group, or because of easier access to specialised cultural provision' (p. 58).

However, the CRE (1987c) put this phenomenon of ethnic minorities adjusting to accommodate racism in a much more negative light. There were 'many, effectively "no-go" areas which have acquired a "name" for racial harassment and where members of ethnic minorities are afraid to accept offers of homes, should they even be offered to them' (p. 20). This geographical differentiation could also be seen as further evidence of the existence of racial discrimination. In the private rented sector, Smith (1989) showed the emergence of a 'dual market' in the private rented sector with ethnic minority tenants predominantly renting from ethnic minority landlords, thereby being restricted to lower quality housing in particular areas of cities. Cater (1981) demonstrated that for owner–occupation, Asian households' reliance on loans from friends and relatives, informal property exchanges and Asian estate agents restricted their housing options to cheaper, older properties in a particular area. In local authorities' housing departments, the CRE (1984c, 1984d, 1989c) exposed perceptions by applicants, staff and tenants of suitable estates for ethnic minority households.

This pattern of geographical segregation continued, as shown by a study of the 1991 Census. Despite revealing that Britain's ethnic minority population had migrated out of inner-city areas, it exposed their concentration into what are termed 'ethnic villages' in the suburbs (Peach, 1996). There was still a difference identified between the ethnic minority groups, with the Black Caribbean population more likely to live in council houses and the Asian population more likely to be owner-occupiers, particularly the Indian and to some extent the Pakistani population, but not the Bangladeshis. The move to the suburbs was most evident among the Black Caribbeans, with a significant move during the 1980s particularly from inner-city areas in London. The highest concentration of Black Caribbeans was in Brent, north London, rather than the more traditional areas such as Brixton and Paddington. However, Wrench *et al.* (1993) pointed out that this pattern of ethnic minority households' migration may be contained by the fact that when moving to more prosperous parts of the country many experienced direct racism, which acted as a deterrent to moving further afield. Phillips and Karn (1992) described this migration as 'characterised by new modes of ethnic minority concentration' (p. 358).

In the 1980s, the government sought to diminish the role of local authorities in owning and renting houses. At the same time, they encouraged and supported the growth of housing associations to take over the role of providing what had come to be called 'social housing' (Harrison, 1995). Many were charities in legal terms, managed by committees of volunteers and employing professional staff. Harrison (1995) was encouraged by the development of the housing association sector and argued that there was the possibility of it providing good-quality provision for ethnic minority households in the greatest housing need. However, despite the National Federation of Housing Associations (NFHA, 1987) claiming that many associations had evaluated their allocations and lettings policy in terms of 'race' issues, including 72 per cent of London associations, they were often viewed as insensitive to the needs of ethnic minorities and inaccessible. Even housing associations working in inner-city areas had an underrepresentation of ethnic minorities on their work force. Julienne (1990) revealed that some housing associations have achieved very little in terms of 'race' equality: 47 per cent were only providing adequate or less access to their housing, more than 20 per cent had no clear policies, monitoring, positive action or targets, and 19 per cent were a cause for concern. The Refugee Housing Association in Bristol was found guilty by the CRE of discrimination against Black Caribbean clients who were turned away because of objections from other tenants (CRE, 1992).

To counter this, an ethnic minority housing association movement developed, which aimed to rectify this situation (NFHA, 1990). However, a reduction in Housing Association Grant meant economic restraints acted against the building of new and larger properties for extended families because value for money was the main criteria for building houses and this was defined in terms of the greatest number of units. Harrison (1992) argued that this 'will disadvantage many black and ethnic minority people, who can then only be housed well away from their community roots and support networks. Safety and security, in terms of racial harassment and victimisation, are not issues in the "value for money" debate'. Law (1996) pointed out that the 1988 Housing Act, which encouraged associations to rely in part on private capital, has led to negative developments, such as rent increases and problems of financial viability for ethnic minority housing associations. This in turn had 'curtailed the optimism about the new role of this sector as an emerging main provider of social housing' (p. 94).

Ethnic minorities are disproportionately vulnerable to homelessness. Dhillon-Kashyap (1994) reported research by the London Housing Unit that found London's ethnic minority households were up to four times more likely to become homeless than other households. Law (1996) argued that: 'The higher proportion of minority ethnic groups leaving care, being unemployed and on low incomes, living in stressful overcrowded conditions and facing racial discrimination when seeking access to rented accommodation is likely to reproduce a persistent level of homelessness amongst these groups' (p. 99). The experience of actual harassment or anticipation of hostility also led ethnic minority families to leave their homes (Black Housing, 1994). Davies *et al.* (1996) found that homelessness was a serious and growing problem for Asian communities. They found that Asian young people faced a higher risk of homelessness than their White counterparts as a result of being more susceptible to unemployment and living in overcrowded conditions. The breakdown in relationships between children and parents was their biggest single cause of homelessness. Studies had shown that single ethnic minority people were over-represented in hostels and bed-and-breakfast hotels and were also much more likely to have previously stayed with friends rather than sleeping rough (Anderson *et al.*, 1993; Randall and Brown, 1993).

Disability

Disabled people were shown to be in an inferior position to most other groups in terms of housing (Borsay, 1986). 'The least satisfactory housing tends to be that inhabited by sections of the population of which disabled people form a disproportionately large percentage, elderly people and people on low incomes' (p. 113). This was because disabled people were denied an equal education, leaving them with poor skill and qualification levels, more likely to be reliant on social security benefits, being widely seen as unemployable, confronted with inaccessible workplaces and, if employed, in lower paid jobs.

Morris (1993c) argued that the government's housing policies directed at an increase in owner–occupation and reduction in council housing 'have been directly against the interests of disabled people, whose economic position and need for housing with particular physical characteristics mean that the private sector has little to offer' (p. 143). Abberley (1993) showed that the vast majority of owner–occupied housing was unsuitable for disabled people, and where disabled people were owner–occupiers they were concentrated in the properties with the poorest conditions because of their lack of income. Therefore, they were reliant on the 'social rented' sector for their housing with 45 per cent of disabled adults living in council or housing association accommodation compared with 31 per cent of the general population (Martin *et al.*, 1988; Gilroy, 1993).

Local authorities have always been the main providers of wheelchair and mobility-adapted accommodation with very little available in all the other forms of housing tenure. However, substantial cuts in local government funding and insufficient funding for housing associations meant that provision is inadequate and often provided on a segregated basis. Disabled people were also finding it increasingly difficult to gain access to local authority accommodation; and homelessness among physically disabled people increased by 92 per cent between 1980 and 1986, compared with 57 per cent for non-disabled households (Morris, 1988). Despite this, Morris (1988) provided figures to show that local authority accommodation was still crucial to disabled people because, although the numbers of adapted properties built declined substantially from the period 1970–81 to 1982–86, they actually rose in terms of the percentage of their total new build. Whereas for housing associations, the alternative provider of 'social rented' accommodation, during their expansion in the 1980s they actually built fewer adapted properties in both real and percentage terms.

However, Morris (1993c) has exposed even local authorities as sadly lacking in their housing service provision to disabled people. A study Morris undertook for Shelter (1990) showed that out of her sample of 21 local authorities, only three housing departments had a written policy on meeting the needs of disabled people. Where they were developing strategies on homelessness, there was no consideration of disabled people's needs such as access to hostel accommodation. They were ill-informed about the level and nature of the needs of disabled people for housing and kept very poor records on the quantity and nature of the adaptations made. Only three had a policy on adaptations; most failed to integrate disabled people into their allocation policies; they were not exerting any influence they might have had on private developers or housing associations; and, despite their obvious role in enabling independent living for disabled people, only two housing departments had regular liaison meetings with their social services department. In the same survey, Morris (1990) also found that within social services departments, residential care is 'still considered as inevitable for many disabled people' (p. 141). The majority used residential care for physically disabled people outside their own community with little knowledge of its quality. She argued that the 'picture that emerges for disabled people is a grim one' (Morris, 1993c, p. 143).

In 1989, completions of adapted local authority and housing association accommodation fell from 4300 to 1200 (Inside Housing, 1991, cited in Gilroy, 1993, p. 130). The number of houses designed to full wheelchair access was about 30 000, whereas the number of wheelchair users was about 80 000 (Gilroy, 1993). Therefore, provision could be seen to be inadequate and the financial situation was not conducive to improving it. Gilroy (1993) also pointed out that all too frequently when considering housing design for disabled people, there was a focus on wheelchair use. It was falsely assumed that other types of disability could be catered for in 'normal' homes. This was not the case and had meant that the needs of other disabled people have had even less recognition than wheelchair users. Most disabled people had other adaptation needs for specific requirements. With six million disabled people in Britain, there needed to be research on the housing needs of disabled people, the development of appropriate models, and the need to gain commitment from housing providers. Finance was a problem. Changes to grant schemes in 1989 promised less complexity, but a means test was applied to grant applications (Morris, 1991b). This was criticized by the Royal Association for Disability and Rehabilitation (RADAR, 1992) for failing to take account of mortgage repayments and the extra costs of being a disabled person, such as special diet, heating, transport, laundry and the purchase of care.

Oliver (1996) argued that some provisions under the welfare state work to deny disabled people their rights. One example he gave was the provision of segregated residential facilities such as Young Disabled Units or Cheshire Homes. He argued that, even done with the best of intentions, these denied disabled people the right to live where they chose because 'to live in such an establishment means that individuals are regarded as being adequately housed; consequently there is no statutory duty on the housing authority to house them' (p. 52). 'The first requirement of disabled people in participating as equal citizens within the community is a home which is suited to them' (Swain *et al.*, 1993). However, a study by the Prince of Wales Advisory Group on Disability reported that: 'The reality of housing and care support options revealed ... is alarming ... few people obtain the flexible, dependable services essential for personal autonomy' (Fiedler, 1988). With the advent of care in the community policies, more people with profound disabilities were coming out of institutional care and looking for independent or assisted independent living.

There were, however, examples of good practice. The Disabled Person's Housing Service formed in 1985 as an agency of Walbrook Housing Association, Derby, was a one-stop shop set up in response to requests from disabled people, which gave advice, and practical help

(Kendall, 1991). Another pioneering example was the Grove Road Housing Collective (Davis, 1981) set up by two disabled people who had experienced living in a residential hostel and were determined to set up an independent living scheme despite opposition and scepticism from professionals. They established a number of accessible ground-floor flats for disabled people with accommodation for helpers on the first floor. The scheme was managed by all the residents. Derbyshire County Council provided a good-practice example of involving disabled people in its funding for a Centre for Integrated Living run by disabled people. Its role included developing initiatives which aided independent living, provided information for disabled people, acted as an advocate when necessary and maintained a register of adapted housing in the district (Morris, 1993c).

Summary

This chapter has examined the social policy areas of health and housing. In the area of health we see that women form the largest group of consumers and providers of health care in Britain. However, the NHS can be seen to be under the control of men and dominated by a male medical tradition. Although women are such a large majority in the NHS labour force, they are mainly in the lower levels of the hierarchy, with ethnic minority women even more disadvantaged than White women. Even in nursing, long seen as women's work, men can be seen to achieve promotion faster and more effectively. The health service can be criticized for having done little to acknowledge and meet health needs as expressed by women themselves, and for not providing adequate or appropriate health care for women. However, because of the 'medicalization of women's lives', women experience a lifetime of interventionist medicine often revolving around their fertility from male doctors who have been criticized for being patronizing and holding stereotypical views of women. Two examples of specific programmes for women, cervical and breast-cancer screening, have been used to demonstrate this.

Ethnic minorities receive a qualitatively and quantitatively worse service from the NHS than White people. This situation continues despite its acknowledgement by the NHS and a substantial increase in research in this area. There has been an over-emphasis on a cultural approach to this disadvantage that has resulted in a failure to examine structures both outside and inside the NHS, which determine the health of ethnic minority communities. Reforms in the control of the NHS, including the setting up of independent trusts and the change to the all-pervading ethos of contracting as suppliers and receivers of services, have done little to improve the situation. There remains an underrepresentation of ethnic minorities at all levels of decision making. Despite being the largest employer of ethnic minorities, the NHS had been exposed as promulgating discrimination and unequal opportunities in the area of 'race' across the many and varied types of jobs within it. This has led to the launching of a programme of action to address barriers facing ethnic minority staff.

The health service stands accused of over-intervention in the area of disability, and taking over the control of decisions from disabled people by dictating the form of intervention in purely medical terms. Medical practitioners can be seen to be the controllers and gatekeepers for disabled people's access, not only to health services, but also to other services and benefits by the over-concentration on medical interpretations of eligibility. The medical model of disability continues to dominate. Medical intervention in disability issues also took the form of striving for 'normality' in behaviour and appearance. This meant a concentration on rehabilitation. It is argued that doctors' training as interventionists, with the demands to diagnose, treat and either cure or admit defeat, is not a suitable model for dealing with disability. Many changes were seen to be needed to ensure an equal service to disabled people – not least an increase in the numbers of disabled workers in the health service, particularly in areas where a special empathy with disabled people is advantageous.

The second section of the chapter deals with housing. During the 1980s and continuing in the 1990s, British housing policy has concentrated on promoting owner–occupation above all other forms of tenure and reducing the resources that are available to social rented housing. This meant that those with higher incomes, savings and capital assets prosper, and those without, such as women without a male partner, ethnic minority communities and disabled people, were forced into private rented accommodation which was generally of poorer quality. The consideration of women's housing needs is becoming increasingly important, because women are outliving men into old age and there is a continuing increase in the breakdown of relationships. It is argued that women need public housing because their housing needs differ from men's. They are more likely to need their housing to accommodate their responsibility for children, and care of disabled, sick or elderly people. Their housing needs also often arise out of an unexpected or sudden life event, pregnancy, relationship breakdown and physical violence. Women's homelessness is hidden and undercounted, because research in this area and policies to deal with it have concentrated on those sleeping rough who were more likely to be men. In addition to the poorer service for women, they are also at a disadvantage in housing employment, being less likely to be managers or represented amongst professional staff.

Ethnic minorities live in poorer quality housing and have a greater housing need than the White population. Racial discrimination has been shown to exist in all sectors of the housing market and all forms of tenure, ranging from blatant exclusion and refusal of mortgagees to the regulation of access to council housing. Although housing tenure varied widely between different ethnic minority groups, overall they live in more overcrowded accommodation than Whites and are to be found concentrated in geographically racially segregated areas, ranging from certain council house estates and whole areas of cities to particular streets. Ethnic minorities are also disproportionately vulnerable to homelessness.

Disabled people hold an inferior position to most other groups in terms of housing. The vast majority of owner–occupied housing is unsuitable for disabled people, and where disabled people are owner–occupiers they are concentrated in the properties with the poorest conditions because of their lack of income. Therefore, they are more reliant on the 'social rented' sector. Local authorities have always been the main providers of wheelchair and mobility-adapted accommodation with very little available in all the other forms of housing tenure. However, substantial cuts in local government funding and insufficient funding for housing associations means that provision is inadequate and often provided on a segregated basis. Even local authorities are sadly lacking in their housing service provision to disabled people.

CHAPTER 8

Conclusion to Part Two

Chapters 5, 6 and 7 of this book have examined the key areas of social policy – education, employment, income maintenance, social services, health and housing – for 'equal opportunities' issues that relate to gender, 'race' and disability. All these areas have been found to be lacking in providing a service to the whole community. In each area, examples are given of where welfare provision falls short of offering equal access to women, ethnic minorities and disabled people, and an appropriate and relevant service for these groups within society. Cain and Yuval-Davis (1990) argued that, certainly in the field of 'race', these services did not meet the needs of particular groups, and that ethnic minority groups shared a common position of marginalization and disadvantage. This criticism can be widened to include women and disabled people too.

It is important to recognize diversity within groups, such as women, ethnic minorities and disabled people, and their different experience of welfare provision. In terms of gender, 'Both post-modernism and feminist theorising point to the dangers of a false essentialism and universalism about the category "women" and thus about women's needs, wants and experiences of welfare' (Hallett, 1996, p. 10). However, Taylor-Gooby (1994) warned that to travel too far down this route of emphasizing diversity and specificity may mean that we lose the politically expedient and empowering categories assigned to the most disadvantaged groups in society: women, ethnic minorities and disabled people. 'If post-modernism denies the significance of such broad developments and substitutes a language of particularism and diversity, the approach may obscure one of the great reversals for the most vulnerable groups in a cloud of detail, may ignore the wood through enthusiasm for bark rubbing' (pp. 388–9). Hallett (1996) agreed that, despite varying experiences at one level based on social divisions, at a deeper level there were shared 'structural factors constituting and affecting those experiences' (Hallett, 1996, p. 11). Also, as Di Stefano (1990) succinctly reported for gender, it is a 'difference that makes a difference' (p. 78). There is certainly evidence in this book of disadvantage in welfare provision across the social divisions of gender, 'race' and disability.

The success of welfare services and provisions should be judged on whether they provide for all groups within society; whether the care provided is satisfactory, relevant and accessible for all. This was not the case in the key social policy areas examined in Part Two of this book.

All too often decisions on the nature of services provided were made by people who do not use them; without consultation with the main users; on the basis of economy and cost-effectiveness; not on the basis of equality but on the basis of misinformation, myths and stereotyped views of the service users. For example, women were available to provide care 24 hours a day; ethnic minority communities care for their elderly and did not want or need support; and disabled people would be cared for by their families and to give them the opportunity for independent living would not be suitable.

The providers of services cannot ignore the social divisions in society on the basis of 'race', gender and disability. Services cannot be provided on a 'colour, sex and disability blind approach'. Women are the main users of welfare services and, like disabled people and ethnic minorities, have the same right as everyone to general services, but also have special needs and requirements. As Williams (1989) argued in the area of 'race': 'Universalism within welfare theories result in inappropriate services to Black people'. This is also true for women and disabled people. This argument is not intended to promote segregation of the services by 'race', gender and disability but, on the contrary, to ensure fair and equal services which meet the needs of all, which is not the case today. As it stands these groups do not have equal access to mainstream services and their special needs are often ignored. This means that welfare services are not fulfilling their responsibility to the whole of society.

Many of the examples of attempts to make services more responsive to all the population have come from local government where developments have occurred in the last decade as a response to the 'equal opportunities' legislation and a political commitment to 'equal opportunities' (Bagilhole, 1994a). Many local authorities set up specialist units and departments to deal with the issues of 'equal opportunities' in employment and across their service delivery areas. The introduction of fair employment policies by local authorities, which led to the recruitment of more women, ethnic minorities and disabled people in service delivery and decision-making jobs, was intended to ensure greater awareness and sensitivity among service providers, as was the training of existing staff. The maintenance of monitoring systems were intended to indicate where services needed to be changed, and to enable a close watch to be kept on those policies which had already been introduced with the intention of achieving that change. The appointment of 'equal opportunities' officers was to facilitate detailed reviews of service delivery, and the use of Section XI funds (see Chapter 3 under Local Government Act 1966 for an explanation of these funds), and processes and structures to consult with their users and clients were to have an influence on the general provision of services, while at the same time meeting the specific needs of women, ethnic minorities and disabled people within the community.

A systematic review of service delivery in all welfare provision areas from an 'equal opportunities' viewpoint was the prerequisite for action in this area. An example of this was action taken by Derbyshire County Council, which produced the first local authority review of all its service provision with individual Equal Opportunities Action Plans for all its departments for gender, 'race' and disability (Bagilhole, 1993a). Each service, after consultation with different groups within the community and service users, came up with a strategy and action plan for change within a given time-scale. The following were the types of questions they asked in their 'equal opportunities' review of their services. What is the effect of current procedures and practices on women, ethnic minorities and disabled people? What are the needs of different groups within the local community and in what ways, if any, are they being met by procedures and practices? Who uses the services? Who needs the services, but does not know about them or does not use them? What changes need to be made to provide services on an 'equal opportunities' basis?

There is an important relationship between the providers and the users of welfare provision. Representation of women, ethnic minorities and disabled people as workers in welfare is essential to increase the likelihood that services will be appropriate, relevant and accessible for these groups. However, the positions that these workers hold is crucial. To have any effect on welfare provision they must be in decision-making positions of power. The area of gender illustrates this well. Fraser (1989, p. 147) described social welfare as a 'feminised terrain'. Women's position as both service users and providers was primary. Women's unequal position and disadvantage in the labour market (Callender, 1996) meant they were over-represented among the poor and reliant on state support (Millar, 1996a) and disadvantaged in the housing market (Woods, 1996). Foster (1996) pointed out that women were the key consumers of health care. Their prime responsibility for child care, family health and other welfare activities also made them the key points of contact between family members and welfare services, education, health care, social security, housing and personal social services (Balbo, 1987, p. 49).

Women were also central as service providers of welfare. This included both formal and informal care of dependants within the family, such as children, the elderly and disabled people (Tester, 1996). Women were predominant in the frontline of service delivery in the statutory, voluntary and private sectors (EOC, 1988; Bagilhole, 1996a). However, women were the lowest paid workers in health, education and social services. They were not in decision-making positions which frame and shape the services. Rather, these services were managed principally by men. Therefore, women could have little effect on services for women. Men control welfare, whereas women are controlled by it. This same analysis can be done in the areas of 'race' and disability. What we find is that, not only are women underrepresented as controllers and decision makers in welfare, but so too are ethnic minorities and disabled people.

It is also important not to simply take an approach to changing services, which concentrates on the service users themselves, either women, ethnic minorities or disabled people, because this can divert attention away from a critical examination of the service itself. Williams (1989), in her consideration of 'race' and anti-racist practices in the discipline of social policy, showed that ethnic minorities experienced services differently to White people, and their entitlement and access to welfare provision was heavily affected by 'race' and nationality. In the past, by taking a cultural approach to explain this difference in experience, racism or lack of 'race' awareness in publicly delivered services was hidden. The ideas of 'Black cultural pathology' and 'Black family pathology' (Lawrence, 1982) were current. This was where the over-representation of ethnic minorities in poverty, inadequate housing, poor health, educational underachievement and higher social-work intervention was blamed on the assumed inadequacy of ethnic minorities themselves and their family formation, thus ignoring structural inequality and past disadvantage. Ethnic minorities were also stereotyped as immigrants unable to speak English and this was given as the prime reason for their lack of use of services. Emphasis was placed on translation and the availability of interpreters (Ratcliffe, 1992; Gilroy, 1993). While all service-delivery organizations need to consider this issue, including the appointment of bilingual staff and the attitudes of staff to clients with little English, access to information is only one issue. Welfare provision has other major problems of the marginalization of 'race' and the existence of racism within it (Gordon, 1986, 1989; Gurnah, 1989). The cultural approach does not address historical or structural inequality and has become a secondary issue, as the proportion of ethnic minorities born in Britain with English as a first language has increased. A study on ethnic minority women in the National Health Service showed that translation of recruitment material would not substantially increase the number of women employed. Asian women did not need or want interpreters in their interviews (Bagilhole and Stephens, 1997a).

Oliver (1996) argued that the welfare state had failed disabled people because it compounded their 'severe economic deprivation and social disadvantage' (p. 64). State education did not entitle disabled children and young people to the same education as the non-disabled. The health service was dominated by the interests of professionals rather than disabled people. Disabled people experienced higher rates of unemployment and, if in employment, they predominated in lower-paid, lower-status work with poorer working conditions. Therefore, the majority of disabled people depended on welfare benefits, which were not adequate to fulfil their needs. This was because welfare provision was based on the approach that concentrated on the service-user rather than social and structural barriers to accessing the service. They took an individual model of disability, the 'personal tragedy' approach, rather than the 'social model' advocated by disabled groups to shift the 'focus away from impaired individuals and on to restrictive environments and disabling barriers' (Oliver, 1996, p. 65).

Oliver (1996) argued that underpinning this failure, which he highlighted for disabled people, was 'the placing of the concept of need at the centre of welfare provision; notably the organisation and delivery of services' (p. 66). This, he argued, could not provide adequate, collective welfare. Oliver (1996) showed that the dominance of a 'needs-based' as opposed to a 'rights-based' approach had been perpetuated through the policy of community care since the 1960s. The assessment of need was an exercise of professional workers' power over disabled people: in other words, the professional's decisions dominated and disabled people's interpretation of their need was denied (Hugman, 1991).

The crucial argument was not that disabled people have failed to receive any benefits from welfare provision, rather that 'the price for those services is usually acceptance of invasions of privacy by a veritable army of professionals and the acceptance of services that the state thinks you should have or is willing to pay for, rather than those that you know you need' (Oliver, 1996, p. 69). Therefore, the effect of the lack of a 'rights-based', 'equal opportunities' approach to welfare can be starkly illustrated for disabled people. This is also true for women and ethnic minorities. While services are determined for disabled people by non-disabled people, they are determined for women by men, and for ethnic minorities by White people, largely without their say or participation. Until this imbalance is altered, little will change in the areas of welfare provision. This is why 'equal opportunities' is fundamental to social policy.

PART THREE

Supporting documents

CHAPTER 9

Documents

Document 1   Summary of important 'equal opportunities' legislation

Legislation	Main Points
Disability Employment	
Disabled Persons (Employment) Acts 1944 and 1958	Introduced register of disabled people and 3 per cent quota system for employers of more than 20 workers.
Companies Act 1985	Annual report on policies for the employment of disabled people for companies with more than 250 employees.
Disability Discrimination Act 1995	Made it unlawful for employers of more than 20 employees to discriminate on the grounds of disability. Contained a right of access to goods, facilities, services and premises; further and higher education; and public transport including taxis, public service vehicles and railways. Established a National Disability Council. Gave disabled people the right to take complaints of discrimination to industrial tribunals with no upper limit placed on compensation awards.
Access to services	
Chronically Sick and Disabled Persons Act 1970 (as amended 1976)	Allowed equal access for disabled people. Allowed equal access for disabled people to new public buildings and places where education took place, and places of employment. Special needs housing and home adaptations. Assessment and

Legislation	Main Points
	register of needs, information on social services. Orange badge scheme.
Education Act 1981	Integration of children with special educational needs.
Building Act 1984	Access for disabled people in building regulations and provisions.
Disabled Persons (services, consultation and representation) Act 1986	Covers education, social services and local authority representation. Representation, information and abilities of carers.

'Race'

Race Relations Act 1965	Outlawed direct discrimination in public places where previously 'Whites only' admittance procedures were legal.
Race Relations Act 1968	Outlawed direct discrimination in housing and employment. Set up Race Relations Board and system of conciliation for complaints.
Race Relations Act 1976	Outlawed direct and indirect discrimination on the grounds of 'colour, race, nationality (including citizenship) or other ethnic or national origins' in 'employment, training and related matters, in education, in the provision of goods, facilities and services, and in the disposal and management of premises'. Set up complainants' right to take cases to industrial tribunals and set up the Commission for Racial Equality as an enforcing agency.

Immigration

Commonwealth Immigrants Act 1962	All holders of Commonwealth passports were subject to immigration control except those who were born in Britain, held British passports issued by the British government, or people included on passports of those

Legislation	Main Points
	not subject to immigration control. Introduced a system of work vouchers, which had to be obtained prior to entry, for other commonwealth citizens.
Commonwealth Immigrants Act 1968	Withdrew African Asians right to enter. Introduced immigration control for Commonwealth citizens who were non-patrials (that is, those who did not have a parent or grandparent born in Britain) and also put a limit on the number of work vouchers issued.
Immigration Appeals Act 1969	Extended the deportation powers of the Home Office.
Immigration Act 1971	Extended the deportation powers of the 1969 Act and abolished the work-voucher system, effectively stopping primary Black immigration. From this time the major form of immigration was restricted to secondary immigration: that is, wives and dependants.
Immigration Act 1988	Revoked the automatic right to be joined by dependants given to men who entered Britain before the enactment date of the 1971 Act, 1 January 1973.
British Nationality Act 1981	Created three classes of citizenship of Britain and Commonwealth: British citizens, British Dependent Territories citizens, and British Overseas citizens. Stated that citizenship could only be acquired by birth, descent or naturalization. Eligibility for citizenship was largely confined to people born of British parents or parents settled here.
Refugee and Asylum Seekers Bill 1996	Extension of the 'white list' of countries, which are considered safe. Refugees and asylum-seekers from these countries are

Legislation	Main Points
	more likely to be viewed as 'economic migrants' and turned away. Restricted the rights of refugees and asylum-seekers to social security benefits.
Religion Fair Employment Protection Act, Northern Ireland 1976 (Amended 1989)	Outlawed direct and indirect discrimination on religious grounds. Required private sector employers with more than ten employees and all public-sector employers to register with the Fair Employment Commission, and to monitor the religious composition of their workforces. All employers must review their employment practices every three years. Failure to do so is a criminal offence. If the review reveals a problem, employers are required to take appropriate affirmative action, and provide targets with a timetable. Also, both government contracts and grants may be removed if employers refuse to comply with the legislation.
Gender Equal Pay Act 1970 (Amended 1983)	Allowed women to claim equal pay with men if they are engaged on like work or work of equal value on an individual case basis. Set up complainants' right to take cases to industrial tribunals.
Sex Discrimination Act 1975 (Amended 1986)	Made discrimination on the grounds of sex or marital status unlawful in employment, training and related matters, education, the provision of goods, facilities and services, and the disposal and management of premises. Set up complainants' right to take cases to industrial tribunals and set up

Legislation	Main Points
	the Equal Opportunities Commission as an enforcing agency.
Employment Rights Act 1996	A woman may claim maternity leave, maternity pay, and the right to return to work providing certain conditions of employment and notification of her intentions to exercise her rights under the Act.

Document 2　Table of categorization of different approaches to 'equal opportunities' in organizations

Based on categories provided by Cockburn (1989); Jewson and Mason (1993); and Kandola *et al.*, (1995).

'Minimalist' position	'Colour, gender and disability blind approach'. Commonly encountered in private industry and among politicians of the right. Assumed that market decisions will maximize fairness, and only individual irrationality and prejudice introduce distortions. Minimalist approach of compliance with anti-discrimination legislation.
'Liberal' perspective	Took on the 'equality of treatment' approach assuming that a 'level playing ground' will ensure 'equal opportunities', and recognizing that institutional discrimination may exist in the form of unfair procedures and practices. 'Equal opportunities' seen as the elimination of barriers to free competition between individuals. Emphasized the development of fair, bureaucratic and formal procedures and rules.
'Radical' perspective	Took 'equal opportunities' on to another plain by adopting the 'equality of outcome' approach. Most often encountered in local authorities and on the political left. Rejected individualistic conceptions of fairness and placed it at the level of the group. Contrasted to the other two approaches. Intervened directly with positive action. Primarily

	concerned with outcome rather than rules and procedures.
Short agenda	Broadly akin to the 'liberal perspective'. Introduced new measures to minimize bias in recruitment and promotion.
Long agenda	Saw need to transform organizations not just tinker with procedures. Highlighted issues of how the power of some groups over others is established and continued. Favoured the 'radical perspective', but went further in looking for a change in power relations.
'Managing diversity'	Acknowledged that the workforce consists of a diverse population. Argued way forward was to 'harness' these differences, value everyone and use all talents. Differed from traditional 'equal opportunities'. Went beyond 'minimalist perspective' of compliance with anti-discrimination legislation by aiming to challenge the culture of organizations. Embraced all individuals, not simply groups targeted by the legislation to avoid resistance from groups outside the focus of 'equal opportunities' policies. Criticized for being individualistic and not addressing the issue of group inequality within an organization.

Document 3   Official classifications of 'race' and ethnicity

Adapted from the Labour Force Survey and the 1991 Census of Population, which used the classification recommended by the Commission for Racial Equality.

Labour Force Survey 1984–91	*Population Census 1991*	*Labour Force Survey 1992*
Black – Caribbean	Black Caribbean	Black Caribbean
African (inc. African Asian)	Black – African	Black African
	Black – Other	Black – Other
Bangladeshi	Bangladeshi	
Indian	Indian	Indian
Pakistani	Pakistani	Pakistani
Chinese	Chinese	Chinese
White	White	White
Mixed and Other	Other	Other (non-mixed)
		Other (mixed)
		Black (mixed)

Document 4 Relevant Articles from the European Social Charter on Fundamental Social Rights in the Areas of Gender and Disability

European Social Charter – Article 19

'Equal treatment for men and women shall be assured. Equal opportunities for men and women shall be developed. To this end, action shall be intensified to ensure the implementation of the principle of equality between men and women in matters of remuneration, access to employment, social protection, education, vocational training and career development. Such action shall imply the development of amenities enabling those concerned to reconcile their occupational and family obligations more easily.'

European Social Charter – Article 29

'All disabled persons, whatever the origin and nature of their disablement, shall be entitled to additional concrete measures aimed at improving their social and professional integration. These measures shall concern, in particular, according to the capacities of the beneficiaries, vocational training, ergonomics, accessibility, mobility, means of transport and housing.'

Document 5 Explanation of the Distinction between the Individual or Personal Tragedy Model of Disability and the Social Model

Oliver, 1996, p. 32.

'There are two fundamental points that need to be made about the individual model of disability. Firstly, it locates the "problem" of disability within the individual and secondly it sees the causes of this problem as stemming from the functional limitations or psychological losses which are assumed to arise from disability. These two points are underpinned by what might be called "the personal tragedy theory of disability" which suggests that disability is some terrible chance event which occurs at random to unfortunate individuals. Of course, nothing could be further from the truth.

The genesis, development and articulation of the social model of disability by disabled people themselves is a rejection of all of these fundamentals (Oliver, 1990). It does not deny the problem of disability but locates it squarely within society. It is not individual limitations, of whatever kind, which are the cause of the problem but society's failure to provide appropriate services and adequately ensure the needs of disabled people are fully taken into account in its social organization.

Hence disability, according to the social model, is all the things that impose restrictions on disabled people; ranging from individual prejudice to institutional discrimination, from inaccessible public buildings to unusable transport systems, from segregated education to excluding work arrangements, and so on. Further, the consequences of this failure do not simply and randomly fall on individuals but systematically upon disabled people as a group who experience this failure as discrimination institutionalized throughout society.

The social model itself can be located within the original UPIAS definition which bears repeating here. 'In our view it is society which disables physically impaired people. Disability is something imposed on top of our impairments by the way we are unnecessarily isolated and excluded from full participation in society. Disabled people are therefore an oppressed group in society.' (UPIAS, 1976, p. 14)

Document 6   A Practical Example of the Social Nature of Disability and Arguments Against Relying Totally on Rehabilitation of Disabled People to Fit Society Rather than Adapting the Social Environment

Oliver, 1996.

'A similar point is made by Ken Davis when he says, "We can elevate the act of walking to an importance higher than engaging in the struggle to create a decent society" (Davis, 1986, p. 4). The point is I hope I have demonstrated, that walking has a significance beyond merely the functional. If it did not have, why should society punish non-walkers for not walking?

After all, we do not punish non-flyers for not flying. In fact, we do exactly the opposite. We spend billions of dollars, yen, deutschmarks and pounds every year providing non-flyers with the most sophisticated mobility aids imaginable. They are called aeroplanes. An aeroplane is a mobility aid for non-flyers in exactly the same way as a wheel chair is a mobility aid for non-walkers.

But that is not the end of it. We spend at least as much money to provide environments, usually called runways and airports, to ensure that these mobility aids can operate without hindrance. Further, hundreds of thousands of people are employed worldwide, in helping non-flyers to overcome their particular mobility difficulties. And finally, in order to provide barrier free environments for non-flyers, we trample on the rights of others, ignoring their pleas not to have their homes bulldozed, their sleep disrupted, or their countryside undisturbed.

'Non-walkers are treated in exactly the opposite way. Environments are often designed to exclude us, transport systems that claim to be public continue to deny us access and when we protest, we are told there is no money. We are also told that giving us access to such systems would adversely affect the rights of others; journeys would take longer and would be more expensive for everyone. Perhaps a useful slogan for the next direct action demonstration could be "equal treatment for non-walkers and non-flyers" ' (p. 108).

Document 7 An Illustration of the Importance of Language in the Field of 'Equal Opportunities'

Oliver (1996) illustrates the importance of language in issues around disability by looking at popular culture. He was stimulated to do this by hearing the reminiscences of a disabled man, who in his youth had been affected by popular songs of the day that mentioned walking – 'He walks like an angel . . . Just walking in the rain . . . Walking my baby back home' (p. 98). For Oliver (1996) he states that; 'Perhaps the song that says it all is one by Val Doonican called "Walk Tall" ' (p. 99).

Oliver (1996) asks us to compare these songs with a poem by Lois Keith (ed.) (1994) *Mustn't Grumble*, The Women's Press, London.

Tomorrow I'm going to re-write the English language
I will discard all those striving ambulist metaphors
Of power and success
And construct new images to describe my strength.
Then I won't have to feel dependent
Because I can't stand on my own two feet
And I will refuse to feel a failure
When I don't stay one step ahead.
I won't feel inadequate if I can't
Stand up for myself
Or illogical when I don't
Take it one step at a time.

I will make them understand that it is a very male way
To describe the world
All this walking tall
And making great strides.

Yes tomorrow I am going to re-write the English Language,
Creating the world in my own image.
Mine will be a gentler, more womanly way
To describe my progress.
I will wheel, cover and encircle
Somehow I will learn to say it all (p. 57)

Document 8 Table on the division of housework by gender

Bagilhole, 1994

This table illustrates the concentration of housework as the responsibility of women. The research was conducted on 100 women civil servants who all worked full time.

Household tasks by gender

	Woman does most or all %	Shared %	Man does most or all %
Washing	89	11	0
Changing sheets	88	11	1
Ironing	86	11	3
Cleaning toilet	80	20	0
Cleaning cooker	81	13	6
Cleaning bath	76	23	1
Cooking for guests	69	28	3
Kitchen floor	70	19	11
Making beds	68	28	4
Dusting	65	26	9
Everyday cooking	63	27	10
Putting clothes away	58	35	7
Car maintenance	4	4	92
Cleaning car	6	25	69
DIY	3	27	70

Source: Bagilhole, B. (1994a) *Women, Work and Equal Opportunity*, Avebury, Aldershot, Tables 5.8 and 5.9

Document 9   Average gross weekly earnings, 1995, £ per week, by sex

New Earnings Survey, 1996.

	Women £	Men £
Managers & administrators	367.80	537.00
Teaching professionals	400.60	482.90
Professional & technical occupations	333.30	442.90
Receptionists, telephonists & related	197.70	305.50
Printing & related trades	235.30	343.60
Catering occupations	158.80	209.50
Sales occupations	199.90	310.30
Plant & machine operatives	201.50	293.70

Source: *New Earnings Survey*, 1996. Crown Copyright 1996. Reproduced by permission of the Controller of HMSO and the Office for National Statistics.

Document 10   Opposing views on 'positive action' for women from: 1. Valerie Amos, Chief Executive of the EOC, and 2. Gillian Shephard, Conservative MP for Norfolk South West

Guardian 1991.
1. 'There is a longstanding debate about the merits and demerits of using positive action or reverse (positive) discrimination to combat

unequal treatment in Britain, yet confusion continues to exist about the difference between the two.

It could be said that we live in a society that has for centuries been characterised by "negative" discrimination. Historically, an environment has existed in which the favouring of individuals from certain groups (e.g. white men) has not been challenged because it has been a norm. So "negative" discrimination, in favour of particular groups, became institutionalised irrespective of individual merit. Its effect has been to make an individual's sex or race a key factor in determining the type and quality of service to which they may have access.

There are some who advocate reverse discrimination as a "quick fix" to eliminate the effects of past discrimination. This may appear an attractive option but its effect is limited, both short- and long-term (for example, quota systems and appointments to jobs purely on the basis of an individual's sex).

In the area of sex discrimination, we have all been conscious of the possible negative impact of a male backlash. If we recognise the reality of unequal treatment, however, and the differential and discriminatory impact on women of some areas of social policy, we must adopt measures aimed at redressing that discrimination.

Positive action, as distinct from reverse discrimination, treats individuals equally according to merit by seeking to identify and remove barriers that prevent their merit from being recognised and rewarded. It seeks to align the culture and the ethos of organisations to the changes in society, to develop better management practice and secure general equal opportunities policies in employment and education.

Positive action has never been more relevant. We have seen the rise in interest in equal opportunities generally but with it has come increasing concern that policy-makers, trade unions and employers do not have sufficient guidance and information about measures that can be taken. This is of particular significance in the context of the single European market and the restructuring of the labour market.

We have come a long way from the days when positive action for women in employment was considered the exception rather than the rule. Positive action is an economic and social necessity, requiring commitment but, more fundamentally, action to make it a reality.'

2. 'Positive discrimination should not be practised in favour of any individual, any group or either sex. It isn't fair and it doesn't work because it lowers the status of the very people it's designed to help. Those who succeed through it may well merit promotion, but they are then seen to occupy their positions by virtue of some factor other than merit – such as colour, sex or age group. This denigrates their contribution: "Don't take too much notice of her – she's only the statutory women".

Women do not want positive discrimination; we are perfectly capable of achieving success through merit. Or are we? We all know the figures. Out of 650 MPs, only 44 are women. Between them, the largest

200 UK companies have approximately 28 women on their boards. There is progress, albeit slow. There are only 48 women in the civil service at under-secretary level and above – but 10 years ago there were just 31.

What we need are equal opportunities – a vital concept that has become blurred by over-use. It means women should be able to compete with men on equal terms.

This is made much easier when positive barriers to our progress are removed. The introduction of independent taxation for married women, for example, was a real step forward. So is the tax relief for those using workplace nurseries, the increasing provision of child care and a national curriculum that ensures all girls now learn science from an early age.

On October 28, Business in the Community launched Opportunity 2000 in which a cross-section of leading companies set themselves goals for increasing opportunities for all women employees. Many government departments are to follow suit; at its launch the Prime Minister expressed his determination to see an increase in the proportion of women holding senior public appointments.

All these initiatives represent positive action to help women – but not positive discrimination. Recent developments in such areas as part-time work, flexi-time and career breaks help women – and men. To acknowledge that the provision of equal opportunities helps both sexes is the best way to help women. We must get away from the assumption that the traditional male career path is the ideal way ahead for everyone and recognise that family concerns are not just women's issues. To assume equality of responsibility in all areas of life leads naturally to equality of opportunity. Positive discrimination assumes a fundamental inequality – and that's fundamentally wrong.'

Document 11   Racial Harassment (CRE, 1997a)

Racial harassment is a serious and continuing phenomenon. The CRE defines racial harassment as verbal or physical violence towards individuals or groups on grounds of their colour, race, nationality, or ethnic or national origin, where the victims believe the aggression was racially motivated and/or there is evidence of racial motivation. Racial harassment includes attacks on property as well as people.

Levels of harassment

- The British Crime Survey (BCS) estimated that in 1991 there were 130 000 racially motivated crimes, with 89 000 against Asians and 41 000 against Black groups. However, as the figure of 130 000 was based on a relatively small sample, the number of incidents could be as high as 170 000.
- Racial incidents are under-reported to and under-recorded by the police. Pakistanis are least likely to report even serious threats to the police; only 15% did so compared with 34% of White and 50% of Indian victims. In 1995/6, the police recorded 12 222 racial incidents in England and Wales, an

increase of 3% over the previous year. Four per cent of these involved serious physical violence.

- The great majority of victims are members of ethnic minority groups, with Asians the most vulnerable. Analysis of the combined 1988 and 1992 BCS data suggests that Pakistanis are the most vulnerable – nearly one-third (31%) of all the crimes they had experienced had been racially motivated (compared with 18% of Indians and 14% of Afro-Caribbeans). For threats this rose to 72%.

The offenders

- Racially motivated crimes against ethnic minorities were committed overwhelmingly by White offenders (98% of those against Pakistanis, 93% against Indians, and 87% against Afro-Caribbeans). Men were responsible for the majority (about 80%). 16–25 year-olds were responsible for over half the racially motivated incidents against Asians, and just over one-third of those against Black people.

Assaults of any kind are covered by the existing criminal law, and most acts of racial harassment will constitute criminal offence under existing legislation. However, there is no specific offence of racial harassment in either criminal or civil law. Existing laws which can and should be used against perpetrators of these incidents include:

- Criminal Justice Act 1991
- Offences against the Person Act 1861
- Criminal Damage Act 1971
- Public Order Act 1986
- Criminal Justice and Public Order Act 1994
- Malicious Communications Act 1988
- Local Government Act 1972
- Race Relations Act 1976

There has been a strong campaign to persuade the Government to give specific recognition to racial motivation in incidents of harassment and violence. Some, including the CRE, say that racial harassment should be a specific offence. Others say that existing laws are adequate. Racial motivation may be taken into account as an aggravating factor by courts when considering sentences. It is a matter of debate, however, whether judges should have a statutory duty to do so.

Document 12   The Criminal Justice System and 'Race' (CRE, 1997b)

Evidence for discrimination?

- After taking account of all relevant factors, Black defendants in the West Midlands were 5–8% more likely to receive prison sentences than White defendants.
- The average prison sentence for Black and Asian offenders were substantially longer than those for White people convicted of similar offences. 17% of

Black adults in the West Midlands and 15% of Asian adults were sentenced to over three years in custody compared with 11% of White adults.

Practitioners in the system.

- Two per cent of prison officers and governors described their ethnic origin as other than White. Eight per cent of probation officers and staff were of ethnic origin.
- Six per cent of all solicitors and barristers were from ethnic minorities. There were believed to be five ethnic minority circuit judges in 1995.

Document 13   Population figures and statistics for ethnic minorities in Britain

According to the 1991 Census, there are just over three million people of ethnic minority origin in Britain, 5.5 per cent of the population. Half the ethnic minority population is South Asian (Indian, Pakistani, Bangladeshi) and 30 per cent are Black (OPCS, 1991), nearly half of whom (46.8 per cent) were born in this country (Owen, 1993a).

The vast majority of Britain's ethnic minorities (97 per cent) live in England, mostly in large urban centres. For example, 45 per cent live in Greater London compared with only 10 per cent of the White population (CRE, 1995a).

Different ethnic groups tend to be concentrated in different regions:

- Of Britain's Black population, high proportions of Black Caribbeans (58 per cent), Black African (79 per cent) and Other Black (44 per cent) people live in Greater London. Sixteen per cent of the Black Caribbean population live in the West Midlands.
- Of the South Asians, most of the Bangladeshi population live in Greater London (54 per cent) and the West Midlands (12 per cent). Pakistanis are concentrated in the West Midlands (21 per cent) and in Yorkshire and Humberside (20 per cent). Indians, while more widely spread, have large concentrations in the South East (53 per cent) and the Midlands (30 per cent).
- The Chinese are concentrated in the South East (53 per cent) and North West (10 per cent) of England, although there are higher proportions in Wales (3 per cent) and Scotland (6 per cent) than any other ethnic minority group.

All the ethnic minority communities have more young people than the White population, with nearly half under 25. Only 14 per cent of the ethnic minority population are over 50, and 3 per cent are pensioners, compared with 17 per cent of the White population (CRE, 1995a).

Ethnic minority populations in Britain 1991

	Number	% of total population	% born in UK
Total population	54 888 844	100.0	93.2
White	51 874 000	94.5	95.9
All ethnic minorities	3 015 050	5.5	47.0
Black Caribbean	500 000	0.9	53.5
Black African	212 000	0.4	37.1
Black Other	178 000	0.3	84.8
Indian	840 000	1.5	42.0
Pakistani	477 000	0.9	50.5
Bangladeshi	163 000	0.3	36.8
Chinese	157 000	0.3	29.2
Other Asian	198 000	0.4	22.4
Other	290 000	0.5	60.2

Different Ethnic Minority Groups as a Percentage of the Total Ethnic Minority Population (CRE, 1995a)

Ethnic Minority Group	Percentage
Indian	28.1
Pakistani	15.4
Bangladeshi	5.5
Other Asian	6.5
Black Caribbean	16.9
Black African	7.1
Black Other	6.0
Chinese	5.0
Other	9.5

Source: 1991 Census

REFERENCES

Abberley, P. (1987) 'The concept of oppression and the development of a social theory of disability', *Disability, Handicap and Society*, **2**(1), 5–19.

Abberley, P. (1993) 'Disabled people and "normality"', in Swain, J., Finkelstein, V., French, S. and Oliver, M. *Disabling Barriers. Enabling Environments*, Sage, London.

Abberley, P. (1996) 'Work, Utopia and impairment', in Barton, L. (ed.) *Disability and Society: Emerging Issues and Insights*, Longman, London.

Abbott, P. and Wallace, C. (1990) *An Introduction to Sociology: Feminist Perspectives*, Routledge, London.

Acker, S. (1992) 'New perspectives on an old problem: the position of women academics in British higher education', *Higher Education*, **24**, 57–75.

Adorno, T., Frenkel-Brunswik, E., Levinson, D. and Sanford, N. (1950) *The Authoritarian Personality*, Harper, New York.

Ahmad, B. (1990) *Black Perspectives in Social Work*, Venture Press, Birmingham.

Ahmad, W. (ed.) (1993) *'Race' and Health in Contemporary Britain*, Open University Press, Buckingham.

Ahmad, W. (1994) 'Consanguinity and related demons: science and racism in the debate on consanguinity and birth outcome', in Samson, C. and South, N. (eds) *Conflict and Consensus in Social Policy*, Macmillan, Basingstoke.

Ahmad, W., Kernohan, E. and Baker, M. (1989) 'Influence of ethnicity and unemployment on the perceived health of a sample of general practice attenders', *Community Medicine*, **11**(2), 148–56.

Allan, M., Bhavani, R. and French, K. (1992) *Promoting Women: Management Development and Training for Women in Social Services Departments*, HMSO, London.

Allen, I. (1988) *Any Room at the Top*, Policy Studies Institute, London.

Amin, K. (1992) *Poverty in Black and White, Deprivation and Ethnic Minorities*, CPAG, London.

Amos, V. and Ouseley, H. (1994) 'Foreword', in Cheung-Judge, M. and Henley, A. *Equality in Action. Introducing Equal Opportunities in Voluntary Organisations*, NCVO Publications, London.

Amos, V. and Parmar, P. (1984) 'Challenging imperial feminism', *Feminist Review*, 17.

Anderson, E. (1979) *The Disabled Schoolchild*, Methuen, London.

Anderson, I., Kemp, P. and Quilgars, D. (1993) *Single Homeless People*, HMSO, London.

Anthias, F. and Yuval-Davis, N. (1993) *Racialized boundaries: Race, Nation, Gender, Colour and Class and the Anti-racist Struggle*, Routledge, London.

Arber, S. and Ginn, J. (1991) *Gender and Later Life: A Sociological Analysis of Resources and Constraints*, Sage, London.

Arnot, M. (1985) *Race and Gender: Equal Opportunities Policies in Education*, Pergamon, Oxford.

Arnot, M. and Weiler, K. (1993) *Feminism and Social Justice in Education*, Falmer Press, London.

Arnot, M. and Weiner, G. (eds) (1987) *Gender and the Politics of Schooling*, Hutchinson, London.

Aronson, J. (1990) 'Women's perspectives on informal care of the elderly: public ideology and personal experience of giving and receiving care', *Ageing and Society*, **10**, 61–84.

Atkin, K. and Rollings, J. (1993) *Community Care in a Multi-Racial Britain: A Critical Review of the Literature*, HMSO, London.

Bagilhole, B. (1986) *Invisible Workers: Women's Experience of Outworking in Nottinghamshire*, Department of Social Administration and Social Work, University of Nottingham.

Bagilhole, B. (1989) *Survey of Adult Day Centres for Disabled People*, Department of Equal Opportunities and Race Relations, Derbyshire County Council.

Bagilhole, B. (1992) 'Liberal excuses', *Social Work Today*, **23**, 47.

Bagilhole, B. (1993a) 'Managing to be fair: implementing equal opportunities in a local authority', *Local Government Studies*, **19**(2), 163–75.

Bagilhole, B. (1993b) 'Survivors in a male preserve: a study of British women academics experiences and perceptions of discrimination in a UK university', *Higher Education*, **26**, 431–47.

Bagilhole, B. (1993c) 'How to keep a good women down: an investigation of the role of institutional factors in the process of discrimination against women academics' *British Journal of Sociology of Education*, **14**(3), 261–74.

Bagilhole, B. (1994a) *Women, Work and Equal Opportunities*, Avebury, Aldershot.

Bagilhole, B. (1994b) 'A tale of two counties' implementation of equal opportunities and race relations policies', *Local Government Policy Making*, **21**(2), 41–8.

Bagilhole, B. (1995a) 'Being different is very difficult row to hoe: survival strategies of women academics', in S. Davies, C. Lubelska and J. Quinn, (eds) *Changing the Subject: Women in Higher Education*, Taylor & Francis, London.

Bagilhole, B. (1995b) 'In the margins: problems for women academics in UK universities', *Journal of Area Studies, Special Edition. Women in Eastern and Western Europe*, 6, Spring, 143–56.

Bagilhole, B. (1996a) 'Kith not kin: women as givers and receivers of voluntary care', *European Journal of Women's Studies*, 3, 39–54.

Bagilhole, B. (1996b) 'Tea and sympathy or teetering on social work? An analysis of the boundaries between voluntary and professional care', *Social Policy and Administration*, **30**(3), 189–205.

Bagilhole, B. (1996c) 'Inequality and discrimination against women academics and its negative effect on higher education', in Watson, K., Modgil, S. and Modgil, C. (eds) *Educational Dilemmas: Debate and Diversity, Volume 3, Power and Responsibility in Education*, Cassell, London.

Bagilhole, B. and Robinson, E. (1996) *Survey of Universities' Policies and Practices on Equal Opportunities in Employment*, Commission on University Career Opportunity, London.

Bagilhole, B. and Stephens, M. (1997a) 'Women speak out: equal opportunities in employment in a National Health Service Hospital Trust', *Social Policy and Administration Journal*.

Bagilhole, B. and Stephens, M. (1997b) 'Management responses to equal opportunities for ethnic minority women in a National Health Service Hospital Trust', *Journal of Health Services Research and Policy*.

Bagilhole, B. and Woodward H. (1995) 'An occupational hazard warning: academic life can seriously damage your health. An investigation of sexual harassment of women academics in a UK university', *British Journal of Sociology of Education*, **16**(1), 37–51.

Baird, V. (1992a) 'We've only just begun', *New Internationalist*, **227**, January, 4–7.

Baird, V. (1992b) 'Difference and defiance', *New Internationalist*, **293**, July, 4–7.

Balarajan, R. and Raleigh, V. (1993) *Ethnicity and Health: A Guide for the NHS*, Department of Health, London.

Balbo, L. (1987) 'Crazy quilts: rethinking the welfare state debate from a woman's point of view', in Showstock Sassoon, A. (ed.) *Women and the State*, Hutchinson, London.

Ball, W., Gulam, W. and Troyna, B. (1990) 'Pragmatism or retreat? Funding policy, local government and the marginalisation of anti-racist education', in Ball, W. and Solomos, J. (eds) *Race and Local Politics*, Macmillan, London.

Banton, M. (1994) *Discrimination*, Open University Press, Buckingham.

Barn, R. (1990) 'Black children in local authority care: admission patterns', *New Community*, **16**(2), 229–46.

Barnes, C. (1991) *Disabled People in Britain and Discrimination*, Hurst & Co., London.

Barrett, M. (1980) *Women's Oppression Today. Problems in Marxist Feminist Analysis*, Verso, London.

Barrett, M. and Phillips, A. (eds) (1992) *Destabilizing Theory*, Polity Press, Oxford.

Barton, L. (1989) *Disability and Dependency*, Falmer Press, Lewes.

Bayley, M. (1982) 'Helping care to happen in the community', in Walker, A. (ed.) *Community Care. The Family, the State and Social Policy*, Basil Blackwell and Martin Robertson, Oxford.

Baylies, C., Law, I. and Mercer, G. (eds) (1993) *The nature of care in a multi-racial community: summary report of an investigation of the support for black and ethnic minority persons after discharge from psychiatric hospitals in Bradford and Leeds*, Sociology and Social Policy Working Paper, University of Leeds.

Beauchamp, K. (1979) *One Race, The Human Race*, Liberation, London.

Beechey, V. and Whitelegg, E. (eds) (1986) *Women in Britain Today*, Open University Press, Milton Keynes.

Begum, N. (1994) 'Mirror, mirror on the wall', in Begum, N., Hill, M. and Stevens, A. (eds) *Reflections. The Views of Black Disabled People on their Lives and Community Care*, Central Council for Education and Training in Social Work, London.

Begum, N. (1995) 'Care management from an anti-racist perspective', *Social Care Research Findings*, 65, Joseph Rowntree Foundation, York.

Benedict, R. (1968) *Race and Racism*, Routledge & Kegan Paul, London.

Benn, S. I. and Peters, R. S. (1959) *Social Principles and the Democratic State*, George Allen & Unwin, London.

Berthoud, R., Lakey, J. and McKay, S. (1993) *The Economic Problems of Disabled People*, Policy Studies Institute, London.

Beveridge, W. (1942) *Social Insurance and Allied Services*, Cmd 6406, HMSO, London.

Bewley, C. and Glendinning, C. (1992) *Involving Disabled People in Community Care Planning*, Joseph Rowntree Foundation, York.

Bhavani, R. (1994) *Black Women in the Labour Market: A Research Review*, Equal Opportunities Commission, Manchester.

Bhopal, R. and White, M. (1993) 'Health promotion for ethnic minorities: past, present and future', in Ahmad, W. (ed.) *op cit.*

Birkett, K. and Worman, D. (eds) (1988) *Getting on with Disabilities. An Employer's Guide*, Institute of Personnel Management, London.

Black Housing (1994) 'Housing Allocation in Oldham', *Black Housing*, **9**(9), 8–10.

Blakemore, K. and Boneham, M. (1994) *Age, Race and Ethnicity*, Open University Press, Buckingham.

Blakemore, K. and Drake, R. (1996) *Understanding Equal Opportunity Policies*, Prentice Hall/Harvester Wheatsheaf, Hemel Hempstead.

Bloch, A. (1993) *Access to Benefits: The Information Needs of Minority Ethnic Groups*, Policy Studies Institute, London.

Borsay, A. (1986) *Disabled People in the Community*, Bedford Square Press, London.

Bourne, C. and Whitmore, J. (1993) *Race and Sex Discrimination*, Sweet & Maxwell, London.

Bourne, J., Bridges, L. and Searle, C. (1994) *Outcast England: How Schools Exclude Black Children*, Institute of Race Relations, London.

Bowler, I. (1993) 'They're not the same as us: midwives' stereotypes of South Asian maternity patients', *Sociology of Health and Illness*, **15**(2), 157–78.

Brah, A. (1986) 'Unemployment and racism; Asian youth on the dole', in Allen, S. Waton, A., Purcell, K. and Wood, S. (eds) *The Experience of Unemployment*, Macmillan London.

Brah, A. (1992a) 'Women of South Asian origin in Britain: issues and concerns', in Braham, P., Rattansi, A. and Skellington, R. (eds) *Racism and Antiracism. Inequalities, Opportunities and Policies*, The Open University/Sage, London.

Brah, A. (1992b) 'Black Women and 1992', in Ward, A. Gregory, J. and Yuval-Davis, N. (eds) *Women and Citizenship in Europe; Borders, Rights and Duties*, Trentham, London.

Brah, A. and Minhas, R. (1983) 'Structural racism or cultural difference: schooling for Asian girls', in Weiner, G. (ed.) *Just a Bunch of Girls*, Open University Press, Milton Keynes.

Brandt, G. (1986) *The Realisation of Anti-Racist Teaching*, Falmer Press, Lewes.

Brion, M. (1987) 'The housing problems women face', *Housing Review*, **36**(4), 139–40.

Brion, M. (1994) 'Women in education and training for housing', in Gilroy, R. and Woods, R. (eds) *Housing Women*, Routledge, London.

Brotchie, J. and Hills, D. (1991) *Equal Shares in Caring*, Socialist Health Association, London.

Brown, C. (1984) *Black and White Britain*, Heinemann, London.

Brown, P. (1992) 'Breast cancer: a lethal inheritance', *New Scientist*, 18 September, 34–7.

Brown, C. and Gay, P. (1985) *Racial Discrimination: 17 Years after the Act*, Policy Studies Institute, London.

Brown, H. and Smith, H. (1993) 'Women caring for people: the mismatch between rhetoric and women's reality?', *Policy and Politics*, **21**(3), 185–93.

Brown, J. and Campbell, E. (1993) *Sex Discrimination in the Police Service in England and Wales*, The Home Office, London.

Bruegel, I. (1989) 'Sex and race in the labour market', *Feminist Review*, 32, 49–68.

Bryan, B., Dadzie, S. and Scafe, S. (1985) *The Heart of the Race: Black Women's Lives in Britain*, Virago, London.

Buchanan, H. and Mathieu, J. (1986) 'Philosophy and justice', in Cohen, R. L. (ed.) *Justice: Views from the Social Sciences*, Plenum Press, New York.

Bull, J. (1993) *Housing Consequences of Relationship Breakdown*, Department of Environment, HMSO, London.

de Búrca, G. (1995) 'The language of Rights and European Integration', in Shaw, J. and More, G. (eds) *New Legal Dynamics of European Union*, Clarendon Press, Oxford.

Burns, B. and Phillipson, C. (1986) *Drugs, Ageing and Society*, Croom Helm, London.

Butt, J. (1994) *Same Service or Equal Service? The Second Report on Social Services Departments' Development, Implementation and Monitoring of Services for the Black and Minority Ethnic Community*, HMSO, London.

Butt, J., Gorbach, P. and Ahmad, B. (1994) *Equally Fair? A Report on Social Services Departments' Development, Implementation and Monitoring of Services for the Black and Minority Ethnic Community*, HMSO, London.

Bynoe, I., Oliver, M. and Barnes, C. (1991) *Equal Rights for Disabled People: The Case for a New Law*, Institute for Public Policy Research, London.

Byrne, E. (1978) *Women and Education*, Tavistock, London.

Cain, H. and Yuval-Davies, N. (1990) ' "The Equal Opportunities Community" and the anti-racist struggle', *Critical Social Policy*, (Autumn), 5–26.

Callender, C. (1996) 'Women and employment', in Hallett, C. (ed.) *Women and Social Policy*, Prentice Hall/Harvester Wheatsheaf, Hemel Hempstead.

Calman, K. C. (1992) *On the State of the Public Health 1991: The Annual Report of the Chief Medical Officer of the Department of Health*, HMSO, London.

Cameron, E., Evers, H., Badger, F. and Atkin, K. (1989) 'Black old women, disability and health carers', in Jeffreys, M. (ed.) *Growing Old in the 20th Century*, 230–48, Routledge, London.

Cameron, I. (1993) 'Formulating an equal opportunities policy', *Equal Opportunities Review*, **47** (January/February), 16–20.

Card, E. (1980) 'Women, housing access and mortgage credit', *Signs*, Spring, 215–19.

Carter, B., Green, M. and Halpern, R. (1996) 'Racialization of migrant labour: USA and Britain', *Ethnic and Racial Studies*, **10**(1), January, 135–57.

Cater, J. (1981) 'The impact of Asian estate agents on patterns of ethnic residence: a case study in Bradford', in Jackson, P. and Smith, S. (eds) *Social Interaction and Ethnic Segregation*, Academic Press, London.

Central Statistical Office (1994) *Social Trends*, 24, HMSO, London.

Central Statistical Office (1995) *Social Focus on Women*, HMSO, London.

Cheeseman, J. (1992) 'Monitoring the rooflessness package in London, February–September 1991', *Homelessness Statistics*, Papers from the seminar of the Statistics Users' Council, December, IMAC Research, Esher.

Cheung-Judge, M. and Henley, A. (1994) *Equality in Action. Introducing Equal Opportunities in Voluntary Organisations*, NCVO Publications, London.

Chevannes, M. and Reeves, F. (1987) 'The black voluntary school movement: definition, context and prospects', in Troyna, B. (ed.) *Racial Inequality in Education*, Tavistock, London.

Chikadonz, G. H. (1983) 'Educating a deaf nursing student', *Nursing and Health Care*, **4**(6), 327–33.

Chinnery, B. (1991) 'Equal opportunities for disabled people in the caring professions: window dressing or commitment?', *Disability, Handicap and Society*, **6**(3), 253–8.

Clarke, J. D. C. (ed.) (1990) *Ideas and Politics in Modern Britain*, Macmillan, London.

Coatham, V. and Hale, J. (1994) 'Women achievers in housing', in Gilroy, R. and Woods, R. (eds) *op cit.*

Cockburn, C. (1989) 'Equal opportunities: the short and long agenda', *Industrial Relations Journal*, **20**(3).

Cockburn, C. (1991) *In the Way of Women: Men's Resistance to Sex Equality within Organisations*, Macmillan, Basingstoke.

Cohen, R. L. (1986) (ed.) *Justice: Views from the Social Sciences*, Plenum Press, New York.

Collier, R. (1995) *Combatting Sexual Harassment in the Workplace*, Open University Press, Buckingham.

Collins, D. (1991) 'Digest: social charter', *Journal of European Social Policy*, **1**(1), 59.

Collins, H. (1992) *The Equal Opportunities Handbook*, Blackwell, Oxford.

Commission of the European Communities (CEC) (1992) *Employment in Europe*, EC Commission, Brussels.

Commission of the European Communities (CEC) (1995) *Fourth Medium-term Community Action Programme on Equal Opportunities for Women and Men (1996–2000)*, COM (95) 381, Commission of the European Communities, Brussels.

Commission for Racial Equality (CRE) (1984a) *Code of Practice for the Elimination of Racial Discrimination and Promotion of Equality of Opportunity in Employment*, HMSO, London.

Commission for Racial Equality (CRE) (1984b) *Birmingham Local Authority and Schools, Referral and Suspension of Pupils: Report of a Formal Investigation*, CRE, London.

Commission for Racial Equality (CRE) (1984c) *Race and Council Housing in Hackney*, Report of Formal Investigation, CRE, London.

Commission for Racial Equality (CRE) (1984d) *Race and Housing in Liverpool, A Research Report*, CRE, London.

Commission for Racial Equality (CRE) (1985a) *Submission in Response to the Green Paper on Reform of Social Security*, CRE, London.

Commission for Racial Equality (CRE) (1985b) *Race and Mortgage Lending: Formal Investigation of Mortgage Lending in Rochdale*, CRE, London.

Commission for Racial Equality (CRE) (1987a) *Employment of Graduates from Ethnic Minorities: a Research Report*, CRE, London.

Commission for Racial Equality (CRE) (1987b) *Formal Investigation: Chartered Accountancy Training Contracts*, CRE, London.

Commission for Racial Equality (CRE) (1987c) *Living in Terror: A Report on Racial Violence and Harassment in Housing*, CRE, London.

Commission for Racial Equality (CRE) (1988) *Report of Formal Investigation into St George's Hospital Medical School*, CRE, London.

Commission for Racial Equality (CRE) (1989a) *The Race Relations Code of Practice in Employment: Are Employers Complying?* CRE, London.

Commission for Racial Equality (CRE) (1989b) *Racial Equality in Social Service Departments, a Survey of Equal Opportunities Policies*, CRE, London.

Commission for Racial Equality (CRE) (1989c) *Racial Discrimination in Liverpool City Council: Report of Formal Investigation into the Housing Department*, CRE, London.

Commission for Racial Equality (CRE) (1989d) *The Race Relations Act 1976: A Guide for Accommodation Bureaux, Landladies and Landlords*, CRE, London.

Commission for Racial Equality (CRE) (1989e) *The Race Relations Act 1976: A Guide for Estate Agents and Vendors*, CRE, London.

Commission for Racial Equality (CRE) (1989f) *Racial Discrimination in an Oldham Estate Agency: Report of a Formal Investigation into Norman Lester and Co.*, CRE, London.

Commission for Racial Equality (CRE) (1990a) *'Sorry It's Gone': Testing for Racial Discrimination in the Private Rented Sector*, CRE, London.

Commission for Racial Equality (CRE) (1990b) *Out of Order: report of a Formal Investigation into the London Borough of Southwark*, CRE, London.

Commission for Racial Equality (CRE) (1991) *Second Review of the Race Relations Act 1976*, CRE, London.

Commission for Racial Equality (CRE) (1992) *Racial Discrimination in Hostel Accommodation: Report of a Formal Investigation of Refugee Housing Association Ltd.*, CRE, London.

Commission for Racial Equality (CRE) (1993) *Housing Associations and Racial Equality: Report of a Formal Investigation into Housing Associations in Wales, Scotland and England*, CRE, London.

Commission for Racial Equality (CRE) (1995a) *Ethnic Minorities in Britain*, Factsheet No. 1, CRE, London.

Commission for Racial Equality (CRE) (1995b) *Housing and Homelessness*, Factsheet No. 3, CRE, London.

Commission for Racial Equality (CRE) (1995c) *Employment and Unemployment*, Factsheet No. 4, CRE, London.

Commission for Racial Equality (CRE) (1995d) *Racial Equality Means Business: A Standard for Racial Equality for Employers*, CRE, London.

Commission for Racial Equality (CRE) (1996) *Appointing NHS Consultants and Senior Registrars: Report of a Formal Investigation*, CRE, London.

Commission for Racial Equality (CRE) (1997a) *Racial Attacks and Harassment*, Factsheet, CRE, London.

Commission for Racial Equality (CRE) (1997b) *Criminal Justice System in England and Wales*, Factsheet, CRE, London.

Commission for Racial Equality/Benefits Agency (CRE/BA) (1995) *The Provision of Income Support to Asian and Non-Asian Claimants*, Commission for Racial Equality, London.

Commission on University Career Opportunity (CUCO) (1994) *A Report on Universities' Policies and Practices on Equal Opportunities in Employment*, CUCO, London.

Cook, J. and Watt, S. (1987) 'Racism, women and poverty', in C. Glendinning and J. Millar (eds), *Women and Poverty in Britain in the 1990s*, Harvester Wheatsheaf, Hemel Hempstead.

Cook, J. and Watt, S. (1992) 'Racism, women and poverty', in C. Glendinning and J. Millar (eds) *Women and Poverty in Britain in the 1990s*, Harvester Wheatsheaf, Hemel Hempstead.

Cook, S. W. (1978) 'Interpersonal and attitudinal outcomes in co-operating interracial groups', *Journal of Research and Development in Education*, **12**.

Cooper, R. (1994) 'Fair employment priorities', *Equal Opportunities Review*, **53** (January/February), 17–18.

Coussey, M. (1995) 'Progress in equal opportunities in the UK and Europe, and the effects governments may have on future progress', *Equal Opportunities Higher Education Network Conference Proceedings*, Higher Education Network, London.

Coussey, M. and Jackson, H. (1991) *Making Equal Opportunities Work*, Pitman/Longman, London.

Coyle, A. (1989) 'The limits of change: local government and equal opportunities for women', *Public Administration*, **67**, Spring, 39–50.

Craig, P. (1991) 'Costs and benefits: a review of research on take-up of income-related benefits', *Journal of Social Policy*, **20**(4), 537–65.

Crawley, C. and Slowey, J. (1995) *Women and Europe, 1985–1995*, Crawley, Birmingham.

Crewe, I. (1983) 'Representation and the ethnic minorities', in Glazer, N. and Young, K. (eds) *Ethnic Pluralism and Public Policy*, Heinemann, London.

Cross, M. and Smith, D. (eds) (1987) *Black Youth Futures: Ethnic Minorities and the Youth Training Scheme*, National Youth Bureau, London.

Cunningham, S. (1992) 'The development of equal opportunities theory and practice in the European Community', *Policy and Politics*, **20**(3), 177–89.

Dale, J. and Foster, P. (1986) *Feminists and State Welfare*, Routledge & Kegan Paul, London.

Daly, M. (1993) *Abandoned: Profile of Europe's Homeless People*, The Second Report of the European Observatory on Homelessness, Federation European d'associations nationales travaillant avec les sans-abri, Brussels.

Daniel, W. W. (1968) *Racial Discrimination in England*, Penguin Books, Harmondsworth.

Dartington, T., Miller, E. and Gwynne, G. (1981) *A Life Together*, Tavistock, London.

Daunt, P. (1991) *Meeting Disability: A European Response*, Cassell, London.

David, M. (1993) *Parents, Gender and Education Reform*, Polity Press, Cambridge.

Davidson, M. J. and Cooper, C. (1992) *Shattering the Glass Ceiling: The Woman Manager*, Paul Chapman Publishing, London.

Davies, B. (1968) *Social Needs and Resources in Local Services*, Michael Joseph, London.

Davies, C. and Rosser, J. (1986) *Processes of Discrimination: A Report on a Study of Women Working in the NHS*, DHSS, London.

Davies, J. and Lyle, S. with Deacon, A., Law, I., Julienne, L. and Kay, H. (1996) *Discounted Voices*, Leeds University, CHAR and Federation of Black Housing.

Davis, A. (1996) 'Women and the personal social services', in Hallett, C. (ed.) *op cit.*

Davis, K. (1981) 'Grove Road', *Disability Challenge*, No. 1, May, Union of the Physically Impaired Against Segregation, London.

Davis, K. (1986) *Developing our own Definitions*, British Council of Organisations of Disabled People, London.

Davis, K. (1993) 'On the movement', in Swain, J. *et al.* (see Harrison, J. 1993).

Deem, R. (1980) *Schooling for Women's Work*, London.

Deem, R. (1996) 'Women and educational reform', in Hallett, C. (ed.) *op cit.*

Deem, R., Brehony, K. J. and Heath, S. (1995) *Active Citizenship and the Governing of Schools*, Open University Press, Buckingham.

Department of Employment (1972) *Take Seven: Race Relations at Work*, HMSO, London.

Department of Employment (1984) *Code of Good Practice on the Employment of Disabled People*, HMSO, London.

Department of Employment (1984) *Labour Force Survey*, HMSO, London.

Department of Employment (1995) *Labour Force Survey*, HMSO, London.

Department of Employment (1996) *New Earnings Survey*, HMSO, London.

Department of the Environment (1993) *Housing in England: Housing Trailers to the 1988 and 1991 Labour Force Surveys*, HMSO, London.

Department of Health (1989) *Caring for People: Community Care in the Next Decade and Beyond*, Cmnd 849, HMSO, London.

Department of Social Security (1994) *Social Security Statistics, 1994*, HMSO, London.

Dhillon-Kashyap, P. (1994) 'Black women and housing', in Gilroy, R. and Woods, R. (eds) (see Gilroy, R. 1994).

Dibblin, J. (1991) *Wherever I Lay my Hat – Young Women and Homelessness*, Shelter, London.

Dickens, L. (1994) 'The business case for women's equality: is the carrot better than the stick?', *Employee Relations*, **16**(8), 5–18.

Di Stefano, C. (1990) 'Dilemmas of difference: feminism, modernity and postmodernism', in L. Nicholson (ed.) *Feminism/Postmodernism*, Routledge, New York and London.

Dominelli, L. (1986) *Anti-racist Social Work*, Macmillan, London.

Dominelli, L. (1989) 'An uncaring profession? An examination of racism in social work', *New Community*, **15**(3), 391–403.

Donald, J. and Rattansi, A. (1992) *'Race', Culture and Difference*, Sage/Open University, London.

Douglas, A. and Gilroy, R. (1994) 'Young women and homelessness', in Gilroy, R. and Woods, R. (eds) (see Gilroy, R. 1994).

Douglas, G., Hebenton, B. and Thomas, T. (1992) 'The right to found a family', *New Law Journal*, **142**, 488–90.

Doyal, L., Hunt, G. and Mellor, J. (1981) 'Your life in their hands: migrant workers in the National Health Service', *Critical Social Policy*, **1**(2), 54–71.

Drake, J. (1989) 'Problem without a name', *Roof*, March and April, 31.

Duffy, K. B. and Lincoln, I. C. (1990) *Earnings and Ethnicity*, Leicester City Council, Leicester.

Dummett, A. (1991) 'Europe? Which Europe?' *New Community*, **18**(1), 167–75.

Duncan, A., Giles, C. and Webb, S. (1994) *Social Security Reform and Women's Independent Income*, Equal Opportunities Commission, Manchester.

Dunn, J. and Fahy, T. A. (1990) 'Police admissions to a psychiatric hospital: demographic and clinical differences between ethnic groups', *British Journal of Psychiatry*, **156**, 373–8.

Dutta, R. and Taylor, G. (1989) *Housing Equality*, CHAR, London.

Earwaker, S. and Todd, M. (1995) 'Services for people with a learning difficulty', in Todd, M. and Gilbert, T. (eds) *Learning Disabilities. Practice Issues in Health Settings*, Routledge, London.

Eley, R. (1989) 'Women in management in social services departments', in Hallett, C. (ed.) *Women and Social Services Departments*, Harvester Wheatsheaf, Hemel Hempstead.

Ellis, K. (1993) *Squaring the Circle*, Joseph Rowntree Foundation, York.

Employment Department (1995) *Equality Pays. How Equal Opportunities can Benefit your Business. A Guide for Small Employers*, Department of Employment Group.

Equal Opportunities Commission (EOC) (1985) *Code of Practice for the Elimination of Discrimination on the Grounds of Sex and Marriage and the Promotion of Equality of Opportunity in Employment*, HMSO, London.

Equal Opportunities Commission (EOC) (1988) *Women and Men in Britain: A Research Profile*, HMSO, London.

Equal Opportunities Commission (EOC) (1991) *Equality Management. Women's Employment in the NHS*, Equal Opportunities Commission, Manchester.

Equal Opportunities Commission (EOC) (1994) *Labour Market Structures and Prospects for Women*, Equal Opportunities Commission, London.

Equal Opportunities Commission (EOC) (1996a) *Facts about Women and Men in Great Britain*, Equal Opportunities Commission, Manchester.

Equal Opportunities Commission (EOC) (1996b) *Maternity Rights: The New Legal Requirements*, Equal Opportunities Commission, Manchester.

Equal Opportunities Review (EOR) (1992) 41 (January/February), 20–5.

Equal Opportunities Review (EOR) (1994a) 'Taking the cap off discrimination awards', *Equal Opportunities Review*, **57** (September/October), 11–13.

Equal Opportunities Review (EOR) (1994b) 'Employment forecasts for women to the year 2000', *Equal Opportunities Review*, **56** (July/August), 20–2.

Equal Opportunities Review (EOR) (1994c) 'Paternity Leave', *Equal Opportunities Review*, **55** (May/June), 14–28.

Equal Opportunities Review (EOR) (1994d) Equal opportunities in the health service: a survey of NHS trusts, *Equal Opportunities Review*, **53** (January/February), 24–31.

Equal Opportunities Review (EOR) (1996a) 'Disability Discrimination Act 1995', *Equal Opportunities Review*, **65** (January/February), 31–50.

Equal Opportunities Review (EOR) (1996b) 'EC fourth equality action programme', *Equal Opportunities Review*, **67** (May/June), 34–5.

Esmail, A., Nelson, P., Primarolo, D. and Toma, T. (1995) 'Acceptance into medical school and racial discrimination', *British Medical Journal*, **310**, 501–2.

European Commission (1994) *European Social Policy. A Way Forward for the Union. A White Paper*, COM(94) 333, Office for Official Publications of the European Communities, Brussels.

Evans, D., Fentiman, I., MacPherson, K., Asbury, D., Ponder, B. and Howell, A. (1994) 'Familial breast cancer', *British Medical Journal*, **308**, 183–7.

Evans, M. (ed.) (1994) 'Introduction', in *The Woman Question*, Sage, London.

Faludi, S. (1991) 'Blame it on feminism', *Mother Jones Magazine*, San Francisco, September/October.

Faulder, C. (1993) 'The nation with the highest death rate debates prevention', *Women's Health Newsletter*, **19**, 12–13.

Fawcett, J. (1988) *Setting the framework for a long-term project*, Social Work Today, **19**(30), 12–13.

Fiedler, B. (1988) *Living Options Lottery: Housing and Support Services for People with Severe Physical Disabilities*, Prince of Wales Advisory Group on Disability, London.

Finch, J. (1984) 'Community care: developing non-sexist alternatives', *Critical Social Policy*, **9**(4), 5–19.

Finch, J. (1986) 'Community care and the invisible welfare state', *Radical Community Medicine*, Summer.

Finch, J. (1989) *Family Obligations and Social Change*, Polity Press, Cambridge.

Finch, J. and Groves, D. (1980) 'Community care: a case for equal opportunities', *Journal of Social Policy*, **9**(4), 487–511.

Finch, J. and Groves, D. (eds) (1983) *A Labour of Love*, Routledge & Kegan Paul, London.

Finger, A. (1992) 'Forbidden fruit', *New Internationalist*, **233**, July, 8–10.

Finkelstein, V. (1980) *Attitudes and Disabled People: Issues for Discussion*, Royal Association for Disability and Rehabilitation (RADAR), London.

Finkelstein, V. (1981) 'Disability and the helper-helped relationship', in Brechin, A., Liddiard, P. and Swain, J. (eds) *Handicap in a Social World*, Hodder & Stoughton, London.

Finkelstein, V. (1993a) 'The commonality of disability', in Swain *et al.*, *op cit*.

Finkelstein, V. (1993b) 'Disability: a social challenge or an administrative responsibility?', in Swain *et al.*, *op cit*.

Foot, P. (1969) *The Rise of Enoch Powell*, Penguin Books, Harmondsworth.

Forbes, I. (1991) 'Equal opportunity: radical, liberal and conservative critiques', in Meehan, E. and Sevenhuijsen, S. (eds) *Equality, Politics and Gender*, Sage, London.

Forbes, I. and Mead, G. (1992) *Measure for Measure. A Comparative Analysis of Measures to Combat Racial Discrimination in the Member Countries of the European Community*, Research Series No. 1, Employment Department, Sheffield.

Ford, G. (1992) (ed.) *Fascist Europe. The Rise of Racism and Xenophobia*, Pluto Press, London.

Ford, J., Mongon, D. and Whelan, E. (1982) *Special Education and Social Control*, Routledge & Kegan Paul, London.

Foster, P. (1996) 'Women and health care', in Hallett, C. (ed.) *op cit.*

Frankena, W. K. (1962) 'The concept of social justice', in Brandt, R. B. (ed.) *Social Justice*, Prentice-Hall Inc., Englewood Cliffs NJ.

Fraser, N. (1989) *Unruly Practices: Power, Discourse and Gender in Contemporary Social Theory*, Polity Press, Cambridge.

French, S. (1986) 'Handicapped people in the health and caring professions – attitudes, practices and experiences', M.Sc. Dissertation, South Bank Polytechnic, London.

French, S. (1993) 'Experiences of disabled health and caring professionals', in Swain, J., *et al.*, *op cit.*

George, V. and Wilding, P. (1994) *Welfare and Ideology*, Harvester Wheatsheaf, Hemel Hempstead.

Gibbon, P. (1993) 'Equal opportunities policy and race equality', in Braham, P., Rattansi, A. and Skellington, R. (eds) *Racism and Anti-racism: Inequalities, Opportunities and Policies*, Sage, London.

Gilbert, T. (1995) 'Empowerment: issues, tensions and conflicts', in Todd, M. and Gilbert, T. *op cit.*

Gill, D., Mayor, B. and Blair, M. (eds) (1992) *Racism and Education: Structures and Strategies*, Sage/Open University, London.

Gill, O. and Jackson, B. (1983) *Adoption and Race*, Batsford, London.

Gilroy, P. (1987) *There Ain't No Black in the Union Jack*, Hutchinson, London.

Gilroy, R. (1993) *Good Practices in Equal Opportunities*, Avebury, Aldershot.

Gilroy, R. (1994) 'Women and owner occupation in Britain: first the prince, then the palace', in Gilroy, R. and Woods, R. (eds) *Housing Women*, Routledge, London.

Ginsburg, N. (1992) *Divisions of Welfare*, Sage, London.

Glazer, N. (1987) *Affirmative Discrimination: Ethnic Inequality and Public Policy*, Harvard University Press, Cambridge, Mass.

Glendinning, C. (1991) 'Losing ground: social policy and disabled people in Great Britain 1980–1990', *Disability, Handicap and Society*, **6**, 3–19.

Glendinning, C. and Millar, J. (1992) *Women and Poverty in Britain*, 2nd edn, Harvester Wheatsheaf, Hemel Hempstead.

Glithero, A. (1986) 'Lending to women: dispelling the myths', *Housing Review*, **35**(6), 202–3.

GLC (1986) *A History of the Black Presence in London*, Greater London Council, London.

Glucklich, P. (1984) 'The effects of statutory employment policies on women in the United Kingdom labour market', in Schmid, G. and Weitzel, R. (eds) *Sex Discrimination and Equal Opportunity*, Gower, Aldershot.

Gohil, V. (1987) 'DHSS service delivery to ethnic minority clients', *Leicester Rights Bulletin*, 32.

Goldberg, D. T. (1993) *Racist Culture: Philosophy and the Politics of Meaning*, Blackwell, Oxford.

Goode, J. and Bagilhole, B. (1996a) *Project on Gender Studies Loughborough University, Gender Studies Research Forum*, Department of Social Sciences, Loughborough University.

Goode, J. and Bagilhole, B. (1996b) 'Whose university? An investigation of the impact of gender on a university campus', Speaking Our Place: Women's Perspectives on Higher Education, Women in Higher Education Annual Conference, University of Central Lancashire, March.

Goode, J. and Bagilhole, B. (1997 forthcoming) 'Gendering the management of change in higher education: collaboration, resistance and transformation', *Gender, Work and Organisations*.

Gooding, C. (1994) *Disabling Laws, Enabling Acts: Disability Rights in Britain and America*, Pluto Press, London.

Gooding, C., Hasler, F. and Oliver, M. (1994) *What Price Civil Rights?*, Rights Now Campaign, London.

Gordon, P. (1986) 'Racism and social security', *Critical Social Policy*, **17**, 23–40.

Gordon, P. (1989) *Citizenship for Some? Race and Government Policy 1979–1989*, Runnymede Trust, London.

Gordon, P. (1991) 'Forms of exclusion: citizenship, race and poverty', in Becker, S. (ed.) *Windows of Opportunity: Public Policy and the Poor*, CPAG, London.

Goss, S. and Brown, H. (1991) *Equal Opportunities for Women in the NHS*, NHS Management Executive, London.

Graham, H. (1993) 'Feminist perspectives on caring', in Bornat, J., Pereira, C., Pilgrim, D. and Williams, F. (eds) *Community Care: A Reader*, Macmillan, Basingstoke.

Green, A. E. (1994) *The Geography of Poverty and Wealth: Evidence on the Spatial Distribution and Segregation of Poverty and Wealth from the Census Population 1991 and 1981*, Institute for Employment Research, University of Warwick.

Gregg, P. and Machin, S. (1993) *Is the Glass Ceiling Cracking? Gender Compensation Differentials and Access to Promotion amongst UK Executives*, Discussion Paper 94–5, Department of Economics, University College London, London.

Gregory, J. (1987) *Sex, Race and the Law*, Sage, London.

Gregory, J. (1989) *Trial by Ordeal: A Study of People who Lost Equal Pay and Sex Discrimination Cases in Industrial Tribunals*, EOC, Manchester.

Grimsley, M. and Bhat, A. (1988) 'Health', in Bhat, A., Carr-Hill, R. and Ohris, S. (eds) *Britain's Black Population: A New Perspective*, The Radical Statistics Race Group, Gower, Aldershot.

Grimwood, C. and Popplestone, R. (1993) *Women, Management and Care*, Macmillan, London.

Groves, D. (1992) 'Occupational pension provision and women's poverty in old age', in C. Glendinning and J. Millar (eds) *Women and Poverty. The 1990s*, Harvester Wheatsheaf, Hemel Hempstead.

Grundy, F. (1992) *Feminism and Computing: What is to be Done?* Proceedings, WIC 92 National Conference.

Guardian (1991) 'Putting women in their place', Tuesday, 3 December.

Guardian (1996a) 'Asylum seekers legislation', Wednesday, 24 April.

Guardian (1996b) 'Girls are doing better than ever in the classroom and the majority of teachers are women, but schools are still run by men', Tuesday, 23 April.

Gurnah, A. (1989) 'Translating equality policies into practice', *Critical Social Policy*, 27, 110–24.

Hall, S., Critcher, C., Jefferson, T. and Roberts, B. (1978) *Policing the Crisis*, Macmillan London.

Hall, S. (1983) 'The great moving right show', in Hall, S. and Jacques, M. (eds) *The Politics of Thatcherism*, Lawrence & Wishart, London.

Hallett, C. (1989) 'The gendered world of the social services department', in Hallett, C. (ed.) *op cit.*

Hallett, C. (1996) *Women and Social Policy: An Introduction*, Prentice Hall/ Harvester Wheatsheaf, Hemel Hempstead.

Hansard Society Commission (1990) *Women at the Top*, Hansard Society, London.

Hantrais, L. (1993) 'Women, work and welfare in France', in Lewis, J. (ed.) *Women and Social Policies in Europe. Work, Family and the State*, Edward Edgar Publishing Ltd., Aldershot.

Harding, N. (1989) 'Equal opportunities for women in the NHS: the prospects of success?' *Public Administration*, Spring, **67**, 51–63.

Harrison, J. (1993) 'Medical responsibilities to disabled people', in Swain, J., Finkelstein, V., French, S. and Oliver, M. (eds) *Disabling Barriers – Enabling Environments*, The Open University/Sage, London.

Harrison, M. (1992) 'Black-led housing organisations and the housing association movement', *New Community*, **18**(3), 427–37.

Harrison, M. (1995) *Housing, 'Race', Social Policy and Empowerment*, Centre for Research in Ethnic Relations/Avebury, Aldershot.

Hartmann, P. and Husbands, C. (1974) *Racism and the Mass Media: A Study of the Role of the Mass Media in the Formation of White Beliefs and Attitudes in Britain*, Davis-Poynter, London.

Hattersley, R. (1965) 'Defending the White Paper', *The Spectator*, 20 August.

Hayden, J. (1991) 'Women in general practice', *British Medical Journal*, **303**, 733–4.

Health Education Authority (1994) *Black and Minority Ethnic Groups in England: Health and Lifestyles*, HEA, London.

Hegarty, S. and Pocklington, K. (1982) *Integration in Action*, NFER/Nelson, Windsor.

Heilman, M. E. (1994) 'Affirmative action: some unintended consequences for working women', *Research in Organisational Behaviour*, 16.

Hennings, J. (1993) *Asian Women's Experience of Maternity Care*, Department of Social Policy and Social Work, University of Manchester.

Hervey, T. K. (1995) 'Migrant workers and their families', in Shaw, J. and More, G. (eds) *op cit.*

Hesse, B., Dhanwant, K. Rai, Bennett, C. and Gilchrist, P. (1992) *Beneath the Surface: Racial Harassment*, Avebury, Aldershot.

Hickling, F. W. (1991) 'Psychiatric hospital admission rates in Jamaica, 1971– 1988', *British Journal of Psychiatry*, **159**, 817–22.

Hilgard, E. R., Atkinson, R. L. and Atkinson, R. C. (1979) *Introduction to Psychology*, Harcourt Brace Jovanovich Inc., New York.

Hills, J. (1995) *Inquiry into Income and Wealth, Volume 2*, Joseph Rowntree Foundation, York.

Hoad, A. (1986) *The Impact of Transport on the Quality of Life and Lifestyles of Young People with Physical Disabilities*, London School of Hygiene and Tropical Medicine, London.

Home Affairs Committee (1986) *Racial Attacks and Harassment*, HMSO, London.

Home Office (1993) *Equal Opportunities in the Police Service*.

Honey, S., Meager, N. and Williams, M. (1993) *Employers' Attitudes towards People with Disabilities*, IMS Report 245, Institute of Manpower Studies, Poole.

Hoods-Williams, J. (1996) 'Goodbye to sex and gender', *The Sociological Review*, **44**(1), 1–16.

hooks, B. (1981) *Ain't I a Woman? Black Women and Feminism*, South End Press, Boston, Massachusetts.

Howe, D. (1986) 'The segregation of women and their work in the personal social services', *Critical Social Policy*, 15, Spring.

Hoyes, L., Jeffers, S., Lart, R., Means, R. and Taylor, M. (1993) *User Empowerment and the Reform of Community Care*, School for Advanced Urban Studies, Bristol.

Hubert, J. (1991) *Home-bound*, King's Fund Centre, London.

Hugman, R. (1991) *Power and the Caring Professions*, Macmillan, Basingstoke.

Humm, M. (1995) *The Dictionary of Feminist Theory*, 2nd edn, Prentice Hall/Harvester Wheatsheaf, London.

Independent (1992) 18, February, 12.

Jackson, J. A. (1963) *The Irish in Britain*, Routledge, London.

Jarrett-Macauley, D. (ed.) (1996) *Reconstructing Womanhood, Reconstructing Feminism. Writings on Black Women*, Routledge, London.

Jencks, C. (1988) 'What must be equal for opportunity to be equal?', in Bowie, N. E. (ed.) *Equal Opportunity*, Westview Press, Boulder, Colorado.

Jenkins, R. and Solomos, J. (1989) *Racism and Equal Opportunities Policies in the 1980s*, Cambridge University Press, Cambridge.

Jewson, N. (1990) 'Inner city riots', *Social Studies Review*, 5(5), 170–4.

Jewson, N. and Mason, D. (1986) 'The theory and practice of equal opportunities: liberal and radical approaches', *Sociological Review*, 34(2), 307–34.

Jewson, N. and Mason, D. (1993) *Equal Employment Opportunities in the 1990s: A Policy Principle Come of Age?*, Faculty of Social Sciences, University of Leicester.

Jewson, N., Mason, D., Dewett, A. and Rossiter, W. (1995) *Formal Equal Opportunities Policies and Employment Best Practice, Research Series No. 69*, Department for Education and Employment, Sheffield.

Jewson, N., Mason, D., Bourke, H. Bracebridge, C. Brosnan, F. and Milton, K. (1993) *Health Authority Membership and the Representation of Community Interests: The Case of Ethnicity*, Faculty of Social Sciences, University of Leicester.

John, D. (1969) *Indian Workers Association in Britain*, Oxford University Press, Oxford.

Jones, T. (1993) *Britain's Ethnic Minorities*, Policy Studies Institute, London.

Joseph, G. and Lewis, J. (1981) *Common Differences*, South End Press, London.

Joshi, H. and Davies, H. (1991) *The Pension Consequences of Divorce*, Centre for Economic Policy Research, London.

Joshi, H. and Davies, H. (1993) *Mothers' Human Captital and Child Care in Britain*, National Institute of Economic and Social Research, London.

Julienne, L. (1990) 'Monitoring H.A.s on race equality issues', *Black Housing*, November/December, (Gilroy (1993), p. 131).

Kandola, R., Fullerton, J. and Ahmed, Y. (1995) 'Managing diversity: succeeding where equal opportunities has failed', *Equal Opportunities Review*, 59, January/February, 31–6.

Kane, P. (1991) *Women's Health: From Womb to Tomb*, Macmillan, London.

Karn, V., Kemeny, J. and Williams, P. (1985) *Home Ownership in the Inner City, Salvation or Despair*, Gower, Aldershot.

Kearns, A. (1991) *Voluntarism, Management and Accountability*, Centre for Housing Research, University of Glasgow.

Kendall, R. (1991) 'Ask us what we want!', *Community Network*, Autumn, 7–8.

King's Fund (1989) *Ethnic Minority Health Authority Membership: a Survey*, Occasional paper No. 5, Equal Opportunities Task Force, King's Fund Publishing Office, London.

King's Fund Final Report (1990) *The Work of the Equal Opportunities Task Force 1986–1990 – A Final Report*, King Edward's Hospital Fund for London.

King's Fund (1991) *Racial Equality: The Nursing Profession*, Occasional Paper No. 6, King's Fund, London.

Klemi, P. J., Joensuu, H., Toikkanen, S., Tuominen, J. Rasanen, O., Trykko, J. and Parvinen, I. (1992) 'Aggressiveness of breast cancers found with and without screening', *British Medical Journal*, **304**, 467–9.

Laczko, F. and Phillipson, C. (1990) 'Defending the right to work: age discrimination in employment', in McEwen, M. (ed.) *Age – the Unrecognised Discrimination*, Age Concern, London.

Lancelot, M. (1990) 'Women in social service departments: not at the peaks', *Community Care*, 28 June.

Land, H. (1982) 'The Family Wage', in M. Evans (ed.) *The Woman Question*, Fontana Paperbacks, London.

Land, H. (1983) 'Poverty and gender: the distribution of resources within families', in Brown, M. (ed.) *The Structure of Disadvantage*, Heinemann, London.

Land, H. and Rose, H. (1985) 'Compulsory altruism for some or an altruistic society for all?', in Bean, P., Ferris, J. and Whynes, D. (eds) *In Defence of Welfare*, Tavistock Publications, London.

Langan, M. (1992a) 'Who cares? Women in the mixed economy of care', in Langan, M. and Day, L. (eds) *Women, Oppression and Social Work. Issues in anti-discriminatory practice*, Routledge, London.

Langan, M. (1992b) 'Feminism, managerialism and performance measurement', in Langan, M. and Day, L. (eds) *Women, Oppression and Social Work Issues in Anti-discriminatory Practice*, Routledge, London.

Larbie, J. (1985) *Black Women and the Maternity Services*, Training in Health and Race, London.

Law, I. (1994) *Sikh Elders and their Carers: A Needs Assessment*, Research Report, School of Sociology and Social Policy, University of Leeds.

Law, I. (1996) *Racism, Ethnicity and Social Policy*, Prentice Hall/Harvester Wheatsheaf, Hemel Hempstead.

Law, I., Hylton, C., Karmani, A. and Deacon, A. (1994) 'The effect of ethnicity on claiming benefits: evidence from Chinese and Bangladeshi communities', *Benefits*, **9**, 7–12.

Lawrence, E. (1982) 'In the abundance of water the fool is thirsty: sociology and black "pathology" ', in Centre for Contemporary Political Studies (CSS) *The Empire Strikes Back*, Hutchinson, London.

Layton-Henry, Z. (1984) *The Politics of Race in Britain*, Allen & Unwin, London.

Leach, B. (1989). 'Disabled people and the implementation of local authorities' equal opportunities policies', *Public Administration*, **67**, Spring, 65–77.

Leonard, A. (1987) *Pyrrhic Victories: Winning Sex Discrimination and Equal Pay Cases in Industrial Tribunals*, EOC, Manchester.

Lester, A. and Bindman, G. (1972) *Race and Law*, Penguin Books, Harmondsworth.

Lister, R. (1992) *Women's Economic Dependency and Social Security*, Equal Opportunities Commission, Manchester.

Lister, R. and Ellis, K. (1992) *Survey of Supported Employment Services in England, Wales and Scotland*, National Development Team, Manchester.

Lonsdale, S. (1986) *Work and Inequality*, Longman, London.

Lonsdale, S. (1990) *Women and Disability*, Macmillan, London.

Lonsdale, S. (1992) 'Patterns of paid work', in Glendinning, C. and Millar, J. *op cit*.

Lorber, J. (1994) *Paradoxes of Gender*, Yale University Press, New Haven, Conn.

Lunt, N. and Thornton, P. (1993) *Employment Policies for Disabled People: A Review of Legislation and Services in Fifteen Countries*, Research Series No. 16, Employment Department, Sheffield.

Lunt, N. and Thornton, P. (1994) 'Disability and employment: towards an understanding of discourse and policy', *Disability and Society*, **9**(1), 223–38.

Lustgarten, L. (1989) 'Racial inequality and the limits of the law', in Jenkins, R. and Solomos, J. (eds) *op cit.*

Lustgarten, L. and Edwards, J. (1992) 'Racial inequality and the limits of law', in Braham, P., Rattansi, A. and Skellington, R. (eds) *Racism and Anti-racism: Inequalities, Opportunities and Policies*, Sage, London.

MacDonald, I. (1983) *Immigration Law and Practice in the United Kingdom*, Butterworth, London.

Maddock, S. and Parkin, D. (1994) 'Barriers to women doctors in the North Western Region', Report for North West Regional Health Authority.

Maes, M. E. (1990) *Building a People's Europe: 1992 and the Social Dimension*, Whurr Publishers, London.

Mama, A. (1984) 'Black women, the economic crisis and the British state', *Feminist Review*, **17**, 21–36.

Mama, A. (1989) 'Violence against black women: gender, race and state responses', *Feminist Review*, **32**, 30–48.

Mama, A. (1992) 'Black women and the British state: race class and gender: analysis for the 1990s', in Braham *et al.*, *op cit.*

Mama, A. (1993) 'Violence against black women: gender, race and state responses', in Walmsey, J., Reynolds, J., Shakespeare, P. and Woolfe, R. (eds) *Health, Welfare and Practice: Reflecting on Roles and Relationships*, Sage, London.

Manning, N. and Oliver, M. (1985) 'Madness, epilepsy and medicine', in Manning, N. (ed.) *Social Problems and Welfare Ideology*, Gower, Aldershot.

Marsh, A. and McKay, S. (1993) *Families, Work and Benefits*, Policy Studies Institute, London.

Marshall, G. (ed.) (1994) *The Concise Oxford Dictionary of Sociology*, Oxford University Press, Oxford.

Martin, J. and White, A. (1988) *OPCS Surveys of Disability in Great Britain. The Financial Circumstances of Disabled Adults Living in Private Households*, HMSO, London.

Martin, J., Meltzer, H. and Elliot, D. (1988) *OPCS Surveys of Disability in Great Britain. The Prevalence of Disability among Adults*, HMSO, London.

Martin, J., White, A. and Meltzer, H. (1989) *Disabled Adults: Services, Transport and Employment*, HMSO, London.

Mason, D. (1990) 'Competing conceptions of fairness and the formulation and implementation of equal opportunities policies', in Ball, W. and Solomos, J. (eds) *Race and Local Politics*, Macmillan, London.

Mason, M. and Reiser, R. (1990) *Disability Equality in the Classroom: A Human Rights Issue*, ILEA, London.

McCarthy, P. and Simpson, R. (1991) *Issues in Post Divorce Housing*, Gower, Aldershot.

McCrudden, C., Smith, D. J., Brown, C. and Knox, J. (1991) *Racial Justice at Work – Enforcement of the Race Relations Act 1976 in Employment*, Policy Studies Institute, London.

McEwen, E. (ed.) (1990) *Age – the Unrecognised Discrimination*, Age Concern, London.

McGovern, D. and Cope, R. V. (1987) 'First psychiatric admission rates of first and second generation Afro-Caribbeans', *Social Psychiatry*, **22**, 139–49.

McIntosh, M. (1981) 'Feminism and social policy', *Critical Social Policy*, 1(1), 32–42.

McIntosh, N. and Smith, D. J. (1974) *The Extent of Racial Discrimination*, Political and Economic Planning, London.

McLaughlin, E. (1991) *Social Security and Community Care. The Case of the Invalid Care Allowance*, HMSO, London.

McManus, I., Richards, P., Winder, B., Sproston, K. and Styles, V. (1995) 'Medical school applicants from ethnic minority groups: identifying if and when they are disadvantaged', *British Medical School*, **310**, 496–500.

McPherson, A. and Savage, W. (1987) 'Cervical cytology', in McPherson, A. (ed.) *Women's Problems in General Practice*, Oxford University Press, Oxford.

McRae, S. (1991) *Maternity Rights in Britain: The Experience of Women and Employers*, Policy Studies Institute, London.

McRae, S. (1996) *Women at the Top. Progress after Five Years*, King-Hall Paper No. 2, The Hansard Society for Parliamentary Government.

Meehan, E. (1993a) *Citizenship and the European Community*, Sage, London.

Meehan, E. (1993b) 'Women's rights in the European Community', in Lewis, J. (ed.) *Women and Social Policies in Europe. Work, Family and the State*, Edward Elgar, Aldershot.

Middleton, S. (1993) 'A postmodern pedagogy for the sociology of women's education', in Arnot, M. and Weiler, K. (eds) *op cit.*

Miles, A. (1988) *Women and Mental Illness*, Harvester Wheatsheaf, Hemel Hempstead.

Miles, R. (1982) *Racism and Migrant Labour*, Routledge & Kegan Paul, London.

Miles, R. (1989) *Racism*, Routledge, London.

Miles, R. and Phizacklea, A. (1984) *Racism and Political Action in Britain*, Routledge, London.

Millar, J. (1989) 'Social security, equality and women in the UK', *Policy and Politics*, **17**(4), 311–19.

Millar, J. (1996a) 'Women, poverty and social security', in Hallett, C. *op cit.*

Millar, J. (1996b) 'Lone parents and social security policy in the UK', in Baldwin, S. and Falkingham, J. (eds) *Social Security and Social Change: New Challenges to the Beveridge Model*, Harvester Wheatsheaf, Hemel Hempstead.

Miller, D. (1976) *Social Justice*, Clarendon Press, London.

Miller, M. (1990) *Bed and Breakfast: Women and Homelessness Today*, Women's Press, London.

Milne, R. (1989) 'Tender topics for the NHS', *Health Service Journal*, 5 January, 16–17.

Mirza, H. S. (1992). *Young, Female and Black*, Routledge, London.

Mitter, S. (1986) *Common Fate, Common Bond: Women in the Global Economy*, Pluto, London.

Modood, T. (1988). ' "Black" racial equality and Asian identity', *New Community*, **14**(3), 397–404.

Moore, J. and Morrison, J. (1988) *Someone Else's Problem*, Falmer Press, Lewes.

Morrell, J. (1990) *The Employment of People with Disabilities. Research into the Policies and Practices of Employers*, Research Paper No. 77, Department of Employment.

Morris, J. (1988) *Freedom to Lose: Housing Policy and People with Disabilities*, Shelter, London.

Morris, J. (1990) *Our Homes, Our Rights: Housing and Independent Living and Disabled People*, Shelter, London.

Morris, J. (1991a) 'Adding injustice to disability', *Inside Housing*, 18 October.

Morris, J. (1991b) *Pride Against Prejudice: Transforming Attitudes to Disability*, The Woman's Press, London.

Morris, J. (1992a) 'Personal and political: a feminist perspective on researching physical disability', *Disability, Handicap and Society*, **7**(2), 157–66.

Morris, J. (1992b) 'Tyrannies of Perfection', *New Internationalist*, **233**, July, 16–17.

Morris, J. (1993a) *Independent Lives: Community Care and Disabled People*, Macmillan, London.

Morris, J. (1993b) *Community Care or Independent Living?* Joseph Rowntree Foundation, York.

Morris, J. (1993c) 'Housing, independent living and physically disabled people', in Swain *et al.*, *op cit.*

Morris, A. E. and Nott, S. M. (1991) *Working Women and the Law: Equality and Discrimination in Theory and Practice*, Routledge, London.

Morris, J. and Winn, M. (1990) *Housing and Social Inequality*, Hilary Shipman, London.

Muir, J. and Ross, M. (1993) *Housing the Poorer Sex*, London Housing Unit, London.

Munroe, M. and Smith, S. J. (1989) 'Gender and housing: broadening the research debate', *Housing Studies*, **4**(1), 81–93.

Myles, G. (1992) *EEC Brief – Volume Three*, Locksley Press, Lisburn.

Nanton, P. (1992) 'Official statistics and the problem of ethnic categorisation', *Policy and Politics*, **20**(4), 277–86.

National Association of Citizens Advice Bureaux (NACAB) (1991) *Barriers to Benefit*, NACAB, London.

National Federation of Housing Associations (NFHA) (1985) *Women in Housing Employment*, NFHA, London.

National Federation of Housing Associations (NFHA) (1987) *Race – Still a Cause for Concern*, NFHA, London.

National Federation of Housing Associations (NFHA) (1990) *Supporting Black Housing Associations*, NFHA, London.

Nationwide Anglia Building Society (1989) *Lending to Women 1980–1988*, Nationwide Anglia Building Society, London.

New Earnings Survey (1996) Part A, HMSO, London.

Newman, J. (1994) 'The limits of management: gender, and the politics of change', in Clark, J., Cochrane, A. and McLaughlin, E. (eds) *Managing Social Policy*, Sage, London.

Niner, P. (1989) *Homelessness in Nine Local Authorities*, HMSO, London.

Nottage, A. (1991) *Women in Social Services: A Neglected Resource*, HMSO, London.

Oakley, A. (1972) *Sex, Gender and Society*, Maurice Temple Smith, London.

Oakley, A. (1980) *Women Confined: Towards a Sociology of Childbirth*, Martin Robertson, Oxford.

Observer (1968) 21 April.

Offen, K. (1992) 'Defining feminism: a comparative historical approach', in Bock, G. and James, S. (eds) *Beyond Equality and Difference*, Routledge, London.

Office of Population and Census Surveys (1991) *Census 1991*, HMSO, London.

O'Hare, C. and Thomson, D. (1991) 'Experiences of physiotherapists with physical disabilities', *Physiotherapy*, **77**(6), 374–8.

Oliver, M. (1981) 'Disability, adjustment and family life: some theoretical considerations', in Brechin, A., Liddiard, P. and Swain, J. (eds) *Handicap in a Social World*, The Open University, Milton Keynes.

Oliver, M. (1983) *Social Work with Disabled People*, Macmillan, London.

Oliver, M. (1988) 'The political context of educational decision-making: the case of special needs', in Barton, L. (ed.) *The Politics of Special Needs*, Falmer Press, Lewes.

Oliver, M. (1989) 'Conductive education: if it wasn't so sad it would be funny', *Disability, Handicap and Society*, **4**(20), 197–200.

Oliver, M. (1990) *The Politics of Disablement: A Sociological Approach*, Macmillan, Basingstoke.

Oliver, M. (1991a) 'Disability and participation in the labour market', in Brown, R. and Scase, R. (eds) *Poor Work: Disadvantage and the Division of Labour*, Open University Press, Buckingham.

Oliver, M. (1991b) 'Reappraising special needs education: a review', *European Journal of Special Needs Education*, **6**(1).

Oliver, M. (1993) 'Disability and dependency: a creation of industrial societies?', in Swain, J. *et al.*, *op cit.*

Oliver, M. (1996) *Understanding Disability. From Theory to Practice*, Macmillan, London.

Ollerearnshaw, S. and Waldreck, R. (1995) 'Taking action to promote equality', *People Management*, **23**, February, 24–9.

Oppenheim, C. (1993) *Poverty: the Facts*, Child Poverty Action Group, London.

Opportunity 2000 (1994) 'International Year of the Family', *Opportunity 2000 Quarterly Update*, Autumn.

Opportunity 2000 (1996) 'Tapping the Talent', *Opportunity 2000 Quarterly Update*, Spring.

Owen, D. (1993a) *Ethnic Minorities in Great Britain: Age and Gender Structure*, Centre for Research in Ethnic Relations, University of Warwick.

Owen, D. (1993b) *Ethnic Minorities in Great Britain: Housing and Family Characteristics, 1991 Census Statistical Paper No. 4*, Centre for Research in Ethnic Relations, University of Warwick.

Owen, D. (1994) *Ethnic Minority Women and the Labour Market: Analysis of the 1991 Census*, Equal Opportunities Commission (EOC), Manchester.

Owens, P. (1987) *Community Care and Severe Physical Disability*, Bedford Square Press, London.

Pahl, J. (1980) 'Patterns of money management within marriage', *Journal of Social Policy*, **9**(3), 313–35.

Parekh, B. (1992a) 'A case for positive discrimination', in Hepple, B. and Szyszak, E. M. (eds) *Discrimination: the Limits of Law*, Mansell Publishing, London.

Parekh, B. (1992b) 'The hermeneutics of the Swann Report', in Gill, D., Mayor, B. and Blair, M. (eds) *Racism and Education. Structures and Strategies*, Sage/Open University, London.

Parkin, D. and Maddock, S. (1995) 'A gender typology of organizational culture', in Itzin, C. and Newman, J. (eds) *Gender, Culture and Organizational Change. Putting Theory into Practice*, Routledge, London.

Parmar, P. (1981) 'Young Asian women: a critique of the pathological approach', *Multiracial Education*, **9**(3), 19–29.

Pascall, G. (1986) *Social Policy: A Feminist Analysis*, Tavistock, London.

Patel, N. (1990) *A Race Against Time: Social Services Provision to Black Elders*, Runnymede Trust, London.

Patel, N. (1993) 'Healthy margins: black elders' care – models, policies and prospects', in Ahmad, W. (ed.) *op cit.*

Patterson, S. (1965) *Dark Strangers*, Pelican, London.

Paul, R. (1991) 'Black and Third World people's citizenship and 1992', *Critical Social Policy*, **32**, 52–64.

Peach, C. (1996) *Ethnicity in the 1991 Census*, Office for National Statistics, London.

Peach, C. and Byron, M. (1993) 'Caribbean tenants in council housing: race, class and gender', *New Community*, April, 407–23.

Pennie, P. and Williams, W. (1987) 'Black children need the richness of Black family life', *Social Work Today*, 12 February, **18**(22), 12.

Phillips, D. and Karn, V. (1992) 'Race and housing in a property owning democracy', *New Community*, **18**(3), 355–69.

Phizacklea, A. (1994) 'A single or segregated market: gendered and racialised divisions', in Afshar, H. and Maynard, M. (eds) *The Dynamics of 'Race' and Gender: Some Feminist Interventions*, Taylor & Francis, London.

Piachaud, D. (1985) *Round About 50 Hours a Week*, Child Poverty Action Group, London.

Pitt, G. (1992) 'Can reverse discrimination be justified?', in Hepple, B. and Szyszczak, E. M. (eds) *Discrimination: the Limits of the Law*, Mansell Publishing, London.

Pollock, S. (1984) 'Refusing to take women seriously: side effects and the policies of contraception', in Arditti, R., Klein, R. and Mindle, S. (eds) *Test-Tube Women*, Pandora, London.

Pozner, A. and Hammond, J. (1993) *An Evaluation of Supported Employment Initiatives for Disabled People*, Research Series No. 17, Employment Department, Sheffield.

Prescott-Clarke, P., Clemens, S. and Park, A. (1994) *Routes into Local Authority Housing*, Department of the Environment, HMSO, London.

Pryde, K. (1991) 'Macho style represses passion', *Social Work Today*, 26 September.

Qureshi, H. and Walker, A. (1989) *The Caring Relationship: Elderly People and their Families*, Macmillan, Basingstoke.

Radical Statistics Health Group (1987) *Facing the Figures: What is Happening to the National Health Service?* Radical Statistics Health Group, London.

Raleigh, V. S. (1996) 'Suicide patterns and trends in people of Indian subcontinent and Caribbean origin in England and Wales', *Ethnicity and Health*, **1**(1), March, 55–63.

Randall, G. and Brown, S. (1993) *The Rough Sleepers Initiative: An Evaluation*, HMSO, London.

Randhawa, K. (1986) 'Late booking: Whose problem is it?' *Maternity Action*, July/August, 9.

Rao, N. (1990) *Black Women in Public Housing*, Black Women in Housing Group, London.

Rapoport, R. and Moss, P. (1990) *Men and Women as Equals at Work*, Thomas Coram Research Unit, Occasional Paper No. 11, Institute of Education, University of London, London.

Ratcliffe, P. (1992) 'Renewal, regeneration and "race": Issues in urban policy', *New Community*, **18**(3) April, 387–400.

Rattansi, A. (1992) 'Changing the subject? Racism, culture and education', in Donald, J. and Rattansi, A. (eds) *'Race', Culture and Difference*, Sage/Open University, London.

Rawls, J. (1971) *A Theory of Justice*, Oxford University Press, Oxford.

Rex, J. (1992) 'Race and ethnicity in Europe', in Bailey, J. (ed.) *Social Europe*, Longman, London.

Rex, J. and Moore, R. (1967) *Race, Community and Conflict*, Oxford University Press, Oxford.

Rex, J. and Tomlinson, S. (1979) *Colonial Immigrants in a British City*, Routledge & Kegan Paul, London.

Rhodes, P. J. (1992) *Racial Matching in Fostering*, Avebury, Aldershot.

Richardson, R. (1992) 'Race policies and programmes under attack: two case studies for the 1990s', in Gill, D., Mayor, B. and Blair, M. (eds) *Racism and Education: Structures and Strategies*, Sage/Open University, London.

Roberts, M. M., Alexander, F. E., Anderson, T. J., Chetty, U., Donman, P. T., Forrest, P., Hepburn, W., Huggins, A., Kirkpatrick, A. E., Lamb, J., Muir, B. B. and Prescott, R. J. (1990) 'Edinburgh trial of screening for breast cancer: mortality at seven years', *The Lancet*, **335**, 241–6.

Roberts, M. (1991) *Living in a Man-made World: Gender Assumptions in Modern Housing Design*, Routledge, London.

Robinson, J. (1981) 'Cervical cancer: a feminist critique', *Times Health Supplement*, 27 November.

Roelofs, E. (1995) 'The European equal opportunities policy', in van Doorne-Huiskes, A., van Hoof, J. and Roelofs, E. (eds) *Women and the European Labour Markets*, Open University, The Netherlands/Paul Chapman Publishing, London.

ROOF (1990) 'New Operators on the old Boys Network', November/December.

Rose, S., Kamin, L. J. and Lewontin, R. C. (1984) *Not in Our Genes: Biology, Ideology and Human Nature*, Penguin Books, Harmondsworth.

Ross, R. and Schneider, R. (1992) *From Equality to Diversity: A Business Case for Equal Opportunities*, Pitman, London.

Ross, S. K. (1989) 'Cervical cytology screening and government policy', *British Medical Journal*, **299**, 101–4.

Rossi, H. in *Hansard*, 28 March 1991.

Roulstone, A. (1993) 'Access to new technology in the employment of disabled people', in Swain *et al.*, *op cit.*

Royal Association for Disability and Rehabilitation (RADAR) (1992) *The Disabled Facilities Grant: Necessary and Appropriate? Reasonable and Practicable?*, RADAR, London.

Runnymede Trust (1992) 'Education round-up', *Runnymede Trust Bulletin*, September, 6.

Sadiq-Sangster, A. (1991) *Living on Income Support: An Asian Experience*, Family Service Unit, London.

Saggar, S. (1991) *Race and Public Policy*, Avebury, Aldershot.

Sainsbury, S. (1986) *Deaf Worlds*, Hutchinson, London.

Sainsbury, S. (1995) 'Disabled people and the personal social services', in Gladstone, D. (ed.) *British Social Welfare. Past, Present and Future*, UCL Press, London.

Sashidaran, S. (1994) 'The need for community-based alternatives to institutional psychiatry', *Share Newsletter*, 7 January, 3–5, King's Fund Centre, London.

Scott, N. in *Hansard*, 28 March 1991.

Secretary of State for Health (1991) *The Health of the Nation*, HMSO, London.

Sexty, C. (1990) *Women Losing Out: Access to Housing in Britain Today*, Shelter, London.

Shakespeare, T. (1993) 'Disabled people's self-organisation: a new social movement?', *Disability, Handicap and Society*, **8**(3), 249–64.

Shakespeare, T. (1994) 'Cultural representation of disabled people: dustbins for disavowal?' *Disability and Society*, **9**(3), 283–300.

Share (1994) 'Race and health care, developments in Liverpool: a positive appraisal', *Share Newsletter*, 9 September, King's Fund Centre, London.

Shearer, A. (1981) *Disability: Whose Handicap?*, Basil Blackwell, Oxford.

Sheehan, M. (1995) 'Fair employment: an issue for the peace process', *Race and Class*, **37**(1), 71–82.

Sheldon, T. and Parker, H. (1993) 'Use of "ethnicity" and race in health research: a cautionary note', in Ahmad, W. (ed.) *op cit.*

Silburn, L. (1993) 'A social model in a medical world: the development of the integrated living team as part of the strategy for younger physically disabled people in North Derbyshire', in Swain *et al.*, *op cit.*

Silburn, R. (1988) *Disabled People: Their Needs and Priorities*, Benefits Research Unit, Department of Social Policy and Administration, University of Nottingham.

Singh, R. (1990) 'Ethnic minority experience in higher education', *Higher Education Quarterly*, **44**(4), 344–59.

Sivanandan, A. (1976) *Race, Class and the State: the Black Experience in Britain*, Institute of Race Relations, London.

Sivanandan, A. (1982) *A Different Hunger*, Pluto Press, London.

Sivanandan, A. (1985) 'RAT and the Degradation of the Black Struggle', *Race and Class*, **xxvi**(4), 1–33.

Sivanandan, A. (1988) 'The new racism', *New Statesman and Society*, 4 November.

Skellington, R. and Morris, P. (1992) *'Race' in Britain Today*, Sage/Open University, London.

Skrabanek, P. (1988) 'The debate over mass mammography in Britain: the case against', *British Medical Journal*, **297**, 991–2.

Smaje, C. (1995a) *Health, 'Race' and Ethnicity: Making Sense of the Evidence*, King's Fund Institute, London.

Smaje, C. (1995b) 'True colours', *Health Service Journal*, 26 January, 28–9.

Smart, C. (1989) *Feminism and the Law*, Routledge, London.

Smith, S. J. (1989) *The Politics of Race and Residence: Citizenship, Segregation and White Supremacy in Britain*, Polity Press, Cambridge.

Solomos, J. (1989) *Race and Racism in Contemporary Britain*, Macmillan, London.

Solomos, J. (1992) 'The politics of immigration since 1945', in Braham, P., Rattansi, A. and Skellington, R. (eds) *Racism and Antiracism. Inequalities, Opportunities and Policies*, Open University Press/Sage, London.

Soper, K. (1994) 'Feminism, humanism and postmodernism', in Evans, M. (1994) *op cit.*

Spelling, P. (1995) 'European Commission legislation, policy and funding on equal opportunity and education', *Equal Opportunities Higher Education Network Conference Proceedings*, EO Higher Education Network, London.

Stacey, J. (1993) 'Untangling feminist theory', in Richardson, D. and Robinson, V. (eds) *Introducing Women's Studies*, Macmillan, Basingstoke.

Stacey, M. (1981) 'The division of labour revisited or overcoming the two Adams', in P. Abrams, *et al.* (eds) *Practice and Progress: British Sociology 1950–1980*, Allen & Unwin, London.

Stalker, K. (1991) 'Missing out', *Social Work Today*, **23**(14), 29.

Stubbs, P. (1993) '"Ethnically sensitive" or "anti-racist"? Models for health research and service delivery', in Ahmad, W. (ed.) *op cit.*

Sumpton, A. H. (1993) 'A difference of culture: assessing the needs of Asian children', *Community Care*, 17 June.

Swain, J., Finkelstein, V., French, S. and Oliver, M. (1993) 'Introduction', in Swain, J., Finkelstein, V., French, S. and Oliver, M. (eds) *Disabling Barriers-Enabling Environments*, Sage, London.

Sykes, R. (1994) 'Elderly women's housing needs', in Gilroy, R. and Woods, R. (eds) *op cit.*

Tanna, K. (1990) 'Excellence, equality and educational reform: the myth of South Asian achievement levels', *New Community*, **16**(3), 349–68.

Taylor, P. (1993) 'Access to higher education: an uneven path?', in Goulbourne, H. and Lewis-Meeks, P. (eds) *Access of Ethnic Minorities to Higher Education in Britain: Report of a Seminar at King's College, Cambridge*, Occasional Paper in Ethnic Relations No. 10, Centre for Research in Ethnic Relations, University of Warwick, Coventry.

Taylor-Gooby, P. (1994) 'Postmodernism and social policy: a great leap backwards', *Journal of Social Policy*, **23**(3), 385–404.

Tester, S. (1996) 'Women and community care', in Hallett, C. (ed.) *op cit.*

Thatcher, M. (1978) Granada Television, 30 January.

Thompson, K. (1988) *Under Siege*, Penguin Books, Harmondsworth.

Thornton, R. (1990) *The New Homeless*, SHAC, London.

Tinker, A. (1981) *The Elderly in Modern Society*, Longman, London.

Tizard, B. (1977) *Adoption: A Second Chance*, Free Press, London.

Todd, M. (1995) 'Ethical issues', in Todd, M. and Gilbert, T. *op cit.*

Todd, M. and Gilbert, T. (1995) 'Policy and intervention', in Todd, M. and Gilbert, T. *op cit.*

Tomlinson, S. (1982) *A Sociology of Special Education*, Routledge & Kegan Paul, London.

Tomlinson, S. (1990) *Multicultural Education in White Schools*, Batsford, London.

Topliss, E. and Gould, B. (1981) *A Charter for the Disabled*, Basil Blackwell and Martin Robertson, Oxford.

Torkington, P. (1991) *Black Health: A Political Issue*, Catholic Association for Racial Justice, London.

Townsend, P. and Davidson, N. (eds) (1992) 'The Black Report', in *Inequalities in Health*, Penguin Books, Harmondsworth.

Ungerson, C. (ed.) (1985) *Women and Social Policy: A Reader*, Macmillan, London.

Ungerson, C. (1990) 'The language of care: crossing the boundaries', in Ungerson, C. (ed.) *Gender and Caring. Work and Welfare in Britain and Scandinavia*, Harvester Wheatsheaf, Hemel Hempstead.

UPIAS (1976) *Fundamental Principles of Disability*, Union of the Physically Impaired Against Segregation, London.

Ussher, J. (1989) *The Psychology of the Female Body*, Routledge, London.

Virdee, S. (1995) *Racial Violence and Harassment*, Policy Studies Institute, London.

Vogler, C. and Pahl, J. (1993) 'Social and economic change and the organisation of money within marriage', *Work, Employment and Society*, **7**(1), 71–95.

Waerness, K. (1984) 'Caring as women's work in the welfare state', in H. Holter (ed.) *Patriarchy in a Welfare Society*, Universitetsforlaget, Oslo.

Walby, S. (1990) *Theorizing Patriarchy*, Basil Blackwell, Oxford.

Walker, A. (1992) 'The poor relation: poverty among older women', in Glendinning, C. and Millar, J. *op cit.*

Walker, R. (1996) 'Understanding social security', *Social Policy Association News*, May/June, 15.

Walker, R. and Ahmad, W. I. U. (1994) 'Windows of opportunity in rotting frames? Care providers' prospectives on community care and black communities', *Critical Social Policy*, **40**, 46–69.

Walker, R., Middleton, S. and Thomas, M. (1994) 'Mothers' attachment to child benefit', *Benefits*, **11**, 14–17.

Ward, L. (1993) 'Race equality and employment in the NHS', in Ahmad, W. (ed.) *op cit.*

Ware, V. (1985) 'Growing up in black and white', *New Internationalist*, **145**, March, 21.

Warner, H. (1984) 'EC social policy in practice: Community action on behalf of women and its impact in the member states, *Journal of Common Market Studies*, **XXIII**, December, 141–67.

Warnock Report (1978) *Report of the Committee of Enquiry into the Education of Handicapped Children and Young People*, HMSO, London.

Watson, S. (1986) 'The marginalisation of non-family households in Britain', *International Journal of Urban and Regional Research*, 10(2), March, 8–28.

Watson, S. (1988) *Accommodating Inequality: Gender and Housing*, Allen & Unwin, Sydney.

Watson, S. and Austerberry, H. (1986) *Housing and Homelessness: A Feminist Perspective*, Routledge & Kegan Paul, London.

Watt, S. and Cook, J. (1989) ' "Another expectation unfulfilled": Black women and social services departments', in Hallett, C. (ed.) *op cit.*

Webber, F. (1991) 'From ethnocentrism to Euro-racism', *Race and Class*, **32**(3), 11–17.

Weiner, G. (1994) *Feminisms in Education*, Open University Press, Buckingham.

Westcott, E. (1996) 'Race matters', *AUT Bulletin*, 202, January, 12–13.

Whitting, G. (1992) 'Women and poverty: the European context', in Glendinning, C. and Millar, J. (eds) *op cit.*

Williams, F. (1989) *Social Policy: A Critical Introduction*, Polity Press, Cambridge.

Wilson, E. (1977) *Women and the Welfare State*, Tavistock Publications, London.

Woods, R. (1996) 'Women and housing', in Hallett, C. (ed.) *op cit.*

Women of Europe Newsletter (1996) 'Romen hosts European week on "Women, Politics and Society" ', *Women of Europe Newsletter*, 62, July/August, 1.

Wrench, J. (1990) 'New vocationalism, old racism and the careers service', *New Community*, **16**(3), 425–40.

Wrench, J., Brar, H. and Martin, P. (1993) *Invisible Minorities: Racism in New Towns and New Contexts*, Centre for Research in Ethnic Relations, University of Warwick.

Young, K. (1990) 'Approaches to policy development in the field of equal opportunities', in Ball, W. and Solomos, J., Race and Local Politics, Macmillan, London.

INDEX